THE
PLANE
TRUTH

THE
PLANE TRUTH

Airline Crashes, the Media, and Transportation Policy

Roger W. Cobb

and

David M. Primo

BROOKINGS INSTITUTION PRESS
Washington, D.C.

9140380

ABOUT BROOKINGS

The Brookings Institution is a private nonprofit organization devoted to research, education, and publication on important issues of domestic and foreign policy. Its principal purpose is to bring knowledge to bear on current and emerging policy problems. The Institution maintains a position of neutrality on issues of public policy. Interpretations or conclusions in Brookings publications should be understood to be solely those of the authors.

Copyright © 2003
THE BROOKINGS INSTITUTION
1775 Massachusetts Avenue, N.W., Washington, D.C. 20036
www.brookings.edu

Library of Congress Cataloging-in-Publication data
Cobb, Roger W.
  The plane truth : airline crashes, the media, and transportation policy /
Roger W. Cobb, David M. Primo.
    p. cm.
  ISBN 0-8157-7198-3 (cloth : alk. paper)
  ISBN 0-8157-7199-1 (pbk. : alk. paper)
  1. Aircraft accidents. I. Primo, David M. II. Title.

TL533.5.C487 2003
363.12'46'0973—dc21   2003000072

9 8 7 6 5 4 3 2 1

The paper used in this publication meets minimum requirements of the American National Standard for Information Sciences—Permanence of Paper for Printed Library Materials: ANSI Z39.48-1992.

Typeset in Sabon

Composition by Stephen D. McDougal
Mechanicsville, Maryland

Printed by R. R. Donnelley
Harrisonburg, Virginia

To Alexandra and Neeta

Contents

Preface

This book grew out of our interest in the politics of the aviation industry and the uses of blame to deflect responsibility when an event with unfortunate consequences occurs. The 1996 crashes of ValuJet flight 592 and TWA flight 800 were of special interest because they highlighted the importance that the media play in aviation safety. The ValuJet crash was used as a symbol of low-cost carriers trading off safety for profits, and the company was forced to reinvent itself under another name. The TWA crash was the year's top news story because of the specter of terrorism raised by the media and investigators.

Another incident that resulted in no loss of life but demonstrated the "blame game" at work occurred during New Year's weekend in January 1999. Blizzard conditions resulted in Northwest Airlines planes being stranded on the runways at the Detroit airport. Northwest Airlines by all accounts handled the situation poorly. Passengers were left on planes for up to eleven hours with no food, drinkable water, or working toilets. On one plane passengers were threatened with arrest when they proposed breaking down the airplane door. Northwest denied responsibility for failing to care for these passengers. Charges and countercharges were exchanged between the airport and the airline, with both eventually blaming the weather. The subsequent furor over the inept management of this situation led to a congressional investigation, the introduction of consumer legislation, and finally, voluntary airline action.

This book was well on its way to completion on September 11, 2001. After the terrorist attacks on that day, we knew that our book would be incomplete without attention to how aviation politics was changed by that event. Our goal was to integrate the new world of aviation security into our larger discussion of how crashes affect policy outcomes. The changes following September 11 fit the pattern of previous attempts at altering aviation regulations.

We would like to thank Alexandra Oleson for reading drafts of our manuscript, Kris Ramsay for excellent research assistance, and anonymous referees for their helpful suggestions. Also, Chris Kelaher and his Brookings colleagues provided valuable assistance.

Finally, coauthored projects require patience, persistence, and compromise. Alexandra and Neeta kept us on course.

THE
PLANE
TRUTH

CHAPTER 1

Plane Crashes and Public Policy

During the week of July 14, 1996, a drunk driver in Indiana died when his car went off the road.[1] A truck driver in Ohio died when he lost control of his big rig.[2] Two sisters and two children were killed in a crash en route to a vacation Bible school.[3] That week 842 people died in motor vehicle accidents, yet none of the accidents was covered by the national media.[4] That same week 230 people lost their lives when Trans World Airlines flight 800 exploded just after takeoff from JFK International Airport and crashed into the Atlantic Ocean. Yet the crash of the airliner, not highway deaths, became the year's top press story, as plane crashes receive media coverage disproportionate to their death toll.[5] Understanding how plane crashes affect airline transportation policy is the focus of this book.

The terror attacks of September 11, 2001, led Jane Garvey, the head of the Federal Aviation Administration (FAA), to order the first-ever national ground stop, which effectively shuts down the domestic aviation system. Aviation security rose to the top of the transportation policy agenda. Despite all the tumult, however, one feature of air travel did not change: It remained an extremely safe way to travel. Fewer than 14,000 individuals have perished in U.S. airline disasters between the beginning of public aviation and the year 2000.[6] Nearly three times as many people lose their lives in automobile accidents *every year*. Yet a Gallup poll commissioned by the Air Transport Association indicates that a plurality of the public views automobiles as the safest mode of transportation.[7]

A dramatic rise in air travel has caused problems, but airline safety is not among them. In 1990 there were nearly 7 million departures. In 1999 that number was nearly 9 million.[8] At the same time, the infrastructure of the national aviation system is crumbling: Air traffic control systems are outmoded, delays have skyrocketed (up 33 percent in the 1990s), and service complaints have risen.[9] Although these problems receive attention from policymakers and the press, the airlines are often able to contain them by promising to make changes voluntarily.

Plane crashes are different. When a crash occurs on American soil, the mass media, the public, and the government focus on it, sometimes, perhaps, out of proportion to its importance. In the era of the twenty-four-hour news cycle, media coverage is immediate and continuous as is media speculation regarding the cause of the crash. Government teams rush to investigate, elected officials offer condolences and promise to find the cause, and sometimes legislation is quickly introduced.

Plane crashes capture our attention because they bring to the fore a fact about flying that is often unexpressed: Once the cabin door closes, passengers are at the mercy of the crew and the equipment. By nature, humans are loath to relinquish control over their fate, but that is precisely what travelers do each time they fly. As a consequence, faith in the air travel system is contingent on the public learning the reason a plane crashed. If there is an explanation, then there presumably is a way to prevent future incidents of a similar nature. Randomness is not a sufficient explanation, even if it is the only one available. "In such a culture," write Eleanor Singer and Phyllis Endreny in *Reporting on Risk*, "the ultimate horror is a disaster without an explanation, an essentially random event."[10]

The Airline Industry at a Glance

In March 1915 the Benoist Company began the first regularly scheduled passenger airline in the United States, offering travel between Saint Petersburg and Tampa, Florida. Less than one year later, the government formed the National Advisory Committee for Aeronautics to support aviation research and assist this nascent industry.[11] In May 1926 President Coolidge signed the Air Commerce Act into law, and the government entered into a regulatory partnership with the airline industry.[12]

Before 1978 the federal Civil Aeronautics Board (CAB) regulated schedules and fares: An airline could not initiate a new route or change fares without approval from the CAB. As the industry grew, such a regulatory apparatus became unwieldy. The last chairman of the CAB, Alfred Kahn, did the unthinkable in Washington: He called for the elimination of his own agency (which was accomplished with the passage of the 1978 Airline Deregulation Act).[13] Suddenly, the fundamentals of air travel changed. The hub-and-spoke system, pioneered by Delta Airlines, became the industry standard.[14] Under this system, airlines use large airports as hubs for flights to a multitude of locations, allowing potentially unprofitable routes to be viable. For instance, the market for a flight from Rochester, N.Y., to San Antonio, Texas, is not very large. However, with the hub-and-spoke system, an airline can offer a flight from Rochester to Chicago, a United Airlines and American Airlines hub with connections to hundreds of cities, including San Antonio. One drawback of the hub-and-spoke system is that it has led to domination of certain airports by one or two airlines, leading to high ticket prices when the hub is the final destination.[15]

Deregulation also spawned no-frills airlines, which often eschew the use of hubs and emphasize point-to-point travel. The most notable example is Southwest Airlines, formed in 1971 to handle intrastate travel in Texas.[16] Southwest has since become a major player by expanding at smaller airports rather than at hub airports controlled by the major airlines. It is one of the few airlines to weather the recent economic downturns of the industry, and competitors now routinely match Southwest's fares on certain routes.

In general, deregulation is lauded for producing lower fares and more options for air travelers. To be sure, there have been calls for reregulation, most notably in 1989, when Senators Howard Metzenbaum (D-Ohio) and Robert Byrd (D-W.Va.) introduced S. 1854, known as the Airline Reregulation Act. The bill never left committee, and most observers agree that the days of government control of airline routes and fares have passed. The economists Steven Morrison and Clifford Winston find that fares dropped 22 percent as a consequence of deregulation.[17] Air travel is therefore now open to more travelers than it was in the 1970s. In 1978 about 25 percent of all Americans took a flight; this measure reached nearly 40 percent in 1997; in 1978 around 65 percent had ever flown on a commercial airliner, reaching 80 percent by 1997.[18]

The effect of deregulation on airline safety is more complicated. Most economists conclude that airline safety has been enhanced or at the very least been unaffected by the change.[19] But the safety benefits of a deregulated marketplace are not immediately obvious. First, when rates and routes were heavily regulated, an airline's competitive edge was through service, which implicitly includes safety.[20] In a deregulated marketplace, however, an airline's competitive advantage comes in large measure from convenience and price. Second, the rise of low-cost airlines like Southwest has increased pressure on major airlines to cut costs, some of which may affect safety. Third, the hub-and-spoke system, which has been generally adopted under deregulation, produces a greater number of stops for each passenger, and accidents occur most often during takeoffs and landings.[21]

Counterbalancing these negatives is the desire of airlines, like most corporations, to protect their brand. Also, lower prices may induce individuals to shift from highway to airline travel, which is safer for longer distances. An airline can weather a single plane crash, but if its planes fall out of the sky regularly or if there is a perception that the airline is unsafe, the company or its management is in dire straits. Even though the effect of a crash on the bottom line is often negligible, the perception that an airline is dangerous can be fatal, and there can be a contagion effect. For instance, after the crash of low-cost carrier ValuJet's flight 592, all low-cost airlines suffered massive declines in their stock, while major carriers (including Southwest) saw a slight increase.[22]

Overall, crashes have been infrequent since deregulation.[23] In 1993, 1998, and 2002 there were no deaths on any major domestic carriers. Yet there is a continual tension between optimal levels of safety and the view that airline travel should be perfectly safe. The Department of Transportation (DOT) and the FAA have both set a goal of zero accidents, a goal that can be met only by grounding all planes.[24] In other words, this objective is unrealistic. Plane crashes are already rare, so the marginal cost of saving an additional life is extremely high.[25] The median cost for every life-year saved by an FAA regulation is estimated at $23,000, which is remarkably low.[26] By way of comparison, the Environmental Protection Agency imposes an average $7.6 million for every life-year saved. If regulations are imposed to address minor risks of air travel, the marginal cost of saving a life will skyrocket. Airlines therefore tangle with the FAA and the National Transportation Safety Board (NTSB) over safety procedures, with the airlines trying to balance safety with other considerations, such as profit. Meanwhile, the NTSB, which has no power to mandate safety measures, is concerned only with learning the causes of crashes and suggesting reforms. Implementation of suggestions falls to the FAA, which until recently had a dual mandate to both promote airlines and regulate their activity.[27]

Although flying is as safe as or safer than it has ever been, there are calls for further regulations. These calls often ignore the fact that airlines and airplane manufacturers already have an incentive to keep their planes safe, if only for purely economic reasons. The economist Nancy Rose writes, "This national preoccupation with airline safety may provide the ultimate explanation for the high safety standards maintained by the U.S. carriers and the immense improvements in air safety over time."[28] And the sociologist Charles Perrow writes,

> The aircraft and airlines industries are uniquely favored to support safety efforts. Profits are tied to safety; the victims are neither hidden, random, nor delayed and can include influential members of the industry and Congress; a vigorous union fights the industry's temptation to call "operator error" and instead looks for vendor and management errors; a remarkable voluntary reporting system exists, experience is extensive, and the repetitive cycle of takeoffs, cruising, and landing promotes rapid training, precise experience with failures, and trials with errors for new designs and conditions.[29]

The Flight Safety Foundation, which publishes a newsletter for airline executives, notes that "poor safety performance equals poor financial performance."[30] The evidence for this claim is not ironclad, but as long as airline executives view safety as an important component of their business, airlines are likely to select the optimal level of safety. It is doubtful, though, that airlines will ever be allowed to make the cost-benefit tradeoffs inherent in safety regulation without some government oversight. There may be some justification for this: Deregulation has increased the competitiveness of the industry but has also led to a challenging business environment (which has only been exacerbated by the events of September 11). The news media influence how the public views political issues, and it helps the public determine what issues are important and evaluate how political officials are managing conflict. The political scientist Bernard Cohen, echoing many others, says that the press "may not be successful in telling the public what to think, but it is stunningly successful in telling its readers what to think *about.*"[31]

The journalist Roger Lowenstein terms the airlines "flying utilities" because of their high fixed capital costs. For example, a new plane can cost in excess of $100 million. This is exacerbated by high labor costs. These factors undoubtedly contributed to the 2002 bankruptcy filings by U.S. Airways and United Airlines. Overall airline financial performance reflects these struggles. From 1995 to 1999, the most profitable five-year period in the industry, major companies made three and a half cents on every dollar; whereas most profitable businesses averaged six cents on the dollar. In the 1990s the return was less than a penny for every dollar earned.[32] Since deregulation the airlines have averaged a 0.3 percent profit margin, or an average annual profit of $255 million.[33]

Profitability in the airline industry is related to what is known as a load factor, or the percentage of seats filled on an airline's flights by paying passengers. The average load factor level has steadily increased since deregulation, rising from 61 percent in 1978 to 72 percent in 2002.[34] The breakeven load factor, the point at which airlines make zero profit, has also increased. The breakeven load factor rose to a record 81 percent in 2002.[35] This figure is even higher for some airlines. In the fourth quarter of 2001, for instance, the breakeven load factor for United Airlines was 96 percent and for American Airlines was around 85 percent.[36] While the airline industry was profitable in each year from 1995 through 2000, the trend reversed in 2001 and continued in 2002. The industry as a whole can expect to be profitable again in 2004, according to the Air Transport Association.[37]

The one ray of light in this otherwise bleak picture is Southwest Airlines, the only carrier to consistently return profits to shareholders by dramatically expanding its routes and flights over time. To minimize costs, on point-to-point routes the carrier uses one type of plane and one passenger class. Pilots fly more hours and planes remain on the ground for shorter periods of time than is true for the major carriers. Union problems are minimized by means of annual cash payments in a profit-sharing arrangement.[38] Other airlines are, however, unlikely to match the Southwest model.

Disaster Stories

Some scholars argue that there are very few news story formats and that only the issues and the names change. Gaye Tuchman writes: "Reports of news events are stories—no more, but no less. . . . Reporters discover events . . . (or are presented with events) in which they can locate themes and conflicts of a particular society. These events get retold as essentially the same story from year to year and even from decade to decade."[39] To understand why plane crashes receive so much media attention, it is important to view a plane crash as a political event with an intrinsic human interest angle.

Certain issues are more media friendly than others. After all, the media operate in a competitive economic marketplace and need viewers or readers to survive and prosper. Robert Entman argues that three principles govern media coverage of stories.[40] The first is *simplification*. To reach the largest audience possible, the story must be boiled down to its simplest and most basic elements. Complexity is to be avoided at all costs. The second principle is *personalization*. Stories must be humanized and framed in terms of an ordinary person's life; people can relate to narratives with a human face. Mention of abstract entities such as organizations and institutions is to be avoided. The third principle is *symbolization*. Stories must be reduced to words, phrases, slogans, gestures, objects, or dramatic actions that readers, listeners, and viewers can identify with. These symbols help frame the story. To shape stories, the media rely on dramatic imagery, a theme of conflict, and novelty. A story that lacks these will have a short life. The time span for most major stories is a few weeks.[41] Normally, objective statistics that show a problem worsening are not sufficient to sustain journalistic interest in a particular story.[42]

A subset of policy news features widespread threats to lives or property. These cases fall under the rubric of disaster news and embody all of the characteristics described above. While not a staple of media coverage, such occurrences dominate the news until the disaster abates or the paucity of new information precludes further coverage. Disasters are characterized by suddenness, lack of warning, impact on many lives, and threat to life and the environment. These events run the gamut from weather problems (hurricanes, floods, forest fires) to geological movements (earthquakes) to those involving human error (oil spills, airline accidents).

There are some common elements in these stories:

—Damage. The immediate angle is numbers. How many were killed? What is the value of the destroyed property? Is the coastline impacted and, if so, how? Numbers usually appear in all stories. Statistics include a dollar estimate of the damage and often feature calls for government aid to deal with the aftermath.

—Victims. The media invest considerable resources on the victim aspect of the tragedy. Those who experienced the disaster firsthand tell their stories; in the case of a disaster in which all victims perish, friends and relatives of the victims are sought out. Hour-by-hour reports of how people dealt with the situation and survived provide the backbone of the early stories. The focus is on people who coped despite overwhelming odds.

They are normally identified as heroes, even though many feel uncomfortable with the designation.

—Cause. Coverage inevitably turns to who or what caused the disaster. The media need a focus of responsibility. This interplay between victims and causes is sometimes referred to as the hero-villain syndrome. While those who survived are portrayed positively, those who might have contributed to the accidents are seen in negative terms. Obviously, some disasters have no human agent, if the cause is natural, and weather or earthquakes do not make convincing villains. In such situations, the only negative portrayal might be of the person who should have seen the event coming and taken more adequate preparations to avoid it. If an accident was caused by an unknown human, such as a camper who accidentally caused a forest fire, he or she is likely to be forgotten. But if the culpable person is a prominent player in the drama (for example, the captain of an oil tanker or a nuclear plant official), attention tends to last longer. The more mystery surrounding the cause, the more attention the press will give to a disaster.

—Cure. The final focus of disaster stories is the reaction of government agencies. Oftentimes this takes the form of public hearings followed by formal actions. Answers to the following questions normally attract media coverage: Are certain people to blame? Have regulations or laws been changed to avoid such calamities in the future? Have certain geographical areas or groups of people been given government funds to prepare for such events in the future? The cure phase may last from a few weeks to several years. Proposals for cures will often be cosmetic and provide questionable "solutions" to intractable problems.

The Role of Experts

Airline crashes place specific safety issues on the government agenda, with the media acting as an integral player in this process. Journalists usually lack the credentials to report on plane crashes with only their own expertise, and they rely on experts in meteorology, geology, chemistry, biology, or engineering to help them translate the story's technological or scientific language. The media encourage the view that experts have consensual views and do not consider that the opinions of their own experts often reflect a particular perspective. The credentials of many of these experts are questionable, and often their speculation spreads misinformation. Jim Hall, the former National Transportation Safety Board chairman, says,

> For me, the biggest disappointment when I review press coverage is the cavalier way some news outlets give their air time away to people who really don't know what they're talking about. You've all seen examples of this. Where once reporters would try to verify stories before putting them on the air, now we constantly hear what can only be called rumors being spread by what are considered legitimate broadcasters. How many times have you heard a reporter say, "This isn't verified but . . . " or "A so-far-unsubstantiated report says. . . ." If it isn't verified, if it isn't substantiated, why are they broadcasting it?"[43]

Story Frames

Slogans, as well as verbal or visual images, anchor a story, but they can be manipulated to give false impressions. E. L. Quarantelli studied a variety of disasters and concludes that media reports of natural disasters "do not reflect reality but are a matter of social construction."[44] Many reporters, for example, prefer the term *toxic dump* to *nuclear disposal facility*.[45] Conrad Smith investigated the television and print coverage of three disasters: the earthquake in Oakland in 1989, the forest fires in Yellowstone Park in 1988, and the Exxon Valdez oil spill in 1989.[46] In each case the coverage promulgated a misconception. Although the earthquake damage was centered in Oakland, reporters relied on images of San Francisco and its 1906 quake to anchor their stories. The forest fire coverage stressed Yellowstone Park as the country's premier pristine national park untouched by external forces and gave the impression that such fires were less frequent than is actually the case. The Exxon Valdez case focused on dying, oil-covered animals, blackened beaches, and Alaska as the last frontier. The prominent symbols were "powerful natural forces, bumbling bureaucrats, anthropomorphized fires, and threatened forest creatures."[47]

Plane crashes are tailor-made for such stories, having all the necessary elements: death, destruction, mystery, conflict, human interest, and tragedy. When a plane filled with German tourists crashed off the coast of the Dominican Republic in 1996, killing all 189 aboard, at least ten major newspapers referred to the crash site as "shark-infested" waters.[48] After the crash of ValuJet flight 592 into the Florida Everglades, reporters said that the plane had landed in "murky" waters "infested" with crocodiles and snakes.[49] Plane crashes fit well into Entman's framework, being easily simplified, personalized, and symbolized. "The way some journalists see it," according to Barry Glassner, "air safety objectively deserves a high level of coverage, not just on account of the drama surrounding plane crashes but because plane wrecks produce lasting effects on people's psyches and on the U.S. economy."[50] The long-term economic effect of a plane crash is actually not as large as journalists believe; nonetheless, the economic effect of a crash is a media focus.

Public Perception and Policy Responses

Airline safety is a political issue due to public anxiety, widespread media coverage, and politicians' attraction to high-visibility concerns, such as crashes. Days after TWA flight 800 crashed in 1996, a CBS News poll showed that 83 percent of regular fliers believed that airlines and government should spend more money on airline safety even if it meant higher ticket prices.[51] In a 1998 Kaiser Family Foundation poll, 65 percent of Americans believed that a lot of regulation was necessary, 23 percent believed that some was justified, and only 10 percent believed that little or none was required.[52] And in a 1999 Gallup poll 55 percent of Americans had "somewhat less" or "much less" confidence in airline safety compared with a few years before.[53] Clearly, an elected official can benefit by promoting safety, especially since airlines (and ultimately customers) bear the costs of additional regulation.

Even if statistics indicate that air travel is extremely safe, each plane crash looms large since news stories focus on them out of proportion to their death tolls. In general, the media tend to exaggerate certain risks. For example, a study in the *American Journal of Public Health* shows that news sources overemphasize deaths from drug use, car accidents, and toxic agents.[54] In a study examining plane crashes, the aviation expert Arnold Barnett shows that, in 1988–89, the *New York Times* gave 8,000 times more coverage (in terms of deaths per thousand people) to plane crashes than to cancer.[55] Further, people tend to overestimate the number of deaths from rare events and to underestimate the number of deaths from common events.[56] They also perceive links between rare events that occur close in time, even if none exists, so that they can avoid accepting that randomness is to blame.[57] Since airline crashes are so unusual, their occurrence is cause for concern and airline safety hence occupies the agenda. Thomas Birkland argues, "The rarity or novelty of the event is important because run-of-the-mill events are unlikely to gain focal power because of their commonness."[58] When an airline crash occurs, government officials are quick to seek out a cause, thereby calming fears. If equipment failure is determined to be a contributory factor, then there may be debate about what action is required to ensure that the same problem does not recur. On a larger scale, a crash reminds policymakers and the public that airline travel carries some risk. According to a RAND study conducted for the NTSB, the crashes of TWA flight 800 and ValuJet flight 592 "shook the foundation of the aviation community. The traveling public was frightened, and media pundits questioned the . . . safety of domestic airline operations."[59] A single mishap often provides very little information about the overall safety of the airline industry. Precisely because they occur with such low frequency, crashes can be thought of as nearly random events that are bound to occur. Airline crashes remind the public and policymakers that airline safety is an issue of interest. Crashes act as triggering events, directing attention to the issue.

Regulatory changes with the aim of improving airline safety are often prompted by plane crashes, which may be misleading indicators of the safety of air travel. Plane crashes draw attention to airline safety, news stories of the crashes publicize the issue, the public then perceives it as a major problem, and political actors address this concern by means of new policy proposals. As we demonstrate in the next few chapters, the multiplicity of actors involved in air safety—all of whom come to the table with different agendas—makes public policy in this area disconnected and fairly chaotic. Airplanes are complex pieces of machinery, and a catastrophic failure may be, after all is said and done, a random event. The desire to find the smoking gun may divert resources and attention from more effective ways of ensuring safety in the skies.

The Rest of the Book

In the remainder of this book we examine the way plane crashes affect public policy. In chapter 2 the players in airline safety are identified, as is the sequence of the events that follow a plane crash. Chapter 3 provides statistics on airline safety, explains the high level of media attention to plane crashes, and notes the way crashes affect public policy. In chapters 4 through 6 three crashes are considered in detail, using media coverage as the lens for analysis. In chapter 7 the effect of the events of September 11 are analyzed in relation to the link between aviation security and safety. In chapter 8 we outline our findings and offer some suggestions for reforming the system.

CHAPTER 2

After the Crash

A natural reaction upon learning that a plane has crashed is, What was the cause? All targets are fair game, and often it is the interaction of a structural problem along with the pilot's response that leads to a mishap. The assignment of blame is largely a legal and political process, because often it is difficult to link a crash to a single causal factor. Public officials, private industry, and the public at large view a plane crash as a tragedy. When such an event occurs, stakeholders in the aviation industry and other relevant parties attempt to protect their interests, and the public views postcrash actions through media coverage. These actions follow a predictable course.

In this chapter, the focus is on the crucial stakeholders in the postcrash scenario. Government officials, passengers, pilots, and the airlines have an interest in airline safety, but some groups are better organized than others. Passengers, for example, are dispersed and fragmented, whereas pilots are a cohesive group. All of these groups are presumably in favor of safe air travel, but there is widespread disagreement over the means to achieve such safety and also over the causes of a plane crash. Conflict over airline safety flows from these disagreements, making it important to understand the motivations of the participants in the policy arena.

The government's role in the aviation industry has varied over time. Until 1978 the federal government regulated all aspects of the business. The Carter era ushered in an antiregulatory stance, which swept over the transportation industry. With respect to aviation, the government removed itself from the regulation of fares, routes, and scheduling. Competition was left to the airlines, and no-frills operations such as People Express appeared. Despite this, the government remained active in aviation, regulating airline safety, airports and air traffic control, and airline mergers and acquisitions.

Given the American government's checks-and-balances system, all three branches influence the aviation industry, each bringing a different organizational perspective to the problem. The major players come from within the executive and legislative branches. The judicial branch becomes involved late in the process, when blame is formally assigned via lawsuits.

The Executive Branch

Normally the president does not devote much attention to transportation concerns, limiting himself to major directives and leaving the rest to policy advisers. After a plane crashes, the president might issue a statement of regret or meet with victims' families. He may also take other symbolic actions, like forming a commission to examine some aspect of airline safety, but he will rarely become involved to any greater extent.

Since the president remains relatively aloof to transportation issues, unelected bureaucrats possess tremendous discretion. They are of two types. Political appointees oversee the operation of government agencies and implement White House directives. Appointees are usually the public faces of the bureaucracy, though the amount of control they have over an agency varies. In addition, their average tenure is thought to be a mere two to three years, with some estimates placing the figure as low as fourteen months.[1] Agency continuity comes from career employees, who are usually experts in their policy area, follow structured promotional schedules, and are not easily fired. These employees play an important role in aviation safety involving extensive technical expertise, but the information they collect and analyze may perish in the political crossfire.

The Department of Transportation

Created in 1966, the Department of Transportation (DOT) is one of the fifteen cabinet-level departments of the executive branch. Its budget is approximately $50 billion, and it employs about 60,000 full-time employees, of which more than 50,000 are Federal Aviation Administration (FAA) employees.[2] The DOT regulates all forms of transportation, from surface to air to water. Its website sets forth its official mission: to "serve the United States by ensuring a fast, safe, efficient, accessible, and convenient transportation system that meets our vital national interests and enhances the quality of life of the American people, today and into the future."[3]

Eleven agencies and bureaus operate under its auspices: the Bureau of Transportation Statistics, the Federal Aviation Administration, the Federal Highway Administration, the Federal Motor Carrier Safety Administration, the Federal Railroad Administration, the Federal Transit Administration, the Maritime Administration, the National Highway Traffic Safety Administration, the Research and Special Programs Administration, the Saint Lawrence Seaway Development Corporation, and the Surface Transportation Board.[4] Each of these subordinate agencies deals with its own stakeholders and transportation mode. The DOT grants fairly wide latitude to these subsidiary agencies. Top-level appointees focus on implementing major initiatives from the president, and by and large the media devote little attention to the DOT proper.[5]

Since most transportation money is allocated by Congress in terms of a formula or is earmarked for individual projects, lobbying for funds is not a primary objective of the DOT secretary, who serves at the pleasure of the president. This leads the department to focus on the big picture of transportation policy.[6] It regularly releases reports on issues, including industry competitiveness and airline safety, thus placing such issues on the agenda. The department finds it awkward to maintain cooperative relations with various transportation players while simultaneously regulating those same parties. As one analyst observes, "Since deregulation, the Transportation Department has had strong powers to police the industry. But it has been reluctant to use them."[7]

The department has an inspector general (IG), who is appointed by the president and confirmed by the Senate. The IG has legal training, often has served as a prosecutor, oversees all operations, and examines problem areas or wrongdoing. The IG's office issues reports to Congress on its findings. Perhaps the most controversial IG in recent years is Mary Schiavo, who began in 1990, resigned in 1996, and subsequently wrote a book on the problems at the DOT and on the dangers of air travel.[8] She argues that the DOT ignored or suppressed her research, especially a report showing that security screenings at U.S. airports were woefully inadequate. DOT officials countered that this was done to protect national security. Regardless of the reason, this incident demonstrates the tensions present when the same agency is responsible for both regulation and promotion.

The Federal Aviation Administration

The tension between regulation and promotion, especially evident at the FAA, led to changes in its mandate. The Federal Aviation Act of 1958 authorized the creation of the Federal Aviation Agency, an independent regulatory unit. In 1966 the agency was stripped of its independent status, renamed the Federal Aviation Administration, and subsumed under DOT. It was given two conflicting objectives (sometimes referred to as a dual mandate). One is safety concerns and regulation. The other is the promotion of the airline business. The first implies oversight of the airline industry, with demands for changes in safety policy. The latter implies a laissez-faire approach, in which airlines would largely be responsible for regulating themselves. The result was an uneasy compromise tilted toward self-regulation. The FAA worked closely with the individual airlines, and often promotion concerns trumped safety regulation. That position was altered, at least symbolically, after a series of accidents in the late 1990s. In 1996, in the wake of the ValuJet flight 592 crash, Congress changed the dual mandate of the agency and emphasized safety over the promotion of aviation.[9]

The FAA had a budget of $14 billion in fiscal year 2002 and employed approximately 50,000 people, most of whom are air traffic controllers. Its administrator is appointed by the president and confirmed by the Senate for a five-year term. This represents a change from the past; before the appointment of Jane Garvey in 1997, the administrator served at the pleasure of the president. The agency is technically under the aegis of the DOT. In practice, however, it has a great deal of autonomy and is responsible for regulating all matters related to commercial aviation. One commentator notes that the agency "largely works independently to oversee aviation safety."[10] Agency administrators manage various subdivisions, including airports, air traffic, aviation standards, logistics, and international aviation.

The FAA tends to receive media attention when something goes wrong. Why? In the 1960s and 1970s the agency had adequate staff, equipment, and monitoring ability, but by 1980 the system began to creak. An air traffic controllers' strike in 1981 alerted the public to problems in the foundation of the system. An ambitious plan to overhaul air traffic control failed. A decade later some key parts were still not working, and much of the equipment was dismantled, leaving the old system still in place.[11] Meanwhile, air travel became more popular and, according to many, congestion began to rule the sky. In the past decade, problems have mushroomed. The FAA has been so slow in responding to changing safety needs that it has been called the tombstone agency (meaning that change comes about only when people die).[12] As the number of people who fly has increased since the early 1980s, passenger complaints have also risen dramatically, and terms like *air rage* have become a part of the national vocabulary. Statistics on the prevalence of air rage are hard to come by, but the press has latched onto it as a problem. A Lexis-Nexis search of major newspapers turned up more than a thousand mentions of air rage in the years 1998 to 2000 and only seventeen in prior years. The term has taken on a more deadly meaning in the wake of September 11.

There has been a steady flow of media articles about the failures and weaknesses of the airline industry in moving passengers. The FAA is always the focus of such articles, because it is this agency that ultimately oversees the safety of planes and has the responsibility for the oversight of airlines. For example, an editorial in *USA Today,* reviewing the performance of the agency, concludes, "Vague excuses are an old story at the FAA, which has a long history of sluggish regulation, failed computer upgrades, and the inability to meet its own objectives."[13]

In addition, there are problems within its organizational culture. In 1998 the General Accounting Office issued a scathing report concerning the status of the FAA's air traffic control system, concluding that there was "unreliable cost information, incomplete architecture, weak software acquisition capabilities, and an organizational culture that did not reflect a strong commitment to the agency's mission focus, accountability, coordination, and adaptability."[14] The report also includes information on an employee survey, showing that many did not understand the agency's goals. They felt that training needed improvement, that problems were not anticipated, and that accurate information was not provided throughout the chain of command.

Public perception of the FAA is either horrible or favorable, depending on the source. One media profile of former FAA head Jane Garvey says she took over an agency that "tends to be about as popular with the public as baseball umpires, tax collectors, and root canals."[15] But in a 2000 Harris poll, 58 percent of respondents said the FAA was excellent or very good in carrying out its duties.[16] This suggests that problems with airline delays and poor service are being blamed on airlines directly and that the public is either unaware or misinformed about the extensive role played by the FAA in transportation policy.

Another reason that the public views the FAA favorably is that people link it with air safety. During the 1990s, though, the agency moved away from a focus on inspecting individual aircraft and pinpointing specific problems.[17] Responsibility for safety was placed more clearly on the private sector. With FAA encouragement, the airlines conduct their own safety checks, ostensibly permitting them to discover potential problem areas more quickly. In late 2000, however, the FAA released a report showing minor safety lapses at a number of airlines. For example, maintenance problems at Alaska Airlines may have contributed to a crash involving eighty-eight casualties in early 2000.[18]

An analysis of airlines' safety records over a fourteen-year period during the 1980s and 1990s finds that the FAA allowed planes that it deemed unsafe to fly anyway. The study does not provide happy news for airline passengers: "Details gleaned from FAA documents such as how many times a plane was flown with a maintenance violation show that tens of thousands of flights flew 'in unairworthy condition' since 1958 because of maintenance problems. The FAA defines unairworthy as 'unsafe for aviation use.'"[19] The FAA responds to such studies by questioning the meaning of the terminology. Problems with aircraft do not mean that the plane should not be in the sky, says the FAA. "The FAA's assistant chief counsel says a plane must be airworthy to fly, but every unairworthy aircraft is 'not an impending accident.' The FAA's director of flight standards says the flying public shouldn't be upset by the fact that thousands of unairworthy planes have carried passengers. 'It doesn't mean there's a lot of unsafe planes flying out there.'"[20]

The FAA has a range of options to use against airlines with a poor safety record. The most stringent is to ground an airline until the particular problem has been addressed. This is an extreme action and rarely taken. The least stringent approach is a warning notice or a letter of correction sent to the offending company. A middle route is a civil penalty, the number of which more than doubled (from 283 to 664) between 1996 and 1998. The airlines and the agency responded to this increase by noting that the number of planes flying has increased, as has the number of flights. If that is combined with a record of few accidents, then the problem is not as severe as initially framed.[21] The FAA is criticized for lax inspection procedures and for allowing the airlines too much discretion in self-policing, and calls to privatize certain agency functions have been frequent. DOT Secretary Norman Mineta has countered that changes such as the creation of a separate air traffic organization within the FAA have made these proposals unnecessary.[22]

Political scientists and economists use the term *capture* to refer to the tendency of agencies to become sympathetic to the economic sector they regulate. Capture theory has fallen out of vogue in political science, but the FAA's recent history suggests that, at a minimum, the appearance of capture is present. The agency was designed to be captured by a dual mandate to promote the industry it regulates. The organizational infrastructure built around promotion and regulation could not be changed overnight with the end of the dual mandate. The FAA faces many cross-pressures from Congress, the airlines, and even the traveling public. The ultimate sanction, the grounding of an airline, would ripple through the entire aviation system and is therefore an unattractive tool for regulatory enforcement. This leaves the FAA with fines and persuasion to enforce its regulations. The agency is put in a difficult position, especially because airlines often choose to pay fines if doing so is more cost-effective than adhering to the regulation. This uneasy position translates into lags in the rule-making process (a problem addressed in chapter 3).

The National Transportation Safety Board

When a plane crashes, the FAA is under pressure to implement changes in response to the crash. Those changes can emanate from Congress, the president, or the National Transportation Safety Board (NTSB). The five-member board was created in 1967, with one member designated as chair. All are nominated by the president and confirmed by the Senate. Terms for board members are five years; the chair serves for two years. The head of the board becomes the government's most visible representative in the investigation of airline crashes. Jim Hall led the board from 1993 to 2001 and through media interviews gave the NTSB more visibility than any of his predecessors. In characterizing the board's findings, he mastered the skill of translating complex technical jargon into ordinary language.

The NTSB is an autonomous agency and can be compared to the Federal Reserve Board in terms of its insulation from political pressure. It is the primary investigative agency when a safety-related transportation incident occurs. One-third of its 400 employees are devoted to the study of airline accidents. The board's budget, currently around $70 million, has increased only modestly since 1980.[23] Unlike the FAA, the NTSB has no power to change existing laws or regulations, despite the fact that it is the agency most directly involved after a plane crash. It can issue reports and suggest changes but lacks rule-making authority. It must rely on the bully pulpit to affect policy.

After a plane crash occurs, the NTSB immediately dispatches a "Go Team" headed by an IIC, or investigator in charge, to the location of the crash. There it begins the laborious process of recovering evidence. The team then prepares a report on the crash for presentation to board members. The IIC gives what is known as party status to the airline, the plane manufacturer, and others with technical expertise regarding the plane involved. By law the FAA is always a party to the investigation. The NTSB directs investigations but uses people and equipment from other government agencies, the pilots' union, and the companies involved in the accident (parties with money or reputations dependent on the outcome of such inquiries). Airlines and pilots provide the NTSB with information and expertise during an investigation. The party system has worked since the 1970s, according to Jane Garvey.[24] Nonetheless, the appearance is that those who have the most to gain or lose from the investigation are directly involved with the inquiry. For the party system to be successful, the NTSB must view information from these interested parties with a healthy skepticism.

The NTSB is often at loggerheads with the FAA and Congress. Since its creation in 1967 until 2001, the NTSB has issued some 11,700 recommendations, over one-third directed at the FAA, with approximately 80 percent being adopted.[25] While that figure appears high, some major NTSB proposals have not been adopted. As a consequence, to obtain more publicity, the NTSB has since 1990 produced its annual most-wanted list of changes. Three items on the 2002 list relate to aviation safety, and one of them—runway collisions or incursions—has been on the NTSB's list since its inception.[26] An NTSB official states, "We've seen some of the same accidents again and again and again. It's extremely frustrating."[27]

When major safety recommendations aimed at the FAA are not implemented, the principal reason is cost. As with all regulatory agencies, the FAA performs a cost-benefit analysis on proposed regulations, and since many will, statistically, save few lives, they may not be implemented. And naturally, airlines do not want to spend money on an expensive suggestion if the probability of the problem occurring is low. For example, the NTSB considers exploding fuel tanks to be a major danger, blaming them for the crash of TWA flight 800 as well as other crashes. But the board's recommendation that the airlines adopt fuel tank inerting has yet to be implemented by the FAA.[28] Sensitive to such criticism by NTSB officials, FAA officials try to place their noncompliance in the best possible light. "We virtually never disagree with the safety intent of an NTSB recommendation," says one FAA official. "Some of the safety objectives are technically very complex and economically very costly."[29] In 1997 the White House Commission on Aviation Safety and Security recommended, however, that cost-benefit analysis not dominate discussions of proposed regulations.[30]

The NTSB's and FAA's seeming "good-cop, bad cop" routine is misleading, though. It is essential for government regulators to place a value on human life and to estimate the risk of death associated with a safety flaw, though economists disagree on the methodology that should be used to calculate these values. Regulations that cost billions of dollars to save one hundred statistical lives may be an inefficient use of scarce resources. FAA regulations "cost" an estimated $23,000 for each life-year saved, one of the lowest among all regulatory agencies. By comparison, the Occupational Safety and Health Administration (OSHA) imposes $88,000 in regulatory costs for every life-year saved, and EPA regulations implicitly value a life-year at $7,600,000.[31] Is the FAA "spending" too little or too much?

The most efficient regulatory regime would promulgate rules such that the cost of saving a life-year would be identical across agencies. But political realities suggest that some agencies will propose more efficient rules than other agencies. Whether the FAA imposes too little or too much regulation is a matter of debate. A different concern is the length of time it takes to implement regulations. In some respects, the decisionmaking process may cast the FAA in a negative light. This time lag may be the source of tension between the FAA and the NTSB. The adversarial nature of their relationship is built into the process, as high-visibility incidents such as crashes put the FAA and the NTSB in opposite corners. The NTSB suggests changes; the FAA evaluates them. One senior executive for a major airline says, "The relationship is legendary for its acrimony. . . . I don't know if the FAA cares any more in its heart about the relationship than it did in the old days. From its inception, the NTSB was resented."[32]

The NTSB has its own problems. In 1998 it sought a review of its activities to find if its objectives were being met. In an independent study completed in 1999, the RAND Corporation found significant management problems at the agency. The results were unsettling; NTSB operations were seen as "nearing the breaking point."[33] The study concluded that the NTSB staff was too small to investigate all aviation accidents and that it lacked adequate facilities and training for its personnel: "There is insufficient assurance that resources currently allocated to the safety board are adequately managed to produce the most efficient and effective results. Arcane management practices and a lack of an independent agency financial system are significantly at fault."[34] The NTSB struggles under the weight of increasingly complex accidents and intense media scrutiny. Since the NTSB's finding of "probable cause" often serves as the basis for assignment of blame and litigation, its goal of merely conducting technical and scientific analyses is threatened.[35]

Another NTSB problem is the dissemination of news after a crash. Board members were reported as "stunned" by "the growing intensity of interest by news organizations after prominent crashes."[36] In response, the NTSB now has a section on its web page informing journalists of how the agency deals with a crash and how the media will be informed of crash-related activity. The NTSB must also face such systemic media changes as the rise of the Internet, television newsmagazines, and cable television. As Jim Hall says, "We have come a long way from footage I saw recently of an NTSB press conference at O'Hare Airport a few days following the crash of American Airlines flight 191 in May 1979, still the deadliest crash in U.S. history. There probably were three or four cameras and no more than fifteen reporters there. Today, you can multiply that by a factor of ten."[37]

Further, the NTSB's tendency to treat lightly airline incidents other than plane crashes is problematic from a safety perspective.[38] From an informational perspective, an airline incident with no deaths is equally as valuable as a plane crash, but such a minor incident is unlikely to create enough pressure on the FAA for corrective action. To the extent that such incidents are given short shrift, NTSB resources are not deployed optimally.

The Legislative Branch

Any authority (or lack thereof) in the executive branch is due to the actions of Congress. Congress relies heavily on committees, which do its business, and on committee chairs, who have wide discretion to place issues on the agenda. The aviation industry falls under the jurisdiction of several committees, including the Transportation and Infrastructure Committee, in the House, and the Science, Commerce, and Transportation Committee, in the Senate.

Three concerns animate most of the legislators who serve on transportation-related committees. First, they seek as many federal dollars as possible for transportation, with an emphasis on parochial spending. Second, regardless of their party affiliation most do not take an adversarial position with respect to the airlines and the government agencies overseeing them. (While they may take the agencies to task, their rhetoric is not matched with action.) Third, they focus on the issue du jour, whether it is airline safety, airline security, or congestion.

The leadership of each committee has some discretion in setting that committee's agenda. The chair, selected by the majority party, has significant though not absolute authority to determine the topics covered, the legislation considered, and the hearings held. Often the ranking minority member (typically the senior member of the opposition party) works in tandem with the chair in setting the agenda. Rarely will major legislation emerge from a committee without the imprint of at least one of these individuals. After major plane crashes, the leadership usually takes the lead in calling for committee hearings. Therefore, the bills introduced by these leaders are a rough measure of legislative interest in airline safety. Before the events of September 11, airline safety and security were not on Congress's radar screen. Instead the delays plaguing the airline industry as well as poor customer service drew its attention. Not coincidentally, these were the issues getting attention from the public and the press. The September 11 crashes shifted the attention of Congress toward aviation security, and concern about delays and congestion disappeared.[39]

Oversight: The House Transportation and Infrastructure Committee

Compared to the intense partisan climate that pervades most House committees, the Transportation and Infrastructure Committee is fairly collegial and nonpartisan. It is the largest congressional committee, composed of seventy-six members, with a party ratio that closely reflects that of the House overall. The primary goal of the committee is to secure funding for all modes of transportation in a bipartisan spirit.

For the period of Republican control between 1994 and 2000, the chair was Bud Shuster (R-Pa.). During his tenure, he was one of the strongest chairs in the House, described as "legendary for his pugnacious way of protecting funding for transportation programs."[40] While he supported more appropriations for all modes of transportation, he was primarily concerned with road construction and was a key player in enacting the 1998 transportation bill known as TEA-21 (at roughly $200 billion, the most expensive domestic capital-spending program ever passed). The Republican leadership had previously negotiated with the White House to keep all domestic spending within budget caps. Shuster overrode the cap by offering committee members $40 million in projects for a favorable vote and all House members $15 million in earmarked funds in return for support. With such tactics he was able to secure funding that overrode legislative budget constraints, preferences of other committee chairs, and the opposition of the White House.[41]

Shuster did make some changes in air industry practices. He was active in getting the NTSB to deal with the needs of victims' families after a plane crash and sponsored legislation giving passengers greater options in dealing with airlines. He legislated unsuccessfully to reform the FAA but was able to change how slots were allocated to airlines at major airports. Facing some ethical concerns and the term limit for committee chairs, he retired in January 2001 and was replaced by Don Young (R-Alaska).

The ranking Democrat from 1995 on was James Oberstar (D-Minn.), who worked closely with Shuster in passing the giant transportation bill.[42] The collegial relationship between Shuster and Oberstar meant generous funding for transportation projects, primarily roads, and minimal interference with airline management. While attentive to the needs of Minnesota-based Northwest Airlines, Oberstar has on occasion criticized the airline industry, and it has usually responded to his concerns.[43] He has pushed for various measures, including prohibition of smoking on all flights, greater restrictions on noncommercial airlines, and an investigation of price-fixing by major carriers. Early in the period he attempted—but failed—to make the FAA an independent agency. His minority party status limited his legislative success.

Table 2-1 shows the legislation introduced by the chair or the ranking minority member in the three congresses, 1995 through 2000. This list does not include reauthorizing legislation and budgetary action or legislation focused on foreign air carriers. In the 104th Congress, the main proposal of these committee leaders was to separate the FAA from the DOT, giving the FAA more freedom and discretion. The proposal failed to pass the Senate, and the committee did not reintroduce the legislation in subsequent sessions. Bipartisan cooperation continued into 2002. Both the new chair, Don Young, and Oberstar criticized the Office of Management and Budget for clipping the FAA budget.[44]

Table 2-1   *Domestic Airline Regulation Bills Sponsored by Chair or Ranking Minority Member (RMM), House Transportation Committee, 104th–106th Congresses*

Legislator and bill number	Intent of bill (legal outcome)
Shuster (chair, 104th)	
H.R. 1036	Change composition and congressional review of Metropolitan Washington Airports Authority
H.R. 3539	Reauthorize FAA, with safety and security reform (P.L. 104-264)
H.R. 3923	Require NTSB and air carriers to address needs of families of aviation accident victims (see H.R. 3539)
H.R. 3953	Require FAA to promote antiterrorism security measures
Oberstar (RMM, 104th)	
H.R. 589	Make FAA an independent agency
H.R. 590	Reform air carrier safety for small planes
H.R. 969	Prohibit smoking on all flights
H.R. 1320	Restrict use of certain special purpose aircraft
H.R. 1545	Require FAA certification for small commuter airports
H.R. 1777	Reform retirement regulations for certain air traffic controllers
Shuster (chair, 105th)	
H.R. 2036/H.R. 4058	Amend aviation insurance requirements (P.L. 105-137 [S. 1193])
H.R. 2282	Require retaliation for limitations on U.S. carrier access to foreign markets
H.R. 4057	Reform FAA
Oberstar (RMM, 105th)	
H.R. 552	Prohibit smoking on all flights
H.R. 728	Modify retirement qualifications for air traffic controllers
H.R. 4547	Amend laws pertaining to the transfer of air carrier certificates
Shuster (chair, 106th)	
H.R. 98	Extend and modify aviation war risk insurance
H.R. 700	Codify air passengers' rights
H.R. 1000	Reform FAA, invest in infrastructure, and change slot restriction provisions (P.L. 106-181)
H.R. 2681	Reform NTSB
H.R. 3072	Require reciprocal slot access for U.S. carriers in EU and U.K.
H.R. 2910	Clarify FBI-NTSB relationship (P.L. 106-424 [S. 2412])
Oberstar (RMM, 106th)	Prohibit operation of certain supersonic aircraft if EU
H.R. 661	adopts certain noise regulations
H.R. 2024	Require U.S. carriers to conduct safety audits of foreign cooperative partners
H.R. 4978	Allow secretary of transportation to investigate suspected price collusion among carriers

Source: Bill sponsorship from the Library of Congress, Thomas website.

Oversight: The House Aviation Subcommittee

The Aviation Subcommittee of the Transportation Committee oversees air travel. It is the second largest subcommittee (next to Highway and Transit) and has forty-four members. Members approach aviation issues from a local perspective in that they want adequate air service to major cities in their districts. Oversight is dependent primarily on events, such as plane crashes, strikes, delays, system failures, or major mechanical problems. The domestic airline regulation bills sponsored by the subcommittee leaders during the 104th, 105th, and 106th Congresses are listed in table 2-2.

The chair from 1995 to 2000 was John Duncan (R-Tenn.), who represents an area of his state that has minimal air access. His principal concern was to aid air travel in districts such as his and to provide more slots in major airports from underserved airports.[45] Other proposals included separating the FAA from the DOT, cracking down on unruly passengers, and reforming pilot hiring practices. The ranking minority member for most of this period was William Lipinski (D-Ill.), whose district includes Chicago's Midway Airport. Lipinsky's main focus was to upgrade that facility and to prevent federal funds from being spent to build a third Chicago-area airport.[46] However, he has supported legislation to change the air traffic system and to protect passengers and whistle-blowers. A self-portrayed champion of consumer interests, he wants more flight information given to the public, limits on the number of carry-on bags, and medical equipment on airplanes to help passengers with heart attacks. While his proposals never came to a vote, the FAA now requires defibrillators to be installed on commercial aircraft.

Duncan served as chair for six years and then was subject to House term limits on subcommittee chairs. His replacement was John Mica (R-Fla.), who has used his committee membership primarily to leverage more funding for light rail in the Orlando area.[47]

Oversight: The Senate Commerce, Science, and
Transportation Committee

The principal Senate committee overseeing aviation is the Commerce, Science, and Transportation Committee, composed of twenty-three members reflecting the partisan division of the chamber.[48] Unlike its House counterpart, which has a distinct focus, this Senate committee has diverse

Table 2-2   *Domestic Airline Regulation Bills Sponsored by Chair or Ranking Minority Member (RMM), Aviation Subcommittee, House Transportation Committee, 104th–106th Congresses*

Legislator and bill number	Intent of bill (legal outcome)
Duncan (chair, 104th)	
H.R. 2276	Establish an independent FAA
H.R. 3536	Require background checks on pilots
Lipinski (RMM, 104th)	
No activity	
Duncan (chair, 105th)	
H.R. 2626	Reform pilot hiring and employment laws (P.L. 105-142)
H.R. 2748	Reform slot allocation laws at high density airports (P.L. 105-277 [title 4, H.R. 4328])
H.R. 2843	Require better first aid equipment on airplanes (P.L. 105-170)
Lipinski (RMM, 105th)	
H.R. 2855	Require collision avoidance systems on air cargo carriers
H.R. 3064	Limit number of carry-on bags
H.R. 3741	Require congressional consent for aviation routes between U.S. and foreign nations
Duncan (chair, 106th)	
H.R. 717	Regulate overflights of national parks (P.L. 106-181 [part of H.R. 1000])
H.R. 951	Reform slot allocation at high density airports to encourage service in smaller markets (P.L. 106-181 [part of H.R. 1000])
H.R. 1052	Increase penalties for unruly airline passengers (P.L. 106-181 [part of H.R. 1000])
H.R. 4529	Restrict who can work security positions at airports
Lipinski (RMM, 106th)	
H.R. 1845	Require congressional review of civil aviation agreements
H.R. 2495	Limit number of carry-on bags
H.R. 5323	Require defibrillators on passenger planes

Source: Bill sponsorship from Library of Congress, Thomas website.

concerns, one of which is transportation. Table 2-3 lists the domestic airline regulation bills sponsored by this committee's leaders.

As in the House, interest by the chair and the ranking minority member is crucial to determining the committee's role in transportation. In the 104th Congress, Larry Pressler (R-S.D.) chaired the committee. He sponsored legislation to reform air traffic management, which passed. Pressler's defeat for reelection in 1996 brought John McCain (R-Ariz.) to the fore. McCain quickly changed the emphasis of the committee to include new

Table 2-3   *Domestic Airline Regulation Bills Sponsored by Chair or Ranking Minority Member (RMM), Senate Commerce, Science, and Transportation Committee, 104th–106th Congresses*

Legislator and bill number	Intent of bill (legal outcome)
Pressler (chair, 104th)	
S. 1994	Reform FAA and air traffic management (P.L. 104-264 [H.R. 3539])
Hollings (RMM, 104th)	
S. 517	Reform Metropolitan Washington Airports Authority
McCain (chair, 105th)	
S. 262	Regulate overflights of national parks
S. 1196	Require foreign air carriers to report plans of action for families of air accident victims (P.L. 105-148 [H.R. 2476])
S. 1331	Propose a slot auction for U.S. airports
S. 2279	Authorize FAA research into effects of national park overflights
Hollings (RMM, 105th)	
S. Amend. 1041 to S. 1048	Extend sharing of pilot employment records to nonscheduled carriers (P.L. 105-66 [H.R. 2169])
McCain (chair, 106th)	
S. 81	Regulate national park overflights
S. 82	Reform FAA and invest in infrastructure (P.L. 106-181 [H.R. 1000])
S. 643	Authorize airport improvement program
S. 2412	Reform NTSB (P.L. 106-424)
S. Amend. 3440 to H.R. 4475	Place conditions on use of FAA non-safety-related funds (P.L. 106-346)
Hollings (RMM, 106th)	
S. 405	Prevent the operation of civilian supersonic aircraft from U.S. airports
S. 545	Reform FAA and aviation law

Source: Bill sponsorship from Library of Congress, Thomas website.

issue areas, particularly air travel, with the stress on competition and service. The committee took a more aggressive stance in pushing the airlines to be accountable for their commercial practices.

McCain was a prominent contender for the 2000 presidential nomination and increased his legislative profile dramatically in the period leading up to his candidacy. McCain successfully proposed legislation that, among other things, reformed the NTSB, limited the FAA's discretion in using non-safety-related funds, and assisted the families of air crash victims. He claims he has taken on the airlines in response to angry constituent reports of failed air service.[49] The companies emerged from McCain's attacks un-scathed, however, by making promises to institute changes voluntarily. And since September 11 the service issue has disappeared from the agenda, although McCain has wrangled with the airlines over aviation security legislation. The ranking minority member during the period was Ernest Hollings (D-S.C.), who has been active in attempting to modernize the FAA and make air travel more efficient.

Oversight: The Senate Aviation Subcommittee

The Senate Aviation Subcommittee has eighteen members. The two most powerful members have been active in pushing for aviation reform. The chair for the 104th Congress was John McCain. As can be seen in table 2-4, in his two-year term he sought to reform the FAA and to require stricter security checks for pilots. When he moved to the chair of the entire committee, his replacement was Slade Gorton (R-Wash.), who sponsored legislation changing the way slots are allocated at major airports. The ranking member in the 104th and 105th Congresses was Wendell Ford (D-Ky.), who was concerned with access to small airports and with re-quiring government personnel to fly on U.S. carriers. Jay Rockefeller (D-W.Va.) replaced him in the subsequent session; he emphasized small-mar-ket service and air traffic management.

Oversight: A Summary

On balance, the oversight committees in Congress have acted to support the transportation industry. Legislators also do not ignore their constitu-ents and quickly respond to a problem identified by a major event (for example, a plane crash) or general constituent discontent (for example, delays and poor service). The political scientists Mathew McCubbins and Thomas Schwartz refer to this as "fire alarm" oversight.[50] The events of September 11 have increased the focus on aviation security, leading to widespread changes (see chapter 7), but this is the exception that proves the rule. Transportation committees can authorize funds but cannot allo-cate them. That falls to the most powerful committees in the House and Senate, the appropriations committees and, most important, their trans-portation subcommittees. These committees are not directly involved in regulation, but their control over the congressional purse strings gives them the ability to place issues on the agenda.

Table 2-4   *Domestic Airline Regulation Bills Sponsored by Chair or Ranking Minority Member (RMM), Aviation Subcommittee, Senate Commerce, Science, and Transportation Committee, 104th–106th Congresses*

Legislator and bill number	Intent of bill (legal outcome)
McCain (chair, 104th)	
S. 288	Abolish Board of Review for Metropolitan Washington Airports Authority
S. 1239	Reform FAA
S. 1461	Require background checks for pilots
S. 1801	Reform FAA
Ford (RMM, 104th)	
S. 682	Require FAA certification of small airports
S. 1037	Require government personnel to fly on U.S. carriers
S. Amend. 4 to S. 2	Prohibit the personal use of frequent flyer miles by members and employees of Congress (P.L. 104-1)
Gorton (chair, 105th)	
S. 1193	Reform aviation insurance (P.L. 105-137)
S. 1358	Authorize FAA research
Ford (RMM, 105th)	
S. 1968	Create office of Aviation Development to promote access to air transport for small markets
Gorton (chair, 106th)	
S. Amend. 1892 to S.82	Reform provisions related to slot allocations for certain airports (P.L. 106-181 [H.R. 1000])
Rockefeller (RMM, 106th)	
S. 379	Improve air service to small markets
S. 1682	Improve air traffic management
S. Amend. 1893 to S.82	Authorize air traffic management reforms (P.L. 106-181 [H.R. 1000])

Source: Bill sponsorship from Library of Congress, Thomas website.

The House Appropriations Transportation Subcommittee

All funding measures, subdivided into thirteen areas, have to pass through the Appropriations Committee. Frank Wolf (R-Va.) chaired the Transportation Subcommittee during the first six years of post-1994 Republican control. He was sensitive to the needs of the Washington metropolitan area and used his position to provide money for the D.C. subway system, a buildup at Dulles Airport, and more road building in the area. In the 105th Congress he supported legislation, as part of an appropriations bill, to protect airline employees who acted as whistle-blowers. In the 106th Congress he introduced legislation to create a commission to review the FAA, but the bill never emerged from the subcommittee. The ranking minority members for this period were Ronald Coleman (D-Tex.) in the 104th Congress and Martin Sabo (D-Minn.) for the remainder of the period.

With subcommittee chairs limited to six years, Harold Rogers (R-Ky.) replaced Wolf in 2001. Rogers reversed Wolf's general stance and, to address customer dissatisfaction with airline performance, was more aggressive toward the airlines and the FAA. He announced that consumer complaints about airline delays and flight cancellations were to be a major priority of his committee. His power superseded the Aviation Subcommittee's authority. Wielding his spending clout, he forced the airlines and the FAA to come up with solutions to passenger complaints about flight delays and cancellations.[51]

The Senate Appropriations Transportation Subcommittee

The chair of the Senate Appropriations Transportation Subcommittee in the 104th Congress was Mark Hatfield (R-Ore.), whose proposals did not affect aviation. Richard Shelby (R-Ala.) was his successor in the subsequent two Congresses. In the 106th Congress, he proposed legislation for consumer protection and enhanced competition among airlines. The ranking minority member for the six-year period was Frank Lautenberg (D-N.J.), who focused on increased funding for Amtrak, high-speed trains, and mass transit. He proposed legislation to ban smoking on domestic flights and to require foreign airlines to provide more disaster assistance to victims.[52] Like other subcommittee members, Lautenberg used appropriations legislation as a vehicle for his issues, which in the 106th Congress included protecting passengers who are bumped from flights.

Nongovernment Interests

Nongovernment interests also play an important role in postcrash investigations, public relations, and lawsuits.

The Airlines

Large domestic airlines are divided by the DOT, based on revenue, into three carrier groups: major, national, and regional. Major carriers include Alaska, America West, American, American Eagle, American Trans Air, Continental, Delta, Northwest, Southwest, United, and US Airways. Although the number of airlines in the three categories approaches 100, the large number belies the market domination by a few. In 2000 major airlines sent 75 percent of all commercial aviation flights into the air. Such domination is more noticeable in passenger load statistics: Major airlines fly larger planes than regional airlines, so nearly 90 percent of all air travelers fly on the planes of major airlines.[53]

Occasionally an airline does not perform all functions within its organization. Typically, smaller or budget airlines outsource some functions to other businesses to lower labor costs and capital expenses. Aircraft maintenance and the placement of shipments on flights, for example, might be handled on a contract basis. Outsourcing received tremendous attention after the crash of ValuJet flight 592 demonstrated shoddy practices on the part of SabreTech, which was hired by ValuJet to handle certain maintenance functions.

After a plane crash, the airline's primary goal is to protect its brand image. A former public relations staffer at United Airlines notes that concern about media coverage trumps even legal considerations: "We recognized that the court of public opinion is an immediate process, while the court of law is slower and more deliberative."[54] In her study of public relations after a plane crash, Sally Ray argues that companies must plan ahead for crises: When a plane crashes, the airline needs to determine its responses to the crash, demonstrate that it is in control of the situation, and understand the needs of the media.[55] Attempts to address the implications of the crash will be effective only if the airline's defenses are consistent with its image and if it is not abandoned by the industry.[56] ValuJet had a reputation for poor aircraft maintenance and, further, was a threat to the major airlines with its low fares. Not surprisingly, when one of its planes crashed into the Florida Everglades, an effective defense could not be mounted, and no other airline came to its aid.

Despite this, the economic evidence suggests that airlines do not suffer an appreciable or sustained loss in consumer demand after a crash.[57] The case of ValuJet is an exception, but this may be due to its lack of a track record and a larger concern about low-cost carriers.[58] However, these results do not imply that airlines overreact after a crash. It may be the extensive public relations and legal maneuverings that maintain confidence in the system after an accident.

Airplane Manufacturers

Airlines have a range of choices in airplanes, and manufacturers clearly have an incentive to build safe ones. During the early 1980s airplane construction was a booming business, involving many companies. American manufacturers such as Fairchild, Lockheed, McDonnell Douglas, and Boeing competed with a number of foreign companies for contracts. However, as a consequence of bankruptcies and buyouts, this number has narrowed substantially. When Boeing absorbed McDonnell Douglas in August 1997, it left only one domestic airplane manufacturer. Boeing's main foreign competition currently comes from Europe-based Airbus. In 1999 Boeing and Airbus built most of the planes for commercial fleets—620 and 295 aircraft, respectively.[59]

Boeing has been the largest producer of commercial jets for some time. Its main product is the 700 line: the 717, the 737, the 747, the 757, the 767, and the 777. Of all commercial designs, the 737 is the most successful. Although the original 737-100 has been phased out, other versions are being produced. More than 12,000 Boeing planes are in service worldwide, or about 75 percent of the world fleet.[60] Almost 80 percent of the U.S. fleet consists of planes built by Boeing or McDonnell Douglas.[61] Boeing is now in a fierce competition with Airbus for the domestic market; Boeing has exclusive contracts with Delta and Continental, while Airbus builds planes for United, Northwest, and America West.[62]

These manufacturers wish to protect their brand. They do not sell to the public, however—their market is the airline industry, a well-informed client that they must keep satisfied. Perhaps manufacturers stand to lose the most after a crash caused by a structural flaw in the plane. In any case, aircraft manufacturers are the parties most knowledgeable about their planes and are valuable (if biased) resources for the NTSB after a crash.

Airline Pressure Groups

The airline industry is populated by a number of trade groups. The most important is the Air Transport Association (ATA), which represents all of the major airlines. It maintains a consistent position: Discourage government regulations and encourage voluntary airline responses to most problems (the only exception being a dramatic incident in which carelessness has led to a major loss of life).

The ATA, in protecting the airlines, may also act in the interests of the flying public. For example, nominees to head the FAA or the NTSB will be criticized if they have little aviation experience. Appointees with no links to the airline industry may be more independent, but they may also want to implement costly regulations.[63] One of the ATA's favorite targets is the hopelessly outmoded air traffic control system.[64] By blaming it for problems, the ATA can deflect blame from individual airlines for flight delays and other service problems.

Air traffic controllers become involved in the investigation after a plane crash if investigators believe their instructions were faulty. Controllers work in a highly stressful job that affects the lives of thousands of people daily. Their union, the National Air Traffic Controllers Association, argues that, to do their job well, controllers need better working conditions and has called for improved equipment, more controllers, shorter hours, and better pay. Controllers strongly oppose the privatization of their jobs.[65] A shortage of qualified controllers looms in the near future, as many current controllers are at or near retirement.[66]

The Air Line Pilots Association (ALPA) is usually a party to crash investigations. Its members fly the planes of all commercial domestic airliners, so the association can provide technical assistance to the NTSB in determining the probable cause of a crash. Its motivation is to help find any cause other than pilot error. If pilots are found to be at fault, ALPA stresses mitigating factors, such as fatigue from previous flights or adverse weather.[67] Directing blame away from pilots helps to maintain the reputation of the profession. This motivation need not work at cross-purposes with the goals of the NTSB.

Crash Victims

While the airlines and related interests must accept plane crash investigations as part of their jobs, there is one group that does not willingly participate. Victims represent the system's failures. This group consists of those who are dead or injured and their friends and relatives. Few have experienced this kind of problem before in their lives. In recent years they have come to the fore, forming alliances and trying to affect public policy. They serve on commissions, testify before Congress, and speak with the media. Many become disillusioned when they realize that economics greatly influences policy responses to a crash.

A poignant example is a commission formed after the crash of TWA flight 800: A family member of one of the victims of a Pan Am flight in the 1980s was chosen to participate but became disenchanted and eventually dissented from the commission's findings. She told a television newsmagazine, "I think that a human life has no price. So I take great offense at people who try—the bean counters who try to decide what your life is worth or what my life's worth or what your child's life is worth."[68]

Such a statement reflects heartfelt emotion, to be sure, but ignores the economic realities. To put into place procedures and equipment that will save lives, a value must be placed on these lives in order to know how to allocate funds among contesting improvements.

Consumer Groups and Personal Injury Lawyers

Airline passengers are a poorly organized group. The benefits of a particular policy change are generally widely distributed, providing little incentive for a given customer to become active on an issue. One group that has overcome this problem—with selective benefits like discounted hotel rooms—is the Air Travelers Association. It lobbies on behalf of airline passengers but, overall, has little clout. Compared with the well-organized airline lobby, consumer groups tend to lose in conflicts over airline issues. In addition, consumer groups can add little to the debate after a plane crash, since they have no expertise on crashes, nor do they have a direct link to the crash (as victims do). However, the association attempts to become involved in the safety debate by releasing an Airline Safety Report Card yearly and by offering views on safety after a crash.[69]

Another passenger group consists of those who sue airline companies through personal injury lawyers. Lawyers' involvement has a private and a public face. Their private role occurs after the crash: They know how to obtain passenger lists and how to contact relatives of the victims. They send brochures to relatives, visit victims' homes, and even attend memorial services. Their public role comes later, in the form of trials or settlements.

After the Crash

While individual crash scenarios may vary by location (water, land, swamp) and by cause (ice, terrorism), a fairly standard sequence of events unfolds after every crash.

Rescue, Recovery, and Sympathy

Immediately after a crash is reported, there are expressions of grief and sympathy by major government officials and the airline (which contacts victims' families and friends and offers to bring them to the crash scene). Local police and rescue teams hunt for the bodies and ascertain if there are any survivors. And the NTSB sends its representatives to the crash site.

The NTSB has become a more prominent actor in dealing with victims. In the mid-1990s Chairman Jim Hall encouraged families to attend NTSB hearings, designating special seating for them at the front of the meeting room.[70] In the past, victims' families have complained about insensitive treatment by airline companies and government officials. The 1996 Aviation Disaster Family Assistance Act has changed that: Each airline is now required to have a plan to get information to families after a crash, including a toll-free telephone number. The airline must provide transportation, lodging, and other assistance at its own expense. The NTSB arranges counseling, plans memorial services, and assists families during the victim identification process.

The Search for the Cause

Once all "souls on board" are accounted for, the major postcrash event takes place—ascertaining cause.[71]

The NTSB's investigation begins soon after the crash. Its mission is to discover the cause of the crash, which involves recovering as much of the aircraft as possible and analyzing it at another site. In addition, finding the "black boxes" (the cockpit recording devices) is of priority, since they can provide important information, such as the pilots' words just before the crash. The NTSB also keeps the media updated on the investigation with news briefings, which can occur daily in the case of a major investigation.

The NTSB investigates about 2,000 accidents and incidents a year. Since its staff is fewer than 500, it relies on outside experts to help with the investigation. The process includes thorough investigations of the following areas: human error, fires and explosions, weather conditions, radar data, flight data recorders, and witness statements. In major investigations the NTSB establishes separate teams to take responsibility for different parts of the inquiry.[72]

The task of the NTSB has become more complex in recent years, as crashes have become more difficult to solve and as high-profile crashes garner such extensive media attention. The average investigation now takes two years, nearly twice as long as in the past. "As the airplane business has matured," says one expert, "all the kinds of accidents you can have, have occurred, and we've done the engineering fixes along the way. The accidents in the future will include ones we haven't seen or anticipated."[73]

The stakes are high for determining cause, as the official determination by the NTSB can affect lawsuits, shape public policy, and focus attention on particular areas of airline safety. Determining the cause of a crash is difficult because aircraft are so complex and because many factors may contribute to a crash. For instance, suppose an engine fails and the pilot makes an error in trying to land the plane.[74] Three options are possible for assessing cause. One attributes the crash to the first event, the engine failing. Another attributes the crash to the last point at which the crash could have been averted, the pilot's error. The third option attributes the crash to both engine failure and pilot error. All of these options are legitimate, but they are biased toward particular conclusions. In this case, the pilot is considered part of the cause in the latter two approaches but not in the first. Clearly, there is room to maneuver when assigning "probable cause" to a crash, as the NTSB is required to do by statute.

The sociologist Charles Perrow has argued that accidents are to be expected in complex systems, yet the tendency is to fix blame on operators, rather than to blame structural causes.[75] This is because the pilot is a natural focal point, even though a far more complex causal chain is likely to be involved. Perrow refers to pilot error as a "convenient catch-all."[76]

Other government officials may also weigh in as to probable cause. For example, a 2000 law gives the U.S. attorney general the authority to make the FBI the lead investigative agency.[77] Certainly if criminal activity is suspected, the FBI will enter the case. Current or former government officials with a variety of motives may also speak out on probable cause. Given their status, their views are covered by the media.

The airline and plane manufacturer involved in the crash also have a stake in the investigation of cause, being concerned with their prestige, the perception of them by the flying public, and their legal culpability. All airlines have crisis communication strategies for dealing with airline crashes and the placing of blame; these strategies focus on providing image-supporting information to the media and on avoiding responsibility for the crash.[78]

Since the official investigation into cause is lengthy and cumbersome, the media will attempt its own investigation, relying in some instances on so-called experts, brought before the cameras or interviewed by the press as to possible causes of the crash. Their remarks soon become a part of the public discussion. Reporters also may use tips from people in the transportation bureaucracy, examine the safety records of the airline in question, discover the extent to which the FAA has issued warnings to this airline, and check performance records and manufacturing problems of the type of plane involved.

Congressional Hearings

A major plane crash offers an opportunity for elected officials to put forth pet proposals regarding airline safety. The type of crash that will occupy their attention will have some unusual element or involve prior egregious behavior by the airline or aviation bureaucrats. Congressional hearings involving a high-visibility crash normally occur several months after the crash but usually before the NTSB hearings. Even if nothing substantive comes out of these inquiries, they may still serve the purpose of deflecting criticism away from Congress.

Legislators often make statements on the House or Senate floor expressing regret or calling for explanations. After the crash of USAir flight 427, Larry Pressler rose on the Senate floor to call for hearings on airline safety. "We should focus on this serious matter and work with our safety agencies to prevent future tragedies," he said. "In my view, we need congressional oversight to be sure that our congressional committees are doing what we are supposed to be doing to promote air safety in this country and protect the safety of the air traveling public."[79] After the crash of TWA flight 800, the Senate passed a resolution expressing condolences to the victims and the hope that a cause would soon be determined.[80]

Symbolic actions like hearings therefore serve at least two purposes: They provide publicity for legislators, and they show that Congress is not ignoring the problem. Given the intense media attention to plane crashes, legislators must create the appearance of action. In some cases, legislation emerges out of crash hearings, so they are not always political theater. Legislators respond to their political environment, and their actions after a crash reflect the tensions they face between the necessity to respond to a crash and the maintenance of a hands-off stance with respect to the airlines. In the final section of this chapter, we delve further into the politics of airline safety.

The NTSB Hearing and Final Report

The NTSB conducts a public hearing after every major commercial plane crash. Normally this takes place within a year of the mishap, although some hearings have been delayed longer than that. The hearing lasts from one day to one week and usually serves three purposes: as a debate on possible causes, as a discussion of broader safety issues, and as a forum for public enlightenment. By the time of the hearing the NTSB has gathered all available information and has made some tentative decisions as to cause.

Representatives from the FAA, the airline, the aircraft manufacturer, and subsidiary operators such as maintenance outsourcers testify. This testimony becomes part of the public record as a basis for the final report, which is issued after the hearing. On rare occasions, a second hearing is convened if additional information is found.

After the hearing is completed, the NTSB staff issues its final report and specifies "the probable cause." This report is discussed at a public meeting in Washington and includes recommendations for changes to avoid such incidents. Often plane crashes are caused by correctable conditions, like flying in adverse weather, equipment malfunction or error, and flaws in the structural design of the plane. Corrective actions may be voluntary or involuntary and can emanate from airlines, airplane manufacturers, FAA regulation and supervision, Congress, or the president.

Legal Action

The last step in the postcrash process is the resolution of legal issues. This involves financial settlements with the families of those who were killed. Victims' families can accept the financial compensation offered by the party responsible for the crash, or they can sue in court.[81] Usually these suits await official assignment of blame. If airline policies are determined to have led to the crash, then the airline is responsible for compensating the families. If the cause is less clear and fractions of guilt are assigned, the resolution process is complicated. Further, NTSB definitions of *cause* may sometimes be at variance with legal definitions. Causality can have many different meanings in legal language.

Lawsuits are normally filed in the federal court district in which the crash occurred or at the home base of the aircraft manufacturer or airline. Most lawsuits end up in federal court because the victims and the defendants come from different states, each with its own procedural rules. The assumption is that the federal arena is the least biased. However, if the plaintiff files in the jurisdiction where the defendant is located, the courts let the case remain in that jurisdiction. Locations vary in their hospitality to such cases. Few lawsuits have been submitted in Washington State, until recently the home of Boeing, as its laws favor the industry.[82]

The Politics of Airline Safety

Why is airline safety such a contentious issue, and why do airline crashes produce so much disagreement as to potential regulatory responses? After all, politicians, bureaucrats, airlines, and passengers all want safe planes. Their definitions of *safe,* however, differ, and beliefs about which organizations or agencies are responsible for safety also differ. Battles over airline safety fall along these two dimensions and often lead to a lack of consensus on the proper course of action. The interest most involved in shaping the debate is the airline industry, which has no well-organized opponents. Support for regulations that emerge after a crash has to come from the NTSB or members of Congress. The airline industry is therefore advantaged in public policy battles over airline safety. Since the airlines have an incentive to maintain safe skies, this is not necessarily a negative component of the policy process. But it is the political reality.

The political scientists Frank Baumgartner and Bryan Jones find that relationships between business and industry varied over the course of the twentieth century. Several decades ago configurations called subgovernments, iron triangles, and policy monopolies predominated. Private businesses and government officials cooperated to provide an environment of business promotion, minimal regulation, government subsidies, and high reelection rates for oversight legislators. Small sectors of the population benefited (for example, farmers, physicians, military contractors) through generous government subsidies and a minimum of government attention. Only when a scandal arose, media attention increased, or an adversarial group challenged the relationship did it alter its structure.[83]

In the world of aviation, a similar subgovernment relationship exists and is threatened each time a plane crashes. In response, legislators may be compelled to take action, potentially leading to a complete unraveling of the relationship. By and large, this has not occurred. Why is this the case?

It is too simplistic to assume that capture theory is the only element present. Certainly the relationship between the FAA and the airlines has been close, with minimal regulatory oversight, and the FAA can ignore NTSB safety recommendations or phase them in slowly. But there are additional elements that capture theory ignores, including public preferences. More people are flying than ever before, and their preferences are clear: They want service to as many locales as possible at a minimum of cost and with minimal or nonexistent delays. Weather problems, hub-based flight patterns, and a complex network of flight interaction means that one small interruption can cause systemwide dislocation. Most changes in safety and security will add to either the cost of flying or delays in boarding. Such developments fuel passenger concern, media coverage, and legislative grumbling. Since plane crashes are rare but routine parts of air travel, additional regulations that may prevent one statistical crash may not be worth the political or economic fallout.

Partisan considerations also come into play. The House of Representatives and the Senate have been under Republican control for much of the period since 1994, and one of the principal partisan objectives has been to reduce regulatory burdens on business. Voluntary compliance, not regulation, has been the order of the day. Such a hands-off view benefits the airlines and certainly does not encourage the FAA to take a more critical view of airline practices.

In addition, safety statistics favor keeping regulations to a minimum. Airline travel is the safest of all forms of transportation, a fact that airlines, aviation officials, and legislators serving on oversight committees trumpet endlessly. Even when accidents occur, the safety statistics are continually repeated and reported by the media. The NTSB attempts to point out specific problems, but the overall picture portrays a system that is fundamentally safe.

Thus subgovernments can be maintained even when industrywide problems need to be addressed; as long as the objective indicators are favorable and public preferences are satisfied, such a relationship is difficult to disrupt. A subgovernment relationship can exist only if the industry can keep the preferences of others from becoming major factors in the calculus of decisionmakers. Keeping planes relatively safe is one way to accomplish this.

As we see in the next chapter, plane crashes focus attention on particular areas of airline safety. These are not necessarily the areas that need the most regulatory scrutiny, but for the reasons described in this chapter and the next, it is not surprising that crashes receive the attention they do.

CHAPTER 3

Death in the Skies
in the 1990s

In this chapter we present a perspective that links airline crashes, media coverage, and policymaking. Several questions merit analysis. What issues besides safety captured press attention in the late 1990s? What did crash coverage look like in the 1990s? How many commercial airliners had accidents that resulted in passenger deaths? How safe is air travel? Based on the answers to these questions, our view is that crashes can be triggers for changes in airline safety. Although crashes are neither necessary nor sufficient for changes in public policy, they focus attention on particular areas of safety, forcing the Federal Aviation Administration (FAA) to address them. Thus the FAA is more than just a "tombstone agency," responding only to death and destruction.

The Media and Government Attention to Airline Problems

The airline industry receives extensive press coverage. Three issues that have captured attention in recent years have been overcrowded skies, customer service, and air rage. While these are distinct policy areas, all are tied to the growth of air travel. As travel expanded through the 1990s, infrastructure development lagged. This led to increases in delays and misdirected baggage as well as other flaws in the system. Each of these problems is tailor-made for extensive media coverage and government attention.

Overcrowded skies are blamed for runway incursions (that is, near misses) and overtaxed air traffic controllers. Congestion is also used as justification for adding runways to major airports and overhauling the nation's antiquated air traffic control system. The FAA is often targeted for failing to implement a new air traffic control system to better manage the skies and allow for a smoother flow of traffic given the current infrastructure. New runways seem like an obvious solution, but invariably there is hostility to such projects, with environmentalists and local citizens objecting to the increased noise and traffic. Runway incursions draw attention to this problem. The media report on near misses because they are stories of death narrowly averted. Also, runway incursions are on the National Transportation Safety Board's (NTSB's) list of most-wanted safety improvements.

A related problem is customer service. Perceptions of poor service are widespread. The event widely attributed with triggering interest in this issue was the decision of Northwest Airlines in January 1999 to leave passengers aboard stranded planes on the runway at Detroit Metro Wayne County Airport. For up to eleven hours during a winter storm passengers had no food, no drinkable water, and no operating toilets. As compensation, Northwest offered the passengers free tickets for future travel. The airline mishandled the situation; its defense focused on the weather and on airport management. The airport in turn blamed Northwest. The airline was promptly sued in a class action lawsuit and eventually (in January 2001) paid $7.1 million to 7,000 passengers.[1]

In February 1999 Senator John McCain (R-Ariz.) cosponsored the Airline Passenger Fairness Act. It called for better service and more passenger rights. The airlines countered with a lobbying blitz. The end result was voluntary guidelines. The reform group Common Cause attributes the airlines' success to their large soft money contributions in that year, while McCain claimed that he had always offered to scale back the bill if the airlines promised voluntary action.[2] The pattern of threatened legislation to produce symbolic voluntary compliance is a familiar one in the airline industry.

Perhaps because of the first two issues, the problem of air rage became an issue of interest. As noted in the previous chapter, air rage jumped from a nonissue to a popular topic with the media, the public, and Congress. In the 2000 FAA reauthorization, Congress raised the top fine for unruly behavior from $1,100 to $25,000 and increased the maximum jail time to twenty-five years. Statistics on air rage are imprecise, at best, ranging from hundreds to thousands of yearly incidents. Senator Dianne Feinstein (D-Calif.), in an attempt to address the issue, has called for a two-drink limit on all flights. While asking for voluntary action, she threatened the introduction of new legislation. In a letter to the chief executive officers, she wrote,

> In view of the 5,000 "air rage" incidents each year, I believe it is time for the airline industry to set standards voluntarily, or else Congress may well step in. To that end, I am in the process of writing legislation that would limit each passenger to two drinks on domestic flights, regardless of the type of alcoholic beverage served. I hope that introducing this legislation will not be necessary and you will be willing to voluntarily set limits on how many drinks a passenger can consume. Absent that, I am prepared to proceed with the legislation.[3]

This is an example of symbolic politics, as many believe that such a limit would not help matters. In fact, the Association of Flight Attendants, the largest flight attendant's union, is against such limits. This proposal provided Feinstein with press attention, was relatively costless, and demonstrated her concern with the problem. In a similarly symbolic move, the FAA in 2001 produced a pamphlet titled "Safety Is Everyone's Responsibility." Before September 11 air rage was not viewed as a security risk, but the issue has since been redefined.

Perception and Risk: Plane Crashes in the 1990s

While an incident of air rage or a near miss on the runway may receive a day of coverage, airplane crashes receive weeks, months, or even years of attention. In its report on the NTSB, RAND notes that the crashes of TWA flight 800 and ValuJet flight 592 tested the public's faith in the air travel system because they occurred within a short time span.[4] Except for temporal proximity, the two crashes had no relationship. There was no rational reason to believe that air travel was less safe in some systemic way after the crashes than before. But the airline industry is similar to the banking industry in that perception matters; a bank that is perceived to be insolvent may collapse if a rush for withdrawals occurs. Similarly, even if air travel is safe, a perception that planes are falling out of the sky could cause damage to the industry.

Social psychologists have studied risk perception and found that people overestimate the deaths caused by rare events.[5] When such events occur, they stand out precisely because they are uncommon. Infrequent large

Table 3-1   *Risk of Death in a Plane Crash, 1990–99*

Year	Q-value
1990	1 in 41.9 million
1991	1 in 6.0 million
1992	1 in 14.1 million
1993	0
1994	1 in 3.0 million
1995	1 in 8.3 million
1996	1 in 3.9 million
1997	1 in 1.0 billion
1998	0
1999	1 in 150.0 million
Average	1 in 11.1 million

Source: Authors' calculations based on NTSB data for passengers traveling on a scheduled domestic part 121 carrier (major domestic commercial carriers are sometimes referred to as part 121 carriers, for the part of the Code of Federal Regulations that governs them).

losses of life are viewed as more severe than frequent small losses, in part due to the catastrophic nature of events leading to many deaths.[6] But risk perception reveals only part of the story. While airline crashes may stand out because they are rare events, the public clearly believes that the benefits of airline travel outweigh the risks. The Bureau of Transportation Statistics reports that from 1990 to 1999 the number of revenue passengers increased from 438,544,001 to 610,628,716, a jump of nearly 40 percent.[7] The FAA anticipates that more than one billion passengers will travel on commercial airliners by 2013.[8] Clearly, Americans continued to fly, despite grumbling about poor service and delays. Even after the 2001 terrorist attacks, Americans returned to the skies.

Is air travel any less safe today than at the beginning of the 1990s? To address that question, a measure of "safety" is required. There are many measures, including deaths per miles traveled, crashes per number of takeoffs, deaths per year, and so forth. We prefer a measure called a Q-value, first proposed in 1979.[9] This measure is the probability of dying on any given flight regardless of length. Since most crashes occur at takeoff and landing, miles traveled do not seem as relevant.[10] The Q-value for major domestic commercial carriers from 1990 to 1999 is presented in table 3-1.[11]

As shown, the probability of dying on a randomly selected flight is virtually zero. Even in 1996, when concerns about air safety reached fever pitch, the chance of perishing on a major domestic carrier was 1 in

3.9 million! Because these measures are so sensitive to even a single crash, the Q-value was calculated for the entire period, 1990 through 1999. The probability of dying in a crash in those years was 1 in 11.1 million. Put differently, a traveler could take a flight each day for more than 30,000 years before expecting to perish in a plane crash. These numbers are meant to demonstrate that air travel is extremely safe and that crashes have now become essentially random events that are unlikely to be eliminated. It is difficult to ascertain whether this pattern is due to safety regulation or in spite of it. Regardless, these figures should give proponents of increased regulation pause; the marginal cost of making air travel any safer is likely to be extremely high.

One reason that air travel is so safe relates to the redundancy and complexity of modern aircraft. For a crash to occur, a series of unfortunate occurrences need to occur simultaneously. The psychologist James Reason developed an apt metaphor: a pile of Swiss cheese slices.[12] Each slice has a solid part, which represents safety systems and security. The holes reflect problems that can exist with respect to a specific factor. A pile of these slices represents a flight. During the flight the holes move around depending on conditions and operator performance. Only when the holes in all slices line up is there a problem. In the case of aviation, there are numerous slices with few holes. As Reason told one reporter, "A modern aircraft system has so many layers of defenses that it is extremely difficult to have a bad disaster."[13]

Of course, positive probabilities of dying imply that planes do crash occasionally. Table 3-2 lists all crashes of commercial airliners between 1990 and 1999 resulting in deaths. The airliners fall into in one of three categories: major commercial domestic airliners, commuter airliners before March 20, 1997 (now classified as major domestic carriers), and foreign airliners either departing from or scheduled to land in the United States. These figures include accidents occurring on the ground as well the air, so a runway collision is considered a crash. Table 3-3 lists the number of crashes and deaths each year, 1990 through 1999. Human error contributed to over half of the crashes in the 1990s. Investigation costs vary widely, as depicted in table 3-4, ranging from tens of thousands to tens of millions of dollars. Factors affecting the cost of an inquiry include where the plane crashes—water or land—and how much testing needs to be done to determine the cause.[14]

The amount of media coverage a crash received varied (see table 3-2 for *New York Times* coverage from 1990 through 2000). Figure 3-1 pre-

Table 3-2 Plane Crashes and New York Times Coverage, 1990–99

Date	Location	Airline	Deaths	Survivors	NYT stories
1/25/90	Cove Neck, N.Y.	Avianca	65	84	49
12/3/90	Romulus, Mich.	Northwest Airlines	7	33	10
2/1/91	Los Angeles, Calif.	USAir	20	63	20
3/3/91	Los Angeles, Calif.	Skywest Airlines	10	0	20
4/5/91	Colorado Springs, Co.	United Airlines	20	0	10
7/10/91	Brunswick, Ga.	Atlantic Southeast Airlines	20	0	12
9/11/91	Birmingham, Ala.	L'Express Airlines	12	1	2
1/3/92	Eagle Lake, Texas	Continental Express	11	0	5
3/22/92	Gabriels, N.Y.	CommutAir (USAir Express)	1	1	0
6/8/92	Flushing, N.Y.	USAir	25	22	38
12/1/93	Anniston, Ala.	GP Express Airlines	2	2	0
1/7/94	Hibbing, Minn.	Express Airlines II	16	0	4
7/2/94	Columbus, Ohio	Atlantic Coast Airlines (United Express)	2	3	1
9/8/94	Charlotte, N.C.	USAir	37	20	13
10/31/94	Aliquippa, Pa.	USAir	127	0	53
12/13/94	Roselawn, Ind.	American Eagle	64	0	26
8/21/95	Morrisville, N.C.	Flagship Airlines (American Eagle)	15	5	8
12/20/95	Carrollton, Ga.	Atlantic Southeast Airlines (Delta)	7	19	4
5/11/96	Cali, Colombia	American Airlines	152	4	25
7/6/96	Miami, Fla.	ValuJet Airlines	105	0	107
7/17/96	Pensacola, Fla.	Delta Airlines	2	140	4
11/19/96	Moriches, N.Y.	Trans World Airlines	212	0	397
1/9/97	Quincy, Ill.	Great Lakes Aviation (United Express)	10	0	2
8/6/97	Ida, Mich.	Comair	26	0	11
9/2/98	Nimitz Hill, Guam	Korean Air	214	23	20
6/1/99	Nova Scotia	Swissair	215	0	40
10/31/99	Little Rock, Ark.	American Airlines	10	129	11
	Nantucket, Mass.	EgyptAir	203	0	64

a. The appendix to this volume presents probable causes of these crashes and the policy changes that followed them. Deaths and survivors are for passengers, not crew.

Table 3-3   *Plane Crashes and Passenger Deaths a Year, 1990–99*

Year	Crashes	Deaths
1990	2	72
1991	6	93
1992	3	28
1993	1	16
1994	5	245
1995	2	159
1996	4	329
1997	2	240
1998	1	215
1999	2	213
Total	28	1,610

Source: Authors' calculations using NTSB data (includes all crashes involving U.S. airlines or foreign carriers on U.S. soil).

sents coverage for the decade by the *Washington Post* along with deaths from airline crashes. The figure demonstrates that media interest is related to, but not dictated by, number of deaths. With the exception of 1993 and 1996, coverage falls within a fairly narrow band. In 1993 no crashes occurred until December, and 1996 saw two major crashes, TWA and ValuJet. This accounts for those two outliers.

Given the low probabilities of a person perishing in a crash, it is not surprising that the studies cited in chapter 1 find that the media coverage of air safety is disproportionate to the risk involved. One defense of the media is that airline safety is intrinsically newsworthy. Every year the FAA issues hundreds of rules, many related to this topic, including technical airworthiness directives that order airlines to fix potentially dangerous defects in planes.[15] Few are sweeping, affecting the entire industry, though there are exceptions. For instance, following several accidents in which airplanes crashed due to ice on the wings, the FAA instituted new rules regarding the deicing process. These modifications are rare, often because industrywide changes impose huge costs that may not be justified by the potential lives saved.[16]

Linking policymaking and airline crashes directly is often not possible. Even the FAA does not keep records of whether a rule was influenced by an airplane crash. The only direct link between a crash and FAA rule making comes from NTSB recommendations stemming from the event.[17] The FAA and NTSB maintain a dialogue on all recommendations; the latter usually classifies them as *open acceptable response, open unacceptable response, closed acceptable response,* or *closed unacceptable response.*

Table 3-4 *NTSB Investigation Costs, Selected Air Crashes, 1994-99*

Date	Location	Airline	Cost ($000ᵃ)
7/2/94	Charlotte, N.C.	USAir	22
9/8/94	Aliquippa, Pa.	USAir	637
10/31/94	Roselawn, Ind.	American Eagle	92
12/13/94	Morrisville, N.C.	Flagship Airlines (American Eagle)	27
8/21/95	Carrollton, Ga.	Atlantic Southeast Airlines (Delta)	25
5/11/96	Miami, Fla.	ValuJet Airlines	2,500
7/6/96	Pensacola, Fla.	Delta Airlines	63
7/17/96	Moriches, N.Y.	Trans World Airlines	> 30,000
1/9/97	Ida, Mich.	Comair	228
8/6/97	Nimitz Hill, Guam	Korean Air	402
6/1/99	Little Rock, Ark.	American Airlines	94
10/31/99	Nantucket, Mass.	EgyptAir	217

Source: NTSB; for TWA 800, estimate is based on published reports and does not include FBI investigation costs.

a. Cost includes direct costs, such as travel and per diem, as well as contractual and nonpay expenses to NTSB only; excludes costs incurred by other federal agencies (not reimbursed by the NTSB, and NTSB employee pay (including overtime) and benefits.

Open and *closed* refer to whether or not the FAA continues to act on the suggestion, and *acceptable* and *unacceptable* refer to the NTSB's view of FAA's action. In keeping with historic trends, the FAA responds acceptably to 79 percent of NTSB recommendations.[18] Also, of the 304 in the data set, about one-third are classified as *open* (see table 3-5).

A report by the General Accounting Office (GAO) shows that the FAA generally accepts NTSB recommendations but that it takes too long to address and implement them.[19] The study finds that the FAA did not act on several recommendations that the NTSB considered closed due to acceptable agency action:

> To improve safety on airport runways, NTSB has made several recommendations to FAA over the years. . . . Of the seven recommendations by NTSB on runway safety that GAO examined, five are listed as having been implemented by FAA in both NTSB's and FAA's tracking systems. However, GAO found that in four of the five cases, the actions necessary to address the problems that gave rise to the recommendations had not been completed by all of the affected airports. For example, in 1991 NTSB recommended that FAA improve its standards for airport marking and lighting when visibility is low;

Figure 3-1   *Deaths in Plane Crashes and* Washington Post *Coverage,
1990–99*

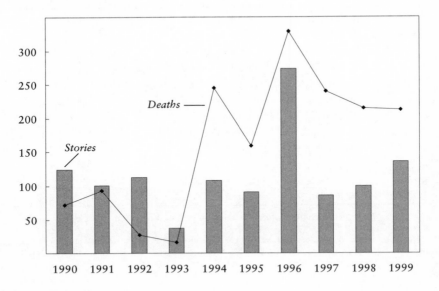

Source: Authors' calculations based on *Washington Post Index*, subject heading "Aircraft Accidents and Safety," various years.

in 1993, NTSB classified the recommendation as "closed" because of an "acceptable action" when FAA issued new standards and guidance that called for airports to develop plans for operating in low visibility by January 1995. However, GAO found that as of July 1996, only 19 of 77 airports that need such plans under these standards had plans that had been approved by FAA, while 23 others had not even formed a working group to develop such a plan.[20]

This trend of dilatory FAA action shows no signs of change. For instance, debate still continues regarding one of the NTSB's most wanted safety improvements: the inerting of fuel to prevent fuel tank explosions like the one that brought down TWA flight 800. Inerting was first suggested in 1974 by FAA employee Tom Horeff.[21] There may be reasons why inerting is not feasible—for instance, it is very expensive—but the FAA delayed a decision by requesting further study.[22]

Table 3-5   *Status of NTSB Recommendations to the FAA*[a]

Status	Acceptable	Unacceptable
Closed	164	40
Open	77	23
Total	241	63

Source: Authors' calculations, based on FAA safety recommendations database, September 2001.
a. The NTSB denotes recommendations *reconsidered* if it decides it will go no further with the recommendations. These are omitted from our data. Additionally, if a recommendation relates to more than one crash, we tabulated it for each crash.

Other examples are worth noting. In June 1999, after American Airlines flight 1420 crashed in part due to pilot fatigue, the FAA promised to vigorously enforce pilot rest rules.[23] Yet a notice of enforcement action was not issued until May 14, 2001, and not implemented until 2002.[24] The FAA took two years to issue a notice to begin enforcing rules that already exist. Another example is the debate over child safety seats. Currently, children under two years old can fly for free if held by an adult. Flight attendants, the NTSB, and others believe that this puts babies at risk. After any crash in which a young child dies, attention is placed on this issue. The former NTSB chairman Jim Hall notes, "I've often said that it doesn't make any sense to me that during take-off, landing, and turbulence, adults are buckled up, baggage and coffee pots are stowed, computers are turned off and put away, but the most precious cargo on that aircraft—infants and toddlers—are left unrestrained."[25] On December 15, 1999, the FAA announced its intention to issue a notice of proposed rule making, news that received coverage in the *New York Times, USA Today,* and other papers.[26] Yet a notice of proposed rule making was not issued until December 2001.[27] These two examples suggest that the FAA can say one thing, do another, and receive credit in the press for taking action.

The FAA's difficulty in implementing or rejecting policy changes in a timely fashion may be related to the fierce battles that occur over safety regulations. Pressure from the airlines, the NTSB, members of Congress, and other interests, combined with the technical nature and uncertain science behind many recommendations, may cause delays in the policy process. Also, the FAA must work with a decentralized group of airports, airlines, and personnel in order to implement any recommendations. This is a possible explanation for why the GAO report indicates that the FAA often receives credit for implementing a recommendation when it is still a work in progress. As long as regulations have financial consequences, there will be battles over them, and the issue becomes how best to manage those conflicts.

When the FAA makes a policy change, it is often difficult to link it to a particular crash. In our search through newspaper databases, NTSB records, and congressional records, it is clear that public policy is affected by plane crashes (see appendix for a list of crashes, probable causes, and resulting policy changes). During the 1990s standards for commuter aircraft were tightened, exit rows were widened, new ground proximity warning systems were implemented, and airport security was tightened. On the other hand, crashes are by no means a guarantee of changes in air safety regulations, nor are all changes linked to a particular crash.

Airline Crashes and Public Policy

As discussed in the last chapter, many interests respond to plane crashes, but only government officials make air safety policy. Specifically, Congress through legislation, the president through executive orders, and the FAA through rule making are authorized to enact new policies. Only the FAA engages in such activity on a regular basis; Congress and the president tend to act only when high-profile safety matters emerge from a plane crash.

The responses of government actors to plane crashes vary according to their area of responsibility. Since bureaucrats are not elected and are more insulated than elected officials from public pressure, they make the difficult decisions. For instance, as a consequence of TWA flight 800, the NTSB recommended major changes in fuel tank wiring (the FAA and the airlines balked due to the cost and also to the uncertainty that such changes would fix the problem). Congress could enact a standard tomorrow, but the controversy precludes that.

Congress (and the president) have the ultimate authority and can overrule agency decisions or nondecisions, but if Congress ignores an issue, the media will focus on the FAA as the legitimate decisionmaker. Because legislators avoid unnecessary conflict and airline safety is a complex area, safety legislation is brought to the floor of Congress only when conflict is minimal. Decisions on airline safety made by Congress will be consensual, and contentious choices will be left to the FAA's rule-making process. As a consequence, Congress will rarely be blamed for failing to enact safety legislation; the FAA will be targeted because inevitably it will reject some NTSB-proposed rules. This is one explanation for the FAA's poor public position. Left to draft regulations on controversial issues, it takes the blame for any failures.

There are two opposing views on this state of affairs: Delegating these decisions to the FAA is efficient, since it can gather information at a lower cost than Congress and can devote a significant portion of time to air safety policy. But this implies that decisions regarding the safety of airlines are being made by unelected bureaucrats who are alleged to be agents of the industry. On major proposals, FAA rule making takes into account the preferences of Congress. Congress has only a limited amount of space on its agenda, so tackling specific regulatory matters is usually not feasible. But if the FAA blocks a popular policy (or enacts an egregious rule) the legislature is likely to act. Knowing this, the FAA usually will not block a rule that commands support on Capitol Hill.

The main way that airline crashes affect public policy is in focusing attention on particular areas of aviation safety, thereby crowding out competing issues. Plane crashes demand a response. A crash caused by x, however, does not mean that x is an imminent threat for future occurrences. Meanwhile, there could be a latent cause y that has not produced any problems but has the potential to do so with far greater damage. To the extent that a focus on cause x crowds out alternative y, airline safety is paradoxically harmed by reflexively addressing the cause of every plane crash. This outcome is magnified by the tendency of recent crashes to be somewhat random and unconnected to a coherent policy area. That said, airline crashes might also have positive policy effects by focusing attention on issues that may otherwise be ignored. For instance, the crash of American Airlines flight 1420 spotlighted pilot fatigue, an issue that had until then received little attention. The key is to differentiate crashes that provide information about systemic problems from those that are caused by idiosyncratic features.

The media affect this process by giving differential attention to crashes. Factors such as the number of deaths affect both policymakers and the media, but the media's role in this process cannot be ignored. For instance, after the fall of ValuJet flight 592, the FAA tried to reassure the public that low-cost airlines were safe and that no action was necessary. Extensive media coverage and investigations overshadowed the FAA's assurances and led to a 180-degree reversal and the grounding of the airline.[28] Since the media focus on events that provide the most compelling drama, attention may lead policymakers to spend time on issues that may not prevent future mishaps.

The mass media are often referred to as the fourth branch of government, as policymakers in Washington factor press attention into the decisionmaking process.[29] The media can focus attention on policy areas that may not be on the government agenda. Media coverage may prompt Congress and the president to propose their own investigations or commissions. These symbolic actions are relatively costless, give the impression of action, and rarely produce change. At best, they may pressure the FAA to act. By the time the investigation or commission completes its work, other issues occupy media attention.

In sum, airline crashes, by forcing policymakers to address their suspected or actual causes, may divert attention from areas of aviation safety that are potentially more important. Media emphasis on crashes, especially dramatic ones, reinforces this tendency. No direct test is possible, but economic reasoning lends support to the idea: Given a fixed regulatory budget and time, attention to particular issues is a zero-sum game. That is, a day or a dollar devoted to a crash is a day or a dollar not devoted to another area of safety. Hypotheses based on this perspective are examined in the next two sections using all crashes in the 1990s.[30]

Hypotheses and Evidence: The Mass Media

The mass media bring certain issues to the agenda by placing them in the spotlight. To the extent that this is true, crash coverage affects government action. The determinants of attention are important. Five hypotheses are discussed, with tests conducted for three.

—The greater the number of deaths, the greater the amount of media coverage. The media thrive on death and destruction. The more passengers that die in a crash, the better the story is for the press. A crash that kills a hundred people may have greater policy implications than one killing two hundred but is likely to generate less coverage. Journalism requires drama, with crashes often framed in terms of the number of people killed.[31] More deaths imply greater drama and media attention.

—The greater the proximity to a major metropolitan area, the greater the amount of media coverage. A crash that is nearer to a major metropolitan area generates more coverage because of greater resource availability, ease of access to the site, and more intrinsic interest to the press. As Conrad Smith shows in a study of disaster news, the media focused disproportionately on San Francisco in its coverage of the Loma Prieta earthquake in 1989 despite the fact that outlying areas suffered greater damage.[32]

—The greater the causal uncertainty regarding a crash, the greater the amount of coverage. Causal uncertainty keeps the media interested because it allows for continued reporting on the crash. A mystery makes a much better story than a crash whose cause is clear-cut, all things being equal.

—A crash in which terrorism or sabotage is suspected will receive more coverage than other crashes. According to an analysis by Todd Curtis, the founder of airsafe.com, the news media give greater coverage to airline crashes dealing with terrorism, hijacking, or military action.[33]

—The presence of political entrepreneurs increases the amount of crash coverage. They have an incentive to keep a crash alive in the press. Since they usually feel passionate about their cause, their activities will likely generate increased coverage.

To test the first three hypotheses, a Poisson regression was used to see whether a change in one variable affected the amount of crash coverage, leaving all other variables unchanged. The dependent variable is media coverage, measured as the number of stories on the crash appearing in the *New York Times*. There are three independent variables of interest: the number of deaths, the proximity to a major metropolitan area, and causal uncertainty. The number of deaths is simply the number of passengers who died as a direct result of the crash. Proximity to a major metropolitan area is coded as 1 if the crash occurred near a major city and 0 otherwise. Causal uncertainty is measured as the number of years between when a crash occurred and an investigatory body (usually the NTSB) issued a final report on the crash.

The results are presented in table 3-6. We conducted two tests, one omitting the crash of TWA flight 800, an outlier in terms of the amount of coverage. The first two hypotheses are strongly supported in at least one of the tests, while the third receives limited support.[34] Note that the three factors that affect coverage are not related to the usefulness of a crash in making air travel safer. For instance, a crash at La Guardia airport in New York City and one in a remote wooded area should affect public policy differently by virtue of their causes, not their locations. To the extent that media coverage influences the amount of attention policymakers give to crashes, limited regulatory resources may be diverted from other uses.

Table 3-6   *Test of Media Hypotheses*[a]

Independent variable	Test 1, all crashes[b]	Test 2, TWA omitted[c]
Number of deaths	.00963*	.00740*
	(.00210)	(.0019)
Proximity to metropolitan area	1.140**	.634
	(.466)	(.409)
Causal uncertainty	.142	.004
	(.093)	(.080)
Constant	1.837*	2.355*
	(.416)	(.345)

* $p < .001$.
** $p < .05$.

a. Dependent variable is number of *New York Times* stories on the crash; Poisson regression calculated in Stata 7.0; robust standard errors in parentheses. One crash—Swissair—did not have a final report as of May 1, 2002, and is left out of the analysis. Adding it in does not change the first test significantly. Adding it into the second test makes proximity to metropolitan area statistically significant. Another crash, the January 3, 1992, CommutAir crash, was not considered a major accident, and is left out of the analysis completely, because an *Aircraft Accident Report* was not issued for the crash.

b. $N = 26$; pseudo-$R^2 = .70$.

c. $N = 25$; pseudo-$R^2 = .37$.

Hypotheses and Evidence: Policymaking

Two counterintuitive hypotheses link airplane crashes and public policy. The first is not formally tested, but qualitative evidence lends support. A statistical test is used for the second.

Hypothesis One

We posit that government policymakers do not necessarily respond to the causes of plane crashes. Officials may use plane crashes to publicize issues not related to the cause of the accident. Their attempts may be more successful if they can link the crash to a particular area of safety. Qualitative evidence supports hypothesis one.[35]

First, the FAA imposed stricter policies on terrorism after the crash of TWA flight 800. Policymakers acted because terrorism was initially suspected in that crash and other terror incidents had immediately preceded the crash. Image trumped reality: The new regulations were mostly cosmetic and did not make the skies safer. In fact in 1999 undercover FAA inspectors were able to sneak onto aircraft through security doors with relative ease.[36]

Second, the FAA's mandate was changed by Congress after the crash of ValuJet flight 592. The FAA would no longer have a dual mandate to focus on promotion of the industry as well as safety; now, regulation was its primary mission. However, it is extremely unlikely that a different decision would have been made on grounding ValuJet even if this mandate were in effect before the crash. But the crash provided an opportunity for members of Congress to claim that action was being taken to redirect the FAA's emphasis.

Third, the FAA paid closer attention to foreign carriers after the crash of Avianca flight 52 in 1990. The Avianca flight failed when the plane ran out of fuel; language problems and lack of familiarity with American emergency procedures were blamed for the crash (there were never accusations that Avianca was an unsafe airline). In response the FAA began its international aviation safety assessment program for evaluating foreign carriers.[37] After its investigation of a subsequent Korean Air crash, the NTSB stated that the program was inadequate to determine whether foreign carriers operating in the United States were safe.[38] This is an example, then, of a crash producing an ineffective policy only tangentially dealing with the cause of the crash.

Fourth, after several small planes crashed in the 1990s, the FAA enacted tighter rules for aircraft flying under commuter rules known as part 135 regulations. But at least one of the crashes that prompted the action already fell under the tighter rules for major domestic carriers.[39] An American Eagle crash was an impetus for those tightened rules, even though they had no bearing on that particular flight.

Hypothesis Two

We posit that the FAA does not respond more favorably to NTSB recommendations after high-profile crashes than those made after low-profile crashes, a hypothesis consistent with our perspective. High-profile crashes (measured by number of news stories) certainly generate a lot of attention from policymakers but do not always translate into more action. The acceptance rate of NTSB recommendations after crashes is remarkably high, so a high-profile incident is unlikely to produce more changes. This hypothesis makes no claims about two separate points. First, high-profile crashes may lead to more attention by the FAA but not to more action. Second, the

Table 3-7   *Test of Policy Hypothesis*

Independent variable[a]	Coefficient (standard error)[b]
Number of *NYT* stories	−.0000424
	(.000951)
Constant	.818*
	(.093)

* p < .001.

a. Dependent variable is one if an FAA response is acceptable and zero otherwise; results are from a grouped probit with robust standard errors, which was run in Stata 7.0 with the bprobit command.

b. $N = 304$; pseudo-$R^2 = 0$.

scope of policy changes may be larger after high-profile crashes. These ideas are hard to quantify and test but are supported by our earlier argument.

To evaluate this hypothesis, a probit procedure for grouped data tests whether high-profile crashes led to a higher percentage of NTSB recommendations being accepted than low-profile mishaps.[40] Since there is a lag between a crash occurrence and FAA action on NTSB recommendations, both open and closed recommendations were considered. If the NTSB decided that FAA action was acceptable, whether open or closed, we considered that an indication of responsiveness. The results are presented in table 3-7. Since the coefficient for stories is not statistically different from zero, we fail to show that high-profile crashes are systematically treated different from others. This result has two implications. First, the FAA is not more responsive to high-profile crashes than to others, at least in terms of the rate at which it accepts NTSB recommendations.[41] Second, to the extent that policymakers focus on, but do not act on, high-profile crashes, other areas of airline safety are neglected.

Conclusion

In this chapter, we present data on airline safety from the 1990s, a view of how crashes affect policy, and tests of hypotheses on the subject. The mass media tend to give coverage to crashes with greater numbers of deaths and proximity to metropolitan areas. To the extent that coverage influences decisionmakers, airline policy may shift toward the sensational and away from substantive concerns. Crashes clearly can affect government responses. High-profile mishaps do not lead to greater FAA responsiveness to NTSB requests, but the time devoted to them most likely diverts attention from more important safety areas.[42] In other words, a rational system of airline safety should not give undue attention to crashes that take more lives or capture more media attention but should focus on areas with pressing regulatory needs.

In the next four chapters, three airline crashes and the effect of the September 11, 2001, attacks are considered. These accounts rely on the official record as well as on press coverage. The case studies highlight some high-profile occurrences, revealing links among crashes, the media, and transportation policy.

CHAPTER 4

The Crash of
USAir Flight 427

> There is nothing I want to accomplish more in my time of service
> on this Board than to find the cause of this crash.
> —*NTSB Chairman Jim Hall*

Establishing a cause after a loss-of-life incident reassures the public that order exists in the world. Absent a definite cause, an individual's sense of order is weakened. Randomness is feared because it does not allow a problem to be "solved." One psychologist observes, "When the issue is unresolved, when there's no known cause, we are left with ambiguity and ambivalence, and our essential rational nature is frustrated. . . . We get a vague sense of powerlessness."[1] The failure to find a cause, however, is not sufficient to sustain media interest in a crash unless there is a continuous supply of new information.

This uncertainty occurred in the case of USAir flight 427. The public and the media expect a cause to be found when a plane falls from the sky. After five years, two sets of National Transportation Safety Board (NTSB) hearings and countless hours of testing airplane parts, no precise cause of that crash was identified. Initial likely culprits were the airline, which was beset with safety problems that year, and Boeing, which had had problems with similar planes. While the specific fault was never identified with certainty, the Federal Aviation Administration (FAA) and Boeing ordered a complete overhaul of the rudder unit. The crash received sufficient press and government attention to prompt significant changes to the design of 737s and demonstrates that crashes sometimes do set the regulatory agenda.

The Crash and Its Immediate Aftermath

On September 8, 1994, just after 7 p.m., a Boeing 737 operating as USAir flight 427 en route from Chicago to Pittsburgh crashed on a hillside outside Aliquippa, Pennsylvania, a few miles from Pittsburgh.[2] All 132 passengers and crew aboard were killed. Planes fly over this area regularly as a landing route for the airport. The weather was clear, winds were calm, and flight conditions were normal. One eyewitness said that the plane made "a popping noise like a muffled backfire," rather than the normal roar, and speculated that it sounded as if the pilot was "trying to restart his engine."[3] Others observed the plane turning over before diving down to earth.[4] One viewer said, "It was a nosedive straight down—a gigantic ball of fire."[5] It landed with tremendous force, leaving only small pieces scattered around a large crater. This was USAir's third fatal crash in three years and its second in three months, and intense scrutiny was sure to follow.

The wreckage was spread over a large remote area. The plane's black box, housing the flight data recorder, was recovered the same day. Emergency workers arrived soon after the crash to begin the grim task of recovering bodies, many of which had been torn apart. Eventually 125 victims were positively identified.[6] USAir officials expressed sympathy to the victims' families. On September 14 the airline announced the possibility of building a memorial at the crash site.[7] It flew family members from around the country to the scene. Some family members told a reporter that "they could not come to terms with the crash until they found out what had caused it."[8]

On the day following the crash, government officials held a press conference near the accident site. Leading transportation officials were present, including David Hinson, head of the Federal Aviation Administration (FAA), and Federico Peña, secretary of the Department of Transportation (DOT). Hinson said that the agency had scrutinized the airline's records as a consequence of its recent accidents and found no reason for alarm. "We deem them to be safe," he said and noted that he would be flying the carrier later that afternoon.[9] Since a USAir accident two years earlier, aviation officials said that they had increased their scrutiny of the company. Peña concurred: "I can tell you that thus far we have found no issues or significant matters that we are concerned about."[10]

A Long Search

As with all aviation accidents, the search for the cause takes precedence once no survivors are found. On the night of the crash, Diane Young, a spokeswoman for USAir, said that the crew had called in before the final approach and that "everything we have would indicate that the flight's descent was proceeding normally."[11] Radar contact with the plane was lost about six miles from the airport at an altitude of approximately 6,000 feet.

Two facts became readily apparent. The crash was the worst accident on American soil since 1987, when a Northwest Airlines plane carrying 156 people crashed on takeoff from Detroit. Second, it was the culmination of a bad period for the airline. Flight 427 was its fifth fatal crash in five years, and the last three fatal crashes of major commercial carriers all involved USAir flights.[12] A company official said that there "was no thread of continuity between the accidents. . . . Five crashes in five years, that's very unusual. We don't believe in jinxes."[13]

An NTSB "Go Team" was sent to investigate the crash. A representative cautioned that several months would pass before any verdict could be announced. However, he indicated that the team already had evidence that the plane's two engines were operating when the plane crashed. The flight data recorder showed that the plane swerved to the left before the crash. Some made the connection between the USAir crash and a 1991 incident in which a Boeing 737 nose-dived to the ground near Colorado Springs. The cause for that accident had not been determined as of 1994. NTSB officials cautioned against drawing any links so early in the investigation.[14] Most of the plane's wreckage was recovered and reassembled for further study.

NTSB investigators have a saying: Never believe anything you hear in the first forty-eight hours.[15] As board member Carl Vogt said a few days after the crash, "It's an axiom in this business that if you say on day two you know what happened, that you're almost unquestionably going to be proven wrong, so we don't do that."[16] Speculation begins the instant a plane crash occurs. The development of round-the-clock news and increased media outlets serves to fuel such theorizing. Statements come from various sources, including government officials, anonymous tipsters, or "experts." For instance, on the night of the crash, a CNN anchor asked a USAir official if the crash was linked to more general problems with the Boeing 737: "So, you do stand behind this airplane—this aircraft—mechanically. There is—the reason I'm pursuing this with you is because there seems to be a lot of confusion and head scratching, among experts even, about the fact that there was possibly smoke and an explosion coming from the plane before it hit the ground."[17]

The battle over cause begins early, and the stakes are high. This case had several prime suspects. The first was the plane. Did a part or a mechanism malfunction or fail? According to Boeing, the 737, first produced in 1965, is the best-selling jetliner of all time. The plane that crashed was part of the 300 series and was delivered to USAir in 1987. It had recently undergone standard maintenance checks.[18] Boeing had a clear incentive to learn the cause of the crash.

The rudder had been a problem for 737 aircraft. A malfunctioning rudder can lead one of the plane's wings to lift and the other to sink, which is consistent with the reported leftward roll followed by a nosedive. Pilots often resolve such problems, but occasionally they lose control of the plane. After a fatal crash in Colorado Springs in 1991, the NTSB recommended that inspections be performed on the 737s' standby rudder mechanism. The FAA initially agreed with that request, proposing inspections after every 4,000 miles of flying. But later it withdrew the recommendation, suggesting that pilots could correct such rudder problems if they happened. Another crash in 1992 led the NTSB to again recommend corrective action. However, the FAA did not act until March 1994, when it ordered periodic inspections for the planes.[19]

Three weeks after the crash, the *Seattle Times* reported that some 737s had leaks in their power control unit, causing rudder malfunction. Between 1974 and 1994, of 550,000 service difficulty reports, 46 indicated problems with the rudder system, 21 of which were linked to leaks in the power control unit. Of those 21, 11 led to unscheduled landings, including 2 emergency descents. Earlier in 1994 the FAA had ordered all airlines with 737s built before 1993 to install new and improved control units by 1999. In April 1993 Boeing began installing these units in new jets.[20]

Engine problems appeared in media speculation within three days of the accident. Thrust reversers are a braking mechanism that slows a plane after it lands by reversing airflow. Six actuators control each engine's thrust reverser. Some actuators on the right engine of flight 427 were found to be in a deployed position, while none of the recovered actuators were found to be deployed on the left engine. This could have led to an unusual force on the plane's right wing, causing it to move sharply. However, the force of impact might have changed the actuator's position. Vogt cautioned against media speculation about this potential problem. "There is, at this point, all too much speculation about this. Speculation about any of this is very premature."[21] Two days later this possibility appeared less likely, as investigators found evidence that the control actuators had been shifted by the force of the impact and not while the plane was airborne.[22]

On September 13 another engine problem appeared in press coverage. Could the right engine have been dislodged from the wing in flight? NTSB investigators had been unable to find the engine's rear mounting. Although the engine was still attached to the wing, it may be been inappropriately attached, causing the plane to dive. Again NTSB officials said that any conclusions were premature.[23] A few days after the crash, this possibility was discounted. The right engine's rear mounts were found and appeared to have separated upon impact.[24]

Evidence of sabotage was also ruled out quickly. There was a report that one of the passengers on the flight was in a witness protection program, that he had spent five years in jail on a drug offense, and that he had been in Chicago to talk with federal prosecutors about his testimony in an upcoming drug trial. Officials said, however, that there was no evidence that this passenger led to the crash or that a bomb caused the accident.[25]

Officials listening to the plane's cockpit voice recorder heard an unusual sound coming from the plane when it was a mile off the ground: a "whoomp, whoomp" followed by a grunt from one of the pilots and a voice saying, "Jeez, what was that?"[26] Speculation about the odd sound continued for three months. In a sworn statement issued in November a USAir pilot reported being a passenger in the cockpit on an earlier leg of the flight between Charlotte and Chicago. While he was on the plane he accidentally moved his leg, turning on the microphone of the public address system. A passenger heard a noise and mentioned it to a flight attendant. The captain was informed, and the cockpit passenger moved his leg away from the public address system. This anecdote suggests that normal movements in the cockpit caused the sounds.[27]

Or could the unusual thump have been caused by a collision with a bird? That view was expounded in the first few days after the crash, after some witnesses reported seeing birds in the area. But no bird remains were found on the wreckage. A small stain on the plane was determined by the Smithsonian Institution not to be bird matter.[28]

In a little over a week the media shifted the theme from naming one possible cause after another to calling it the mystery crash. Press reports stressed that investigators had ruled out most plausible causes. The *New York Times'* headline read, "With Factors Ruled Out, USAir Crash Emerges as a Puzzle."[29] The imprint of *mystery* had been firmly planted on the USAir disaster.

Blame Avoidance and Strategic Responses

With the crash unsolved and some causes ruled out, three blame targets were in the line of fire: USAir, Boeing, and the plane's pilots.

USAir probably had the most at stake in the crash outcome, since it was losing money, was heavily in debt, and was suffering from a downgraded bond rating. Culpability could irreparably harm the airline. The location of the accident also put the company in an awkward position. Its operations are headquartered in Pittsburgh, and air travel is a major component of the area's economy. The airline was already in financial trouble before the crash. Five crashes in as many years did not communicate confidence to the flying public, even if they were not evidence of systemic problems.

The safety record of the company was in question. A press investigation revealed that FAA inspectors had found more than forty problems in USAir flight operations and pilot training programs. Ten days before the accident, FAA officials and company executives met to discuss improving training and safety operations. The airline was put on notice to make improvements in both areas. A former NTSB chairman said, "From the issues of pilot training and cockpit discipline, you could potentially have a connection between three [accidents] there. The NTSB members are failing to do their job if they fail to look at those lines and see if they make a picture."[30]

An alternative approach is to take the broader definition of flying mishaps, which, along with crashes and loss of life also include events that are less serious. This broader category—classified as *accidents*—include in-flight occurrences such as a person breaking a bone by falling or being hit by a piece of equipment. If this measure is used, USAir had the most occurrences in the period between 1989 and the crash (fifteen: United and American had twelve each). Similarly, USAir ranked third in pilot deviations (in-flight actions that violate FAA regulations) between 1989 and the crash date.[31]

The financial plight of the company also raised concerns. The press intimated that there was pressure on employees to keep the planes running at all costs. The *New York Times* reported that in the five years leading up to the crash the airline had resisted modifications to make the cabin more fire retardant; had flown with too little fuel, necessitating emergency landings; and had not made required repairs.[32]

The media had found a frame for their stories: This crash was part of a larger pattern of unsafe practices at USAir. The company had no choice but to respond, and forcefully, but it was caught in a dilemma. If the pilots were blamed, that would reflect badly on the airline. If Boeing were blamed, USAir would have the problem of reassuring passengers that all of the 737s in its fleet were safe. As a result, USAir defended its safety record and avoided the blame game. For example, executives strongly defended the safety record of the airline in response to the *New York Times* report, and they distributed these defenses widely, making three points.

First, the accidents were not connected, and the airline's economic plight did not contribute to the crashes. USAir's CEO Seth Schofield said, "When it comes to safety, we are well within the mean range and better than some. The reality is that if I thought the airline was unsafe, I would ground every plane."[33] Second, the *Times* was criticized for engaging in data mining: trying to find patterns in a large set of data. James Lloyd, USAir executive vice president, said, "Any time you have millions of takeoffs and landings and 45,000 employees and you put them under a microscope, you will find some irregularities. But this does not mean the company is lax."[34] Third, company officials noted that USAir had 2,500 daily flights, more than any other American carrier. Its pilots spent more of their flight time in the most dangerous part of flying, takeoffs and landings. Accounting for that, its crash record was much better than others.

In addition to defending itself in the press, the airline took other symbolic actions to deflect blame. In October 1994 Schofield wrote a letter to every USAir frequent flyer member (more than a million), assuring them that its "45,000 employees are personally and professionally committed to ensuring that our high safety standards are met on each of our nearly 2,600 daily flights. Safety never has been, nor ever will be, compromised at USAir." Even that strategy was criticized, as one skeptic noted that move reflected cost-cutting tactics. "It's much less expensive than taking out a full-page ad in newspapers across the country."[35]

Company leaders were buttressed by support from prominent government officials. Anthony Broderick, associate administrator at the FAA, said that the airline's safety record was not a problem. "I think they've had a real string of bad luck here, and a number of these crashes are not their fault and could have happened to anybody."[36]

USAir made a number of internal changes. In November, the company brought all of its pilots in for one full day of retraining at several locations around the country. The month-long effort cost the company $2 million. A spokesman said, "It is essential to stress the importance of following basic procedures and review all the steps that have been taken over the past several months."[37] In addition, the company brought in retired Air Force general Robert Oaks to oversee its safety procedures in the air and on the ground. A company representative said, "We had come to the decision several months before the crash that we wanted to have one person in charge of all safety operations—both ground and air." The current head of safety and compliance on the ground retired. On the same day, experts were also hired to reevaluate the airline's safety policies and procedures. Schofield said the audit team "can go anywhere, ask anyone anything. There are no limits."[38]

On November 21 USAir began a new national advertising campaign focusing on its commitment to safety as part of the continuing effort to restore public confidence. In full-page ads that ran in newspapers like the *Wall Street Journal* and the *New York Times,* Schofield wrote in part, "We who are airline professionals know our system and our planes are safe. This is validated each and every day by federal regulators who fly with us, inspect our maintenance facilities, and review our records. . . . We will not rest until each and every member of the flying public shares in the certainty of our commitment to be the safest of airlines."[39]

Like USAir, Boeing's financial stakes were enormous. If the 737 were indicted by the crash investigation, sales for the world's most popular jet in commercial aviation could plummet. Nearly half of all the planes the company made were 737s.[40] Initial concerns regarding the thrust reverser and the engines had been dismissed, but issues related to the rudder lingered. This provided fodder for media scrutiny.

When the charge was made that the older 737s had faulty rudder systems, the company responded that these accusations were based on raw reports collected by the FAA and were not sufficient to determine whether rudder unit performance was related to flight problems. A Boeing representative said that it had "no data in hand to support . . . [the *Times*] survey and baseline account of the problem."[41] The company's position throughout the investigation was that such a rudder movement did not occur and that the plane was not at fault. The company spent $1.5 million on rudder testing, with nearly a hundred employees devoting more than 40,000 hours to the investigation. The rudder system has a built-in redundancy: Every lever in the power control unit has a backup lever that moves with it in case the main lever should malfunction. The valve is powered by two hydraulic systems in case one does not work. In repeated tests, the rudder system passed inspection.[42]

This outcome led Boeing to push an alternative cause: human error; that is, the pilots. Boeing's chief engineer listened repeatedly to the voice recorder. Nothing indicated that the plane failed to perform satisfactorily. He concluded that the pilots were surprised by something and then incorrectly responded to the problem. The rudder was never mentioned. He focused on the head pilot's statement, "pull, pull." He concluded that the pilots were surprised and mistakenly pushed on the rudder mechanism to correct the problem. Then they pulled back on the control column, stalling the plane and leading to the subsequent crash.[43] When Boeing officials thought that NTSB staffers were assembling evidence that rejected the pilot theory, they assembled their own report, "Boeing Contribution to the USAir Flight 427 Accident Investigation Board," which concluded that the pilots had caused the crash. The NTSB, however, rejected the report, seeing it as an attempt to override its own findings.[44]

Even though Boeing never publicly acknowledged that its plane or rudder mechanism was the cause of the crash, company officials announced in September 1996 a design change in new 737 models that would limit how far the rudder could move if an in-flight problem emerged. This change would not affect planes currently flying or in production. Boeing officials said the change was made for technical, not safety, concerns.[45]

Media charges were then leveled against the company that it had known about problems with the rudder system for several decades before the USAir accident. An October 1996, five-part investigative series by reporter Byron Acohido in the *Seattle Times* focused on a pattern of deception and avoidance by Boeing in dealing with the rudder system on its most popular airplane. Acohido found that airline pilots had filed hundreds of reports of 737s suddenly altering their course as if the rudder had a life of its own.[46] Boeing followed with an industry advisory calling for the inspection of some 737 rudder control systems. The FAA then issued an emergency directive making the company inspection order mandatory for all 737s.[47]

Boeing's target for deflecting blame from itself was the pilots, and the existing data provided them with a decent argument. Though statistics vary, pilot error is thought to contribute to a large proportion of fatal crashes. While the pilots' union was not economically liable for the crash, it had its reputation at stake. Boeing and this group had fought in the past. After 737s took to the air, the union demanded and got a third pilot in the cockpit for safety reasons, even though Boeing had government approval for a two-person crew. The company interpreted the union's demand as a move to show that its planes were unsafe and as a means to employ more pilots.[48] In previous crash investigations, Boeing defended the plane, and the union defended the pilots.

Needless to say, the pilots' representative who listened to the same tape discussed above reached a very different conclusion about the cause. The pilots were startled and had no idea what had happened. As a result, there must have been a malfunction in the plane's operations.[49] The pilots and Boeing were clearly at odds. To deflect blame, each criticized the other.

Congress and the Department of Transportation

Congress remained mostly silent about the crash: no committee hearings, no legislation, no floor discussions. Senator Larry Pressler (R-S.D.), chairman of the Commerce Committee, made the only floor statement on the crash:

> I point no finger of blame at anyone for this most recent crash. I do not know all the facts. Indeed, the NTSB and FAA are working hard to determine its cause. However, we should focus on this serious matter and work with our safety agencies to prevent future tragedies. In my view, we need congressional oversight to be sure that our congressional committees are doing what we are supposed to be doing to promote air safety in this country and protect the safety of the air traveling public.[50]

In the House, Peter DeFazio (D-Ore.), a long-time critic of the FAA and a member of the House Transportation Committee, cited the series from the *Seattle Times* and called on Congress to hold hearings on the issue of the safety of all 737 aircraft. He further requested that the FAA take immediate action in changing the design of the rudder system to make it safer.[51]

Meanwhile, because there were four plane crashes in the last four months of 1994 killing more than 200 people, Peña held an "emergency" conference on airline safety in January 1995. Many of the proposals that emerged from the conference had previously been delayed by the FAA. One official said that his group's recommendations were the same as those "in a host of studies that just needed to be dusted off and acted upon."[52] Hall repeated his standard refrain that the FAA takes too long to act on NTSB recommendations after an accident. However, the highlight of the conference was in a speech by Peña in which he called for a "zero-accident aviation environment. We have to get out of the mind-set of saying, 'No matter how hard we try, we will have accidents' and into 'We will not have accidents.'"[53] This is an example of symbolic politics, designed to reassure the flying public that air travel is safe and will be even safer in the future.

NTSB Hearings, Part 1

On January 23, 1995, a few weeks after the emergency conference, the NTSB opened weeklong hearings to investigate the cause of the crash. Approximately thirty witnesses testified.[54] Normally a hearing leads to a consensus as to the cause, but this was not the case for the USAir crash. In his opening statement the head of the NTSB said that the hearings would not establish a definitive cause.

Witnesses discussed the possibility of a wake vortex encounter, in which a plane flies into the path of another plane and is affected by the spinning air that plane leaves in its wake. There was general agreement that this was unlikely. Then the focus shifted to the rudder. The plane's rolling dive could be traced to a full swing of the rudder to the left. The rudder had been recovered, however, and was found to be nearly straight. Even so, an FAA test pilot who had performed a number of examinations on a simulator testified that the rudder could have caused the rolling dive.

The next focus was the power control unit (PCU) regulating the rudder. The servo valve, which is the size of a soft drink can, could have jammed due to a small contaminant. However, in tests conducted by Boeing, the PCU was found to be operating properly after the crash. No markings that would have been left by contaminants were present. A Boeing engineer testified, "I have come to the conclusion that this rudder PCU on this aircraft did what the rudder power control system told it to do."[55] There is no evidence that the rudder had moved, since its wrecked remains were found to be within two degrees of the norm.

Boeing came under criticism from the NTSB chair for not being forthcoming about prior incidents involving its 737 jets, information that might be relevant to the USAir crash. When the company was asked to provide a list of incidents involving flight control problems that might include the rudder, it provided a list of 187, which proved to be only a partial list when Air France offered other instances. Hall said that such shoddy record-keeping on the part of Boeing threatened the credibility of the investigation.

Attention was also focused on the flight data recorder. The one involved in this crash was an older version, which did not have as much information as more recent types that record the condition of up to a hundred separate parts of the plane, including the rudder. Hall said that Boeing should not have shipped off boxes that recorded only thirty-one pieces of information (the minimum FAA requirement). The NTSB had long urged the FAA to require more advanced mechanisms for all 737s. However, the agency and the airlines had balked, as the planes would have had to be removed from service for too long a period of time.

The hearings ended without consensus on the cause of the crash, and though the focus was for the most part on the rudder, Jim Hall promised to consider all possible causes. Months followed with no new information. Endless repetitions in a flight simulator, testing interactions between altered variables, produced no new theories. The FAA's director of aircraft certification said, "We're going to do whatever we can to solve it, we're going to keep reviewing and re-reviewing and re-re-reviewing until we find it. I probably won't sleep a full night until we do."[56]

NTSB Hearings, Part 2

In November 1995 the NTSB conducted an unusual second set of hearings into the crash.[57] They lasted three days and focused on the airworthiness of the 737, the rudder, and the possibility of pilot error. According to Hall the NTSB had devoted 50,000 person-hours to investigating the crash, and the precipitating factor was still unknown. He admonished those speaking to the press who claimed that the NTSB knew that rudder problems had caused the crash but was withholding information.

One question posed during the hearing was whether the FAA should have certified the plane in the first place. It had conducted a critical design review to reexamine the initial certification of the 737 and "to give us a measure of where or what the certification basis was for those airplanes with regard to today's requirements."[58] Michael Zielinski, the head of the research team that studied the 737's design, said a single failure was acceptable if its occurrence was only once in a billion flying hours. An "engineering judgment" was made that the aircraft met this standard. Board members raised the possibility that such a determination was flawed. Further, newer design versions had been approved in 1984. A modification to an existing aircraft does not need to go through an entirely new certification process.

The focus then shifted from mechanical problems to human error. Officials of the FAA and Boeing testified that if pilots had increased their air speed and not held their altitude they could have pulled the out of the sudden swing. However, a senior pilot at Boeing reported that pilots are not trained for such eventualities: "We don't train for events that don't occur."[59]

As with the first hearings, no conclusion was reached as to the cause of the crash. Instead they provided an opportunity for parties to the investigation, including Boeing, USAir, and the pilots, to defend themselves against claims that they were responsible for the accident.

Interim Actions

After the hearings, no final report was issued. Action, however, seemingly was still warranted, what with two unsolved plane crashes with similar circumstances surrounding them. The NTSB, citing the popularity of the 737 and the possible problems indicated by the Pittsburgh and Colorado Springs crashes, issued recommendations for changes in training and equipment on these aircraft. "Unusual attitude" training was to teach pilots how to react in unexpected circumstances, and a cockpit indicator system would note rudder surface position and movement.[60]

Meanwhile, Al Gore inserted himself into an area not normally characterized by vice presidential interest. After two noteworthy crashes in 1996 (ValuJet and TWA), an international summit on aviation safety and security was convened in Washington in January 1997 under his leadership. Several aviation problems were discussed, including the rudders of the 737. Gore made a major speech covering a variety of aviation topics and specifically noting forthcoming action on the rudder:

> Today, I'm pleased to announce an important new government industry initiative to improve safety. As you know, the investigations into the crashes of Boeing 737s in Colorado Springs and Pittsburgh have not yet been closed. But those investigations have identified improvements that could help eliminate the chance of rudders playing a role in future accidents. These changes can and should be made without delay. And with today's announcement, they will be. Boeing has developed modifications to the rudders of older 737s that will improve safety. And they are going to begin retrofitting those planes largely at their own expense and without waiting for a government mandate. Under a schedule to be developed by the FAA, these improvements will be made throughout the next two years. This is a major action. It affects some 2,800 planes worldwide, 1,100 of them

here in the United States. Like all the other examples I have given, the beneficiaries of this action are the millions of passengers who will fly on these planes. And I want to say a special word of thanks to everyone at Boeing and at the NTSB and FAA for this step that is being taken today.[61]

For years Boeing had argued that changes in the rudder were not required. Now it was willing to take two years and to spend upward of $100 million to change the mechanism on all of its 737s. This step indicates the pressure that Boeing was under to take some action with respect to its 737 plane. The NTSB was "encouraged" by the proposed modifications, but it joined the Air Line Pilots Association in saying they did not go far enough.[62]

The NTSB Final Crash Report

After nearly five years had passed, in March 1999 the NTSB finally concluded its investigation into the crash of USAir flight 427. Following intense internal battles, the nearly 400-page report was issued. It states that a rare rudder malfunction was the likely cause of the crash. However, the language was conditional, as the determination was made based on circumstantial, not direct, evidence. But in so many technical words, the agency was blaming a malfunction for causing the crash. In the words of the NTSB,

> The National Transportation Safety Board determines that the probable cause of the USAir flight 427 accident was a loss of control of the airplane resulting from the movement of the rudder surface to its blowdown limit. The rudder surface most likely deflected in a direction opposite to that commanded by the pilots as a result of a jam of the main rudder power control unit servo valve secondary slide to the servo valve housing offset from its neutral position and overtravel of the primary slide.[63]

The board made ten recommendations to the FAA, focusing on three areas: improving pilot training programs, upgrading flight data recorders, and creating a more reliable rudder system. Additional training in flight simulators was suggested to deal with jammed rudders with varying speeds. New planes were to have upgraded recorders by July 31, 2000; older ones were given an additional year. The report demanded that all 737s and future planes have "a reliably redundant rudder actuation system."[64] One of the favorite phrases of aviation officials is "reliable redundancy."[65] If one aspect of a mechanism fails, another will correct the problem. This is what the NTSB recommended with respect to the rudder mechanism. Such implementation would involve a considerable cost outlay by Boeing.

The NTSB criticized the FAA for responding either too slowly or not at all to previous recommendations it had made regarding this occurrence.[66] The implicit tone of the report blamed the FAA and Boeing for creating conditions that led to the crash. The FAA was responsible for failing to demand up-to-date flight recorders on all aircraft. Boeing was guilty of failing to develop more reliable rudder systems for the 737.

With respect to flight recorders, the final report notes:

> The Federal Aviation Administration's failure to require timely and aggressive action regarding enhanced flight data recorder recording capabilities, especially on Boeing 737 airplanes, has significantly hampered investigators in the prompt identification of potentially critical safety-of-flight conditions and in the development of recommendations to prevent future catastrophic accidents.

With respect to rudders, the report says,

> Rudder design changes to Boeing 737 next-generation-series airplanes and the changes currently being retrofitted on the remainder of the Boeing 737 fleet do not eliminate the possibility of other potential failure modes and malfunctions in the Boeing 737 rudder system that could lead to a loss of control. . . . The results of this investigation have disclosed that the Boeing 737 rudder system design certificated by the Federal Aviation Administration is not reliably redundant.[67]

Hall emphasized that all parties to the investigation believed that the cause was a mechanical malfunction. There was the one exception: Boeing, which still held to the view that pilot error may have caused the accident. NTSB staff members, however, said that for Boeing's view to be accurate the pilot would have to hold the rudder in the wrong position for ten seconds while the copilot acquiesced.[68] After the issuance of the final report, Hall held a press conference and indicted the FAA for failing to act: "The Federal Aviation Administration failed in its responsibility to the flying public. I'm kind of tired of pulling the FAA. It's their turn to lead."[69]

Legal settlements took longer than usual, in part because of battles over cause. Families of forty-eight victims settled without filing a lawsuit, while eighty-four filed suit, eighteen in Illinois and sixty-six in Pennsylvania. Winning an award in Pittsburgh was likely to be more difficult. This was the home of USAir, a major employer in the area, and juries were thought to be less charitable in viewing the claims of the families of those who died. The flight's originating point in Chicago offered a different scenario. Cook County juries were known for awarding large damage claims in crashes. All lawsuits in Illinois ended before trial, while four in Pennsylvania went to trial.[70]

Policy Change and Safety Reform

Throughout the period, Boeing continued to make improvements to the 737, all the while maintaining that the theory of pilot error had not been ruled out. It did make modifications in the 737 rudder, but they fell short of what the NTSB recommended. In September 2000 the FAA announced that it was planning to order all Boeing 737 planes to be outfitted with a new rudder system, and Boeing officials held a press conference to announce a voluntary rudder redesign, pending extensive testing. Pilots would begin receiving training in how to handle jammed rudders immediately. New rudder control systems would be installed beginning in 2003. The process was to be completed by 2008.[71] In October 2002 the FAA issued a final rule mandating this change. The FAA estimated the cost of a new system at $364 million for the 2,000 existing 737s affected by the requirement.[72] This is considered by most to be a success in aviation safety policy but also supports the claim of slow movement: Nearly fifteen years will have passed before the problem that most likely brought down USAir flight 427 is completely fixed.

The FAA also proposed changes to flight data recorders, which contained too little information in the USAir crash and made the investigation more difficult, but this suggested change fell short of what the NTSB desired.[73]

"The Unforgivable Sin"

An airline crash involving the loss of more than a hundred lives was certain to attract media attention. But how much? There was intense interest when the crash occurred, but that interest quickly dissipated. After the initial few weeks, coverage was minimal. Only with the NTSB hearings the following January did articles reappear. After that there was infre-

Box 4-1   New York Times *Coverage of USAir Flight 427, 1994–2000*

1994: 32 stories (3 front page)
   September: 25 stories (2 front page)
   October: 2 stories
   November: 3 stories (1 front page)
   December: 2 stories
1995: 12 stories (6 in January)
1996: 3 stories
1997: 1 story, front page
1998: 1 story
1999: 4 stories
2000: none
   Total: 53 stories (4 front page)

Source: Authors' calculations based on *New York Times Index*, various years.

quent interest in the crash. Front-page attention in the *New York Times* was limited (see box 4-1).[74]

More than five years passed before an official resolution was reached, with press accounts reporting every major step of the story. It had elements that attract media attention: a dramatic loss of life, the failure of the world's most popular jetliner, and the mystery surrounding the cause. Here there were no smoking guns in terms of weather problems, pilot error, or a dramatic failure of a specific aircraft mechanism. Investigators focused on the rudder as the likely candidate, but this speculation was based on circumstantial evidence.

Press coverage focused on the lack of an explanation. While the loss of life in any crash is always horrible, this investigation was driven by the parallel unsolved crash of a 737 in Colorado in 1991. As Hall said when he launched the first public hearings in 1995, "It is no secret that the aviation community is concerned about this accident, not just because of the great human tragedy it represents, but because this is the second accident in nearly four years involving a Boeing 737 for which as yet no cause has been readily identified."[75] All investigators assume that accident causes can and should be uncovered by thorough, exhaustive research. An FAA official commented, "Unexplained accidents are something that just cry for somebody to explain them. . . . It's just not acceptable as far as I'm concerned."[76] "The unforgivable sin in aviation," another observer says, "is not killing a planeload of passengers—it is killing two planeloads because of the same cause."[77]

Crash Oversight and Change

The crash of flight 427 in September 1994 resulted not only in the death of more than a hundred people but also in a loss of credibility for parties associated with the investigation. Once the plane went down, many assumed that the cause would be determined quickly. It had been a clear night with no weather problems, and the plane's recording equipment was recovered.

First, the status of the NTSB, as the agency whose mission is to investigate air disasters and inform the public about them, was challenged and weakened. After exhaustive, expensive testing and the passage of five years, all that was produced were conclusions based on circumstantial evidence. If that were not enough to damage the board's reputation, there was the troubling matter of precedent. Three years before flight 427's demise, a plane crashed in Colorado with many comparable elements. That case was not fully resolved, either. Yet all parties concluded that the cause was related to a malfunctioning rudder.

Second, Boeing faced a challenge to its reputation for building safe planes. Reports were afloat that the plane had had rudder problems for some time before this incident. Due to the cost of designing an alternative, however, the company focused on minor changes and stonewalled the criticism by insisting on the plane's safety. When this strategy began to falter, Boeing pointed to the pilots as the culpable party. Years passed with no major redesign of the rudder. Finally the local Seattle newspaper published an investigative series alleging decades-long cover-ups by the company. Only then did Boeing call for an inspection of all of its rudder systems. Some six years after the accident, the aircraft giant agreed to replace existing rudders starting in 2003.

Third, the FAA provided minimal regulatory oversight and for several years supported Boeing in its resistance to changes in the rudder system. It either refused to act on NTSB recommendations or responded with minor modifications in existing policy. Protection was provided to the company responsible for building the most popular commercial plane. Minor changes to the rudder and to the flight data recorders were supported, but both modifications stopped far short of NTSB requests. Only after intense pressure was action taken on the rudder control system.

Fourth, prominent politicians reversed roles in their reaction to the crash and its aftermath. Individuals normally not astute in matters of aviation became involved. Both the vice president and the DOT secretary held conferences in which changes in aviation practices were announced. These changes, however, were either delayed or subsequently reformulated. Yet others who would be expected to respond with calls for oversight did not. Members of Congress expressed concern about what happened that night in September 1994, but no hearings were held and no legislation was proposed. This was a crash that could be tied to others, had implications for an entire fleet, and involved backbiting between pilots and the airline, yet it received a fraction of the attention given to the TWA flight 800 disaster. No congressional hearings focused on flight 427, media coverage was higher than for most but not near the levels of the ValuJet or TWA incidents, and no commissions were formed as a result.[78]

The reason for the low level of concern is suggestive of airline safety policy more generally: Without an unusual or unique element, plane crashes are handled within the regulatory apparatus of the FAA and the NTSB and are free from extensive media or congressional scrutiny. While the number of airline crashes is (fortunately) too low for systematic analysis, it does not appear that the *significance* of policy outcomes is enhanced by intense media scrutiny or by extensive congressional attention. If anything, these factors may detract from public policy, as such attention often leads to symbolic rather than substantive action, allowing actors to delay even further the implementation of significant safety changes. Major changes to the 737 were implemented as a result of the crash, albeit at a delayed pace, and the media coverage that occurred, while limited, had an impact.

This is an important point: Airline safety is not necessarily improved by high-profile cases. The TWA case received more attention for reasons unrelated to airline safety. USAir flight 427 was just as mysterious but received far less attention from the press and policymakers. This was a long investigation, which ultimately led to the problems with rudder reversal on Boeing 737s being addressed. Given the link to at least two crashes, it was not an insignificant problem. But because the issues involved were highly technical, media coverage was sporadic, even though higher than with most crashes. Ultimately, a crash that received less attention led to more concrete action.

Conclusion

One of the most thorough, expensive, and lengthy crash investigations in the history of commercial aviation concluded with a somewhat unsatisfactory result. After much debate, the NTSB's final view was based on circumstantial evidence: The rudder that provided vertical stabilization to the aircraft moved in the opposite direction from that which the pilots had instructed it to take.

Changes to the 737 were eventually imposed as a consequence of the crash, but following past trends, these changes will take many years to be fully implemented. Media coverage was limited, because the crash had no unusual elements except for the fact that it was a "mystery." However, media coverage did bring to light potential problems with the 737, so it did have an impact. Whether the investigation and the subsequent adjustments were efficient uses of limited funds is an open question. But undoubtedly the USAir crash raised the rudder issue to a prominent place on the safety agenda.

The following themes are highlighted in this chapter:

—Mystery will guarantee initial media interest but cannot sustain it.

—After the initial interest, the press spotlight only reappears when prior or new problems with the aircraft are found.

—If there is no bureaucratic malfeasance and a major airline is involved, congressional interest is minimal.

—The FAA, the airline, and the plane manufacturer will resist expensive changes in plane construction.

5

The Crash of
ValuJet Flight 592

ValuJet Airlines was founded and operates daily upon the
principle that SAFETY is by far our most important responsibility.
Accordingly, it is the commitment of ValuJet's Board of Directors,
its management personnel, and all permanent, temporary,
contract, and non-contract employees to place safety above all
other company objectives.

—ValuJet Standard Practice 0001

ValuJet Airlines was set to be the airline success story of
the 1990s. The Atlanta-based company began flying in late 1993 under
the direction of experienced aviation managers Robert Priddy, Lewis Jordan, and Maurice Gallagher and represented a new breed in the industry.
It operated on a no-frills basis, targeting cost-conscious customers and
beginning with service from Atlanta to three southeastern cities. The fleet
grew from a single plane to fifty-one planes by May 1996, and ValuJet
expanded its low-cost service to thirty-one cites in nineteen states, primarily in the South and East.[1] Profits increased rapidly, and its growth was
unprecedented in the industry. Stock value increased 366 percent in 1995,
with net income totaling $67.8 million and an industry-leading net profit
margin of 17.3 percent.[2]

How was this accomplished? ValuJet stressed low fares, minimum frills,
and a variety of cost-cutting strategies, especially with respect to labor.
Pilots and flight attendants received some of the lowest salaries in the
industry.[3] Many pilots had failed to obtain jobs with major carriers, and
all had to pay $10,000 for their own training and certification.[4] ValuJet
relied on older equipment; its planes were twenty-six years old on average, the oldest fleet in the industry.[5] Only one type of aircraft was used,
the McDonnell Douglas DC-9. Equipment was in almost constant use, as
there were no hubs and most routes were nonstop. Planes were emptied
and filled quickly, maximizing the number of flights a day for each aircraft. Maintenance was outsourced, leading to large cost savings. Accord-

ing to the Federal Aviation Administration (FAA), ValuJet's oversight of these operations was limited.

Meanwhile, cheap travel had political benefits. President Clinton was extremely supportive of encouraging low-cost carriers as a way to lower airfares and satisfy the public.[6] Political advisers in the White House saw a partisan advantage in encouraging the Department of Transportation (DOT) to do everything possible to provide additional price competition for the major carriers, with ValuJet being the prime example.[7] In a study released on April 23, 1996, Federico Peña notes that consumers were saving over $6 billion annually due to low-cost service. This development was, according to Peña, "in large part the outgrowth of President Clinton's effort to support new-entrant carriers."[8]

The government emphasis was on promotion, not on oversight. In the process, ValuJet developed a flight record that was less than spotless. A National Transportation Safety Board (NTSB) report showed that, since 1993, it had accumulated accident and incident reports at a rate four times that of Delta, American, and United.[9] Mishaps included aborted take-offs, skidding off the runway, and landing gear failure.[10] This record would soon capture media attention.

In this chapter, the crash of ValuJet flight 592 and the subsequent fall-out is examined. This start-up airline initially changed the nature of competitive pricing in various airline markets. After the crash of flight 592 government officials praised the company and its safety record. However, such positive endorsements proved premature. While the crash cause was identified quickly, the rancor in the postcrash debate cast a negative aura over all the affected actors. ValuJet airline officials, SabreTech maintenance providers, and FAA regulatory oversight were all found to be at fault.

The Crash and Its Immediate Aftermath

On May 11, 1996, a ValuJet DC-9 operating as flight 592 was en route from Miami to Atlanta under ideal weather conditions. At 2:10 p.m., about ten minutes after take-off, the pilot reported smoke in the cockpit. He turned the plane around and planned to return to Miami. Radar contact was lost at 2:13 p.m. One witness reported that the plane went into a near-vertical dive position as it crashed into the Florida Everglades. All 105 passengers and 5 crew members perished in the swamp.[11]

Rescue teams arrived shortly after the crash, but access was difficult. They saw bodies floating in the water but could not reach them; flammable aviation fuel covered the surface of the water. In addition, the location complicated matters. The Everglades is a marsh of more than 5,000 square miles in southern Florida. It contains poisonous snakes and alligators, making recovery even more difficult. The crash site was accessible only by air and helicopter. Within one day, the hunt for survivors was called off; the search for bodies continued, but no remains were recovered. After flying over the site in a helicopter, a detective for the county police department said, "The average person would not have known a plane went down in that location."[12]

After a tragic plane incident, officials rush to reassure the public that they care about those who are lost and that such an occurrence will not be repeated. On the day of the crash, ValuJet president Lewis Jordan held a press conference in Atlanta and said, "Our thoughts and prayers and sincere emotion go out to the people on board and their families, loved ones, and friends. It is impossible to put into words how devastating something like this is."[13]

The next day, DOT secretary Federico Peña flew over the crash site and met with the families of the victims. He conducted a news conference near the scene and asserted that ValuJet flights were safe: "Whenever we have found any issues, ValuJet has been responsive, they have been cooperative, they have in some cases even exceeded the safety standards that we have." Peña reinforced the point later in the conference: "I've flown ValuJet. ValuJet is a safe airline, as is our entire airline system."[14] Two days after the crash, FAA administrator David Hinson appeared on ABC's *Nightline* program and said, "I will tell you and our viewers, the airline is safe. I would fly it. And I will leave it at that."[15]

A Challenging Crash Scene

Immediately after the crash, the NTSB sent a "Go Team" to investigate the site, but the Everglades did not lend itself to detailed inspection. Vice Chairman Robert Francis said, "The site was the most difficult scene that we have ever encountered for the recovery of an aircraft."[16] Major pieces of the plane were eventually recovered, including the tail, portions of the wings, and the two engines.[17] The flight data recorder and cockpit voice recorder were also retrieved. The flight data recorder indicated significant drops in altitude and pressure inconsistent with what was recorded on radar, suggesting that an event on the plane caused incorrect readings. The cargo manifests indicated that fifty to sixty oxygen canisters (used for emergency masks on planes) were in the forward cargo hold. When mixed, the chemicals in these canisters give off heat up to 500 degrees. The shelf life of the canisters had expired, and they were being shipped from Miami to Atlanta for disposal. Such oxygen canisters had exploded on two previous ValuJet flights, and in one incident an idle DC-10 was destroyed.[18]

Six days after the crash, further details were released. ValuJet had asked workers for the maintenance company, SabreTech, to place the canisters (which had been removed from two other ValuJet planes in Miami) in boxes. More than a hundred of these canisters were packed into five boxes, which were marked "COMAT," or company materials, but which lacked the required warning that the materials were hazardous. An employee for SabreTech, a maintenance company contracted by ValuJet, did not realize that the generators were unsafe and labeled the boxes as empty, signifying that the canisters had been discharged and were inert. However, some canisters has not been discharged and therefore were still flammable.[19] Discovery of the canisters was a major step in pinpointing the cause of the crash. On May 23 the DOT issued a temporary emergency order banning chemical oxygen generators from passenger airlines until January 1, 1997.[20]

While the NTSB's investigation proceeded, the media search began, focusing first on the aircraft itself. Was it too old? Was its safety record flawed? The plane, originally owned by Delta, was twenty-seven years old, a year older than the average for the ValuJet fleet. That number was within the range of equivalent planes flown by competitors, and many believed that age was not as relevant as its maintenance record. This now became the initial media focus, as the plane operating as flight 592 had been forced to return to the airport seven times in the past two years for a variety of problems, ranging from an oil loss due to a defective cap to a malfunctioning hydraulic pump.[21]

However, press coverage of the event changed dramatically within a few days. The daily releases of prior FAA records and memos covering its oversight of ValuJet in the past months and the airline's imperfect performance record altered the reporting. There was fertile ground for investigative coverage, as the spotlight shifted to the interplay between the regulator and the regulated. This focus was aided by political entrepreneurs who viewed the ValuJet crash as an opportunity for publicizing the issue of airline safety.

Dissension in the Ranks

When an air tragedy occurs, retention of public confidence requires that all personnel speak with one collective voice. There should be no contradictions, minimal inconsistencies, and a firm control over the situation as it evolves. If any cracks in the official armor appear, the media will seize upon them and the public may become less confident not only of air travel but of official oversight. Occasionally, an issue entrepreneur or whistleblower will appear and transform an investigation into a larger issue. The ValuJet crash was such an instance.

The DOT inspector general (IG) oversees all of the agency's operations and is primarily concerned with uncovering problematic or unlawful behavior. This person traditionally works behind the scenes and maintains a low public profile. The IG at the time of the crash was Mary Schiavo, who had been appointed to the office by President Bush six years before the crash. She had been a prosecutor in Missouri before coming to Washington. Many IGs have had an auditing background, which did not lend itself to a public role. Having been a prosecutor, Schiavo took a more public approach to aviation security.[22] She saw herself as the protector of the flying public and was determined to unearth and solve safety problems. Though she had little background in aviation oversight, she acquired a reputation for blaming aviation officials for problems in the skies. Paul Light of the Brookings Institution wrote in 1994 that Schiavo's selection represented the politicization of the appointment process, an assertion used by at least one reporter in describing her.[23]

In previous congressional testimony, Schiavo argued that the FAA was lax in enforcement of airline safety regulations and indicated her frustration at its lack of action. The FAA and the DOT, she said, had failed to monitor start-up airlines more closely because they were more concerned about fostering competition than protecting the flying public. Three months before the ValuJet crash, she had warned FAA officials that ValuJet was having severe safety problems.[24] Her concerns were ignored. The crash of ValuJet flight 592 represented an opportunity to publicize her message. By all accounts, she succeeded. Before the crash, the Lexis-Nexis database of major newspapers records 72 articles that mention Schiavo. The number from May 11, 1996, until the end of 2001 is 412.

On the same night that David Hinson appeared on *Nightline,* Schiavo also appeared, stating that "it's not my job to sell tickets on ValuJet. I would not fly ValuJet." She produced FAA statistics showing that

ValuJet's record was fourteen times worse than other major carriers. By chance, she authored a guest column for *Newsweek* for the week following the ValuJet crash.[25] However, once the disaster occurred, she quickly rewrote her piece to focus on that particular tragedy, negatively portraying the company and the FAA.

The FAA was Schiavo's target because it had overlooked her recommendations concerning airline safety during her entire tenure. She called it the "tombstone agency," that is, not taking action unless people died. These comments appeared in all the major papers and received wide television coverage as well. Such remarks were a public relations nightmare for the FAA and ValuJet.

Schiavo had few friends in Congress. She claimed that she had issued warnings in prior congressional testimony, but legislators felt she should have alerted them to the ValuJet problem. This time, instead of warning Congress, she made her case to the public via the media. "One of the most important things you can do is bring about change. . . . I don't think that necessarily happens in the dark. Sometimes the public has to know or you don't get any change."[26]

These accusations shattered the rosy scenarios painted by the FAA, the DOT, and ValuJet. After all, here was a DOT official who not only criticized the airlines and their overseers but also would not even travel on some of them. Even worse, these carriers tended to be the low-cost airlines, which were—at least until ValuJet—the success stories of the industry. Frustrated by her lack of success within the aviation community, Schiavo moved her case to the public arena. On July 8 she resigned her position with the DOT and subsequently wrote a book about airline safety, *Flying Blind, Flying Safe*. Schiavo's concerns were partially reinforced by the grounding of ValuJet on June 17, 1996. *Nightline* aired Hinson's statements immediately after the crash and contrasted them with his statement on the day ValuJet was grounded, making the FAA look inconsistent.

Blame Avoidance and Symbolic Actions

Immediately after the crash, there were three natural targets of blame. The first was the airline, ValuJet, and its possibly lax practices and procedures. The second was the oversight agency, the FAA, which had been aware of the airline's record. The third was the support company, SabreTech, which the airline had hired for maintenance.

ValuJet was faulted soon after the crash by Schiavo, and then the flood-gates opened. The written record of the FAA became a major component of the blame game. When an airplane crashes the media usually search for previous problems with the plane. Aircraft reports are part of the public record and are usually released during the investigation period. These reports, including the following, were particularly damaging:[27]

—May 14: ValuJet had to make emergency landings eight times in the previous two years with the plane that crashed.

—May 15: Since its inception in 1993, ValuJet reported 284 "service difficulties" to the FAA.

—May 16: A "senior DOT official" said that ValuJet might have broken the law in carrying hazardous cargo.

—May 20: A February 14 memo showed that officials at the FAA field office in Atlanta suggested a recertification of ValuJet's planes (that is, shutting down the airline).

—May 20: An April 3 FAA report said that ValuJet had made progress in solving problems but that "many corrective actions being implemented will take time to have a positive effect."

—May 20: An FAA analysis dated May 2 showed that ValuJet had the second-highest accident rate of the fourteen low-cost carriers.

The release of these memos was a double-edged sword for the FAA. While they indicate that ValuJet had safety problems, they posed the question, What was the FAA doing to correct them before allowing its planes back in the air? The agency was heavily criticized for appearing to do nothing about the airline's problems, even as its own findings suggested that action was warranted. On May 17 Anthony Broderick, an FAA associate administrator, defended the agency, stating, "In large airlines and large companies you will find individual pockets of noncompliance. . . . We judge people in a binary fashion: Either you do meet our standards or you don't. . . . If they do not meet the standards at any time in the future, we will not let them fly."[28]

Within a few days after the crash, attention focused on the canisters. In a cost-cutting move, ValuJet had outsourced all maintenance to local companies in host cities. In Miami that was SabreTech. Since its employees handled the canisters and put them in boxes ready for the flight, SabreTech's handling of the canisters became a target of criticism.

While media coverage continued, ValuJet and SabreTech were faced with legal, financial, political, and regulatory fallout. The FAA was depicted as inept. Under such circumstances, the best posture for a potentially offending party is to adopt a twofold policy. First, avoid negative portrayals and deflect responsibility by blaming an alternative target. Second, place your operation in as positive a light as possible and engage in symbolic actions when necessary. Both of these strategies were used with varying degrees of success in the aftermath of the crash. The postcrash period can be separated into three phases: the immediate aftermath lasting until mid-June, the set of events transpiring near the congressional investigation in late June, and the period surrounding the NTSB hearings in late November.

One of the oldest maxims is, The best defense is a good offense. Finding someone else to blame for the disaster is a viable strategy, particularly when it removes the spotlight from one's own actions. This is what each of the three parties attempted to do from the moment that attention was focused on their shortcomings. Despite ValuJet's less-than-stellar safety record, its president never admitted responsibility for the crash, except for a general statement saying that he was ultimately in charge of the airline and responsible for its performance. Lewis Jordan otherwise moved aggressively to blame others; he had both a major and a minor target. The major culprit was SabreTech. First, he claimed that SabreTech ignored ValuJet's and the federal government's procedures for properly handling the oxygen canisters. He expressed anger: "I am outraged by SabreTech's complete lack of regard for the truth in acknowledging any responsibility for shipping the generators."[29] The canisters had been mislabeled by employees of SabreTech as empty, so naturally the ValuJet crew would not know that they were hazardous when they placed them on the plane.

However, the notion of responsibility is somewhat clouded in legalisms. ValuJet claimed that when SabreTech officials gave the boxes to ValuJet, Valujet became the shipper and was obligated by federal law to handle them properly. If the canisters had been labeled as hazardous waste, however, as required by law, Jordan claimed that ValuJet would never have accepted them. Instead, the shipping ticket marked them as company property and as empty oxygen containers. SabreTech countered that it was ValuJet's responsibility to know what it was shipping.[30]

The airline's second target was the FAA. As FAA memos critical of ValuJet's past practices were published, Jordan indirectly criticized it for unfairly pointing the finger at his company. No other airline, he felt, had ever been subject to the same level of scrutiny by the FAA as ValuJet had in the wake of the crash. This strategy was used primarily in May and June, before congressional hearings; subsequently it was used less frequently.

To provide a positive company portrayal, Jordan took several steps to protect ValuJet's brand. Its image had to change quickly or the company would suffer financial losses due to passenger apprehension. On May 17 Jordan announced on CNN's *Larry King Live* the appointment of retired Air Force general James Davis to oversee safety at the airline. In addition, he ended Valujet's relationship with SabreTech in June, citing the primary importance of safety. Overall, he engaged in a multifaceted public relations campaign to save the company from financial ruin.

Meanwhile, the FAA was in a bind. It was part of a policy subsystem in which the aviation industry was given great freedom with little oversight. FAA officials refrained from negative characterizations of airlines, the only exception being ValuJet's shutdown on June 17. Even that was couched in vague administrative language. However, by releasing reports critical of ValuJet's operation, the FAA provided the media and others with the ammunition to blame the company for the crash. This strategy allowed the FAA to appear both supportive of the industry and also critical of ValuJet. This tack deflected blame from the agency to some degree, though the release of the memos had the downside of making the FAA appear derelict in oversight duties before the crash.

Corrective action could salvage the FAA's reputation in part. Shortly after the crash, it began an intense thirty-day investigation of the airline's operations; its more than 2,000 inspections represented the equivalent of four years' work. The FAA now appeared to be serious about safety, and ValuJet would be subject to severe scrutiny before it could fly again. After the investigation was completed, the FAA decided to ground ValuJet on June 17, 1996.

Issuing a written statement and holding a press conference, the FAA's David Hinson announced the airline's grounding and referred to "several serious deficiencies." Further, ValuJet had failed to establish the "airworthiness" of some of its aircraft, and "multiple shortcomings" had been found in the airline's supervision of maintenance contractors. None of these vague terms—*serious deficiencies, airworthiness, multiple shortcomings*—was spelled out in either the press conference or the written statement. About half of ValuJet's operations had been shut down since the crash and the flight schedule greatly reduced in order to allow FAA inspections to proceed. Hinson said that ValuJet accepted the new, total shutdown and that all of the problems mentioned in the press statement had to be resolved before it could resume operations.[31]

The next day Secretary Peña repeated his oft-cited assertion that the American skies were "the safest in the world." Defending his earlier, premature, endorsement of ValuJet operations, he said those remarks were based on the information available at the time. But after "an exhaustive top-to-bottom inspection of the airline, the FAA is no longer confident in the airline's ability to operate at the required highest levels of safety." He made a symbolic gesture by announcing that Congress would be asked to eliminate the FAA's dual mandate. "I am urging that Congress change the FAA charter to give it a single, primary mission: safety. Let me say this as clearly as I can: There should never be another question about the top priority of the FAA."[32] The notion of divided or multiple loyalties would be permanently removed, at least symbolically.

On June 18 the FAA followed a classic political strategy of scapegoating. Often when an agency makes a mistake, the easiest way to signal to others that policies have been changed is to remove a key individual who headed the operation. This scapegoat can give public credence to the seriousness with which the agency views the matter and a sign of its resoluteness to change directions. In this case, that man was Anthony Broderick, the top FAA official responsible for safety, who had worked at the agency for twenty years. His removal was not as ominous as it initially appeared. He had planned to retire in six months, and that date was effectively moved forward to the present.

His letter of resignation emphasized the need for change following a disaster: "The events of the past weeks mandate that you make major visible changes to improve the public confidence in the safety of our air transportation system and the quality of FAA oversight of the airlines. My leaving will provide you with the maximum amount of flexibility to make those changes."[33] Many praised him for past efforts at the agency. Representative James Oberstar (D-Minn.) commented, "Somebody made a decision that heads had to roll, and he is the chief person in aviation safety within the agency. . . . He was sacrificed."[34]

Throughout this period, SabreTech defended its performance by focusing on the ineptness of others. Outsourcing is a common strategy used by airlines to save money. However, there is always the possibility of misunderstanding. Here, the maintenance company had a serious problem: It had handled the canisters on the ground at Miami. But its president took an aggressive stance from the outset. Steven Townes, president of SabreTech, never accepted responsibility for the crash throughout the period. The company line was that ValuJet was responsible for the accident, that it had never given orders to SabreTech employees to get rid of the canisters, that it instead had asked them to put the canisters into boxes. Although SabreTech employees mislabeled the boxes, they did not put them aboard the plane. Airline personnel performed that task. Since it was ValuJet's decision to ship the boxes, it became the shipper of record, meaning that it was responsible for the packing and marking of the boxes. The validity of such an explanation depends upon the tenuous separation of activities at the terminal and those related to placing materials on the aircraft.[35]

Congressional Action

Before the congressional hearings on the disaster, scheduled for June 25, the three main actors—ValuJet, the FAA, and SabreTech—all attempted to use blame strategies to deflect responsibility for the crash, with the airlines and the FAA engaged in activities to salvage their reputations. Many of the FAA's actions on June 17 and 18 were taken in anticipation of the congressional hearings. The parties to the dispute thus had a small window of opportunity to present their best possible face to Congress before what were likely to be contentious exchanges.

The hearings (held on June 25, 1996, before the Aviation Subcommittee of the House Transportation and Infrastructure Committee) are here discussed in detail to demonstrate how Congress engages in "fire alarm" oversight of the aviation industry.

The subcommittee had twenty-seven members plus two ex officio members—the chair and the ranking minority member of the full committee. Two members from each party dominated the hearings. The Republican protagonists were Bud Shuster (R-Pa.), the committee chair, and John Duncan (R-Tenn.), the subcommittee head. On the Democratic side were James Oberstar (D-Minn.), the ranking minority member for the full committee, and William Lipinski (D-Ill.), with the equivalent status on the subcommittee. They were the only members permitted to make opening statements, with others active only in the question phase after these four had aired their concerns. In deference to the Senate, one member appeared to make an opening statement. William Cohen (R-Maine) was chair of the Senate Governmental Oversight Subcommittee and had held hearings twice in the previous year concerning airline safety.[36]

The legislators made their positions clear in their opening statements. The Republicans stressed the safety of air travel but questioned the FAA's oversight role. Lipinski focused on inconsistency of statements from Mary Schiavo, Anthony Broderick, and Federico Peña. While critical of the FAA, he singled out Broderick for special praise. Cohen pointed to the shortcomings of all major parties: ValuJet for its shoddy maintenance record, the FAA for lax oversight, and the DOT for its rosy assessments. The organizational culture within the FAA precluded it from effective oversight: "One of the problems we have had in dealing with the FAA is it seems to have a culture that denies a problem exists, that defends the status quo, and then seeks to deflect public criticism."

Four witnesses, representing the relevant government units, appeared in the first group: Jim Hall, chairman of the NTSB, Mary Schiavo, David Hinson, and Anthony Broderick. Government officials attempted to defend their respective positions. Hall stressed the airline's safety record, cited the problem with the canisters although the investigation was not complete, and then mentioned the NTSB safety recommendations languishing at FAA headquarters. "We may not just have a ValuJet problem here; we may also have an FAA problem." Schiavo attacked the safety record of ValuJet and the improperly executed oversight role of the FAA. Hinson stressed the safety record of the airline industry, ValuJet's rapid growth, and the financial difficulties of the FAA that had precluded the performance of its functions.

When the questioning phase began, Shuster first praised the job that Hinson had done at the agency but then focused on partisan dynamics. He demanded a detailed description of a June 17 White House briefing concerning the ValuJet matter. Present at that briefing were officials of the FAA and the DOT. Had administration officials pressured the FAA as to its handling of the ValuJet crash? Specifically, did White House officials tell Hinson to fire Broderick? Both Hinson and Broderick denied that interpretation of events, and Broderick asserted that he had left of his own volition.

The Democratic response came from Oberstar. He reviewed the same briefing to stress that there was no high-level Democratic interference. Turning to a February 14 internal FAA memo raising questions about ValuJet's performance, he wanted to know if FAA officials had seen it. Hinson reported that he had not seen the memo but that no action would have been taken had he seen it. His defense focused on his interpretation of a sentence in the memo, "Consideration should be given for corrective action," as meaning that the airline should not be grounded. Oberstar criticized the FAA for an inadequate inspection program, and Hinson agreed.

Duncan questioned the main witnesses. He praised both Hinson's work and the industry's safety record. His question was whether more FAA inspections would have solved the ValuJet problem, or would they have simply been no more than added paperwork. Hinson assured the chair that the FAA's inspection process was real and involved on-site investigation of the planes.

Lipinski asked Hall if the FAA's reluctance to enact NTSB recommendations was due to industry costs. Hall concurred. Puzzled about the sequence of reports, Lipinski asked why ValuJet was shut down in June if the same facts were present months earlier. Broderick said that four months of study were necessary to assess the airline's operations; only when it was completed was it obvious that the airline had to be closed down. Lipinski pressed Schiavo for names of other unsafe airlines, since her earlier statements implied their existence. When she demurred, he asked if the ValuJet matter had been discussed with either Hinson or Peña. Hinson had not been contacted, but her staff had reached FAA officials in Atlanta, she answered. She would not discuss contacting Peña due to the ongoing investigation.

Other committee members covered the same ground as the leaders. Separating the individual and agency roles, several praised either Hinson ("greatest respect for your ability," "brought a professional element to the agency"), or Broderick, or both. Legislators negatively portrayed the FAA, however, by focusing on its reluctance to oversee ValuJet's flight performance records. Hinson's and Broderick's defenses took the following forms:

—The FAA could not or should not interfere with an airline company's desire to expand.

—FAA investigations of ValuJet's safety record were ongoing at the time of the crash but were not yet complete.

—There is a need to raise the standards for subcontractors.

—There must be equality of treatment across airlines with respect to regulation.

—New carriers are safe. Until the ValuJet accident, "new entrant carriers" had never had an accident.

—Response time varies, depending on the situation, and can range from a few months to a few decades. By law, the FAA must respond to an NTSB recommendation in ninety days; the average for the first response is sixty-eight days.

The next group of witnesses was from outside government, including Steven Townes, the president of SabreTech; Lewis Jordan, the president of ValuJet; and Martin Bollinger, the vice president of Booz-Allen and

Hamilton. Townes took a conciliatory approach in his testimony. He was apologetic for past errors, sympathetic to the families' anguish, and desirous of change, saying there is "a tragic thin line of human errors." Greater attention should be given to handling hazardous materials in flight with more training for ground personnel, he said, and SabreTech had conducted its own thorough review of the situation. As a result, new stringent safety procedures had been installed.

The president of ValuJet also began by expressing sympathy for the victims' families. He repeated in detail how his company was not responsible for the mishandling of the canisters but did not mention SabreTech as the culprit. Since the shutdown, FAA teams of inspectors had carefully examined his planes, he said, as ValuJet had become the target of unprecedented scrutiny. "We have had four years of inspections in a four-week period."

Finally, the executive from Booz-Allen, which had done a survey of FAA certification procedures in 2000, concluded that its management strategy should shift from local or regional autonomy to national control and that its rule-making process should be simplified.

These positions were then subject to committee scrutiny. Shuster focused only on probing the president of ValuJet about whether the shutdown was politically motivated in that the directive came from the Clinton administration. Jordan said he had no such knowledge. Duncan then honed in on one aspect of the crash: the incorrect labeling of the boxes of canisters. SabreTech's president changed his tune from previous months and now used the phrase "shared responsibility" but hedged about what could have been done differently. He could not comment, he said, until the NTSB investigation was completed. After continued rephrasing of the same question by the committee member, he said, "I am absolutely committed not to use this forum to turn into a blame-lobbing session." Duncan asked Jordan if he thought ValuJet would have been shut down with the same circumstances if it were not a start-up airline. The reply was, "I cannot imagine that I would have even gotten anywhere near the same amount of attention. . . . I am quite frankly, very baffled by what has happened."

Oberstar asked Jordan if ValuJet's rapid growth caused the company to lose control of its maintenance oversight. Jordan pointed to Southwest as a model for outsourcing heavy maintenance with no problems. Oberstar praised ValuJet's record. "Safety responsibility starts at the corporate board room. . . . You've certainly demonstrated an attitude of compliance. Every time the FAA has made recommendations, suggestions, you have done it. I think that's much to your credit."

Lipinski focused on the work order relating to the disposition of the canisters, specifically with respect to capping, discharging, and placing them on the airliner. Townes said manuals were available but that the specific work order did not refer to how to discharge and dispose of the canisters. The work order "doesn't go to that detailed specification, and we're required to work to those types of written engineering instructions; we have a problem that goes beyond one incident and should be fixed industrywide." When asked if ValuJet was responsible for making that work order comprehensible, Townes avoided the question, saying it was a "broader responsibility."

In this session, the real culprit turned out to be Schiavo, who had testified earlier in the day. Several members were puzzled as to why Schiavo had not spoken to FAA and DOT officials if she had been so worried about ValuJet and airline safety. They wondered how she could be so responsive to the media and not to official and committee concerns. Some members typecast her as the uncooperative witness.

Overall, the hearings allowed members of Congress to address the ValuJet crash in more detail, which kept attention focused on the disaster. While they produced no major changes, agency officials took corrective action in anticipation of their testimony. On September 26, a little more than three months after ValuJet had been grounded and long after the hearings, the DOT gave ValuJet permission to resume flying on a limited basis. The company had to agree to reorganize its management and to recast safety operations.

NTSB Hearing

On November 18 the NTSB hearing convened in Miami with approximately twenty witnesses scheduled to testify over five weekdays. More reports and testimony were gathered for this hearing than any up until that time.[37] Initial witnesses testified about the technical aspects relating to handling oxygen generators, the heat of the fire, and the time required to start the fire. However, other developments captured media attention.

A renowned fire expert, Merritt Birky—whose expertise had been used by the NTSB after other crashes—simulated the aircraft explosion in the laboratory. Two videotapes were made of the test and were shown during the hearings. SabreTech officials had objected strongly to the viewing, at one point during the proceedings handing around a letter stating their objections. A hearing officer threatened to remove company officials for disturbing the hearing.[38]

There was also a conflict with Jordan, who disputed the FAA statistics showing that ValuJet had had fifty-nine unscheduled landings in the five months preceding the crash. He argued vociferously that the numbers were a statistical anomaly and were misleading, since most of these incidents were minor. At the conclusion of his testimony, Jordan had to be escorted from the room by a security guard.[39]

Despite such passion, ValuJet and SabreTech officials refused to criticize one another during the hearing. They did not cross-examine each other's witnesses about the handling of the canisters, because the employees who had actually handled them were not on the stand. These employees refused to testify, invoking their Fifth Amendment rights. Combined with similar stances at the congressional hearing, the apparent nonaggression pact was a shift from the charges levied against one another immediately after the crash.[40]

The hearing also focused on whether ValuJet's behavior with respect to the oxygen canisters was the exception rather than the rule. During the hearings, Delta and TWA admitted that they had shipped oxygen generators, though both stopped after the ValuJet crash. Both airlines maintained that such actions were legal. As the TWA representative said, "It would not be unusual that we have [a] difference of opinion over government regulations."[41]

The principal purpose of NTSB hearings is to identify the cause of a crash and hold culpable parties responsible for their actions. The main focus of this one was to interrogate officials of ValuJet, SabreTech, and the FAA as to their role in the events that preceded the crash. These exchanges were detailed and lengthy. John Gentry, a ValuJet vice president, defended the airline's oversight of SabreTech under questioning from board member John Goglia, but he ultimately conceded that ValuJet has final responsibility for what comes onto its planes.

SabreTech representatives explained how a clerk mislabeled the canisters without realizing their contents. On the day before the crash, a stock clerk was preparing for an inspection visit from Continental Airlines, a potential customer, and quickly arranged the canisters inside five cardboard boxes and taped them shut. A SabreTech truck driver delivered the canisters, along with tires, to a ValuJet ramp agent and said, "The tires and boxes could go out" on flight 592. Townes admitted that errors were made and said, "What we should do is resolve that this should never happen again."[42]

A parade of FAA officials came forth on the last two days of the hearing to answer questions about their lax attitude toward problems at ValuJet. What emerged was that problems existed at various levels in the agency, which when combined were a recipe for trouble. Three months before the crash, John Tutora, the supervisor of maintenance inspectors, found problems with the airline's performance. He thought a shutdown was required but, instead of taking action, wrote a memo to his boss. In the event Tutora's superior was ever questioned, this communication would protect him. Goglia said, "Mr. Tutora, this smells, this really smells, when you have an internal report with such pointed findings, and it's done in preparation or posturing for hearings or investigations."[43]

The NTSB Final Crash Report

In August 1997 the NTSB released its final report on the accident. The cause stressed the oxygen generators being improperly carried as cargo. The report separated causal responsibility for conditions leading to the accident from the accident itself. Three culprits were identified.

For conditions leading to the mishap, two targets were singled out:

The failure of the FAA to adequately monitor ValuJet's heavy maintenance programs . . . and to adequately respond to prior chemical oxygen generator fires . . . and ValuJet's failure to ensure that both ValuJet and contract maintenance facility employees were aware of the carrier's "no-carry" hazardous materials policy.[44]

For the accident itself, three parties shared the blame:

The failure of SabreTech to properly prepare, package, and identify unexpended chemical oxygen generators. . . . The failure of ValuJet to properly oversee its contract maintenance program to ensure compliance with maintenance and hazardous materials requirements and practices. . . . The failure of the FAA to require smoke detection and fire suppression systems in class D cargo compartments.

There were no surprises in the report. The NTSB now formally chastised the three parties that blamed one another and that had been targeted in hearings by both members of Congress and the NTSB.

Policy Change

Overall, the NTSB hearing and the resulting media coverage cast all parties—ValuJet, SabreTech, and the FAA—in a bad light, one that further harmed ValuJet's chances for revival. The final report portrayed no party favorably, either. In the time between the NTSB hearing and the issuance of this document, airline companies assumed the offensive.

Three weeks after the NTSB hearing, industry officials announced a voluntary compliance measure in which all planes would be retrofitted with fire detectors in cargo holds, at an estimated cost of $400 million. However, none of the companies committed to equipment that would extinguish such fires. At a December 12, 1996, press conference attended by airline executives, Vice President Al Gore endorsed this measure as the beginning of a new joint commitment of the private and public sector to airline safety:

> It's important not just because it will mean improved fire detection but also because it signals the beginning of a change in how government and this industry work together to achieve safety goals. We're working to craft a relationship that will allow us to implement safety improvements more quickly and at less cost and with a lot of the unnecessary adversarial conflict that for too long has characterized the government-industry relationship.[45]

President Clinton also made a statement at the press conference, noting that "by putting smoke detectors in every cargo hold of these carriers, we take another step to make our people and our skies safer."[46]

In anticipation of the NTSB hearing, the FAA on November 14 had issued a directive banning airlines from carrying *any* oxidizing materials that can feed fires. On December 30, 1996, this rule was formalized and was amended in mid-1997. However, despite that edict, such materials continued to be transported by some airlines. At least fifteen illegal shipments of oxygen generators occurred in the year after the ValuJet tragedy. Further, NTSB investigators said those were only the ones they knew about, raising suspicions that others existed.[47] A newspaper investigation in 1998 turned up other examples of such shipments. The FAA imposed fines for such acts, but a former security inspector said, "It appears to be quite easy to succeed if you want to illegally introduce hazardous materials. What's wrong is that no controls are being applied."[48] Others asserted some of the traffic was unintentional, but such shipments continue.

Another NTSB recommendation called on the FAA to require smoke detection and fire suppression equipment in cargo holds. New-model planes already have these systems, but this recommendation required an addition to 3,700 older planes.[49] Fire safety had been an issue for years: The NTSB had wanted a stronger response since 1988, when a cargo fire created a problem for an American Airlines plane en route from Dallas to Nashville. However, the airlines and the FAA resisted such actions due to cost. In February 1998 the FAA instituted this rule.

Within a few months of the crash, Congress passed a $19.5 billion, two-year package reauthorizing the FAA. A provision of the law eliminated the FAA's dual mandate. The package included money to hire 410 additional workers (controllers, pilots, and safety inspectors) and 140 hazardous materials inspectors, provisions that did not raise partisan rancor.[50] There were no significant changes to the regulatory apparatus governing airlines. Instead, members stressed the strong safety record of the aviation industry. As John Duncan noted, "If we totally overreact, we can just about shut down the airlines."[51]

Business and Legal Fallout

Ultimately, neither SabreTech nor ValuJet would survive the crash. SabreTech closed its Miami office in January 1997 and soon after ceased all operations. SabreTech and its employees were accused of criminal liability for the crash, the first time in history that had occurred. The company was convicted on nine charges and ordered to pay $9 million in restitution and a $1.5 million fine. On October 31, 2001, a federal appeals court overturned the convictions and reversed the fines, and state murder charges were dropped in exchange for a donation to promote flight safety.[52] Both the airline and the maintenance company dealt with victim lawsuits as well.

ValuJet could not overcome the effects of the crash. In an attempt to remake its image, a new $8 million advertisement campaign was introduced in October 1996, soon after the resumption of operations. In the past, the company conveyed a "fun" image, using the slogan Good Times, Great Fares. Now the emphasis changed to cost, with the slogan Low Fares, Everyday, Everywhere We Fly. "ValuJet is now stressing safety, company pride, and low prices over fun," wrote one observer.[53] On November 5, 1996, Joseph Corr, a former executive with Continental Airlines, was hired to oversee ValuJet's daily operations. Jordan removed

Box 5-1   New York Times *Coverage of ValuJet Flight 592,*
  1996–2000

1996: 85 stories
  May: 33 stories (8 front page)
  June: 26 stories (3 front page)
  July: 5 stories
  August: 5 stories
  September: 3 stories
  October: 1 story
  November: 10 stories
  December: 2 stories
1997: 9 stories
1998: 3 stories
1999: 10 stories (1 front page)
2000: none
  Total: 107 stories (12 front page)

Source: Authors' calculations based on *New York Times Index,* various years.

himself from the day-to-day operations of the company and became the company's chairman.[54]

In July 1997 the airline began a facelift by initiating merger talks with AirTran, which served twenty-two cities. The airlines merged, and in September 1997 ValuJet formally changed its name to AirTran. Headquarters were shifted from Atlanta to Orlando. Analysts argued that the airline needed to change its image of being disaster prone.[55] In addition, $40 million was spent to repaint thirty-three planes and, in the process, to remove the smiling logo.[56] AirTran ultimately survived, but ValuJet did not.

The Implications of the Crash

The crash of ValuJet flight 592 kept the attention of the media. Consider the coverage patterns of the *New York Times* (see box 5-1).[57] The postcrash period received significant attention for the first two months and then ebbed until the end of the year, when it reemerged with the NTSB hearings. Why the focus on ValuJet? Several possibilities emerge.

First, the principal development in commercial aviation in the mid-nineties was the growth of cheap, no-frills airlines. In this regard, ValuJet was the unquestioned leader in market impact and growth rate. It was symbolic of the new upstart ready to challenge established companies. Second, the crash occurred over a dangerous wetland, the Everglades, making it a natural media event. The difficulty in recovering bodies from a swamp built drama into the episode. Third, lax oversight by a government agency brought the adversarial nature of the media into play. The "watchdog" of the public interest had a field day when incomplete but critical FAA reports trickled out. The media emphasized the FAA's inefficiency, lack of coordination, deference to industry, and disregard for safety.

Normally, uncertainty would pique media interest. Lack of a cause could fuel speculation as to the various possibilities. However, that was not the case in this crash. The likely culprit appeared within days of the tragedy. While it took the NTSB more than a year to formally state its conclusion, the issue early on shifted from what caused the crash to who was responsible. Three possibilities emerged: two private companies and a government agency. Let us consider briefly how the sequence of events played out.

In the first month, the major parties first expressed sympathy for the victims and then, when the cause emerged, attempted to avoid liability. ValuJet and SabreTech blamed one another for the crash. However, shortly thereafter, when the spotty regulatory oversight of the FAA became known, the agency emerged yet again as a target of the NTSB.

The overriding response of the companies and government agencies involved was to reassure the public, with a major emphasis on the symbol of safety. At every stage, key participants declared what an aberrant event a crash was and how safe the system was. In fact the only problem occurred when, immediately after the crash, the heads of the FAA and the DOT attached the symbol of safety not only to the whole airline industry but to ValuJet in particular. Within days that was found to be inaccurate, and the credibility of these officials suffered. Then the DOT disappeared from view with respect to the crash, and all parties referred only to the industry's safety, not to ValuJet's. That link was not made until the recertification process had been completed.

Public oversight came in the form of two hearings. A House subcommittee spent part of the time bickering over the involvement of the Clinton White House in aviation matters. Beyond partisan dynamics, committee members adopted a dual strategy. They praised the individuals overseeing safety in the skies, particularly Broderick and Hinson, yet found fault with agency procedures. Even the heads of ValuJet and SabreTech did not receive harsh criticism. FAA, ValuJet, and SabreTech officials downplayed the culpability of other actors and basically admitted to shortcomings. The individual weathering most of the committee's scorn was Schiavo, who was criticized for seeking out the media rather than agency personnel with her concerns.

The NTSB hearings changed that tone. Board members did not lavish praise on the individuals involved. Instead the emphasis was on the shortcomings of the three actors: ValuJet was overwhelmed by the company's success and growth; SabreTech officials had neither the information nor the equipment to handle the canisters; and FAA officials, although they had met their responsibilities, had been undercut by poor communication and interoffice coordination. Paperwork intended to prevent problems ironically caused them.

There were consequences of the crash: ValuJet changed everything about its operations, from the color of its planes to its leadership and its name. Congress enacted a law adding money to the FAA budget for additional inspectors and eliminating the FAA's dual mandate. The agency passed a few new rules precluding passenger planes from carrying oxygen canisters in their cargo holds and requiring them to carry equipment to detect and prevent fires. However, oxygen generators continued to be shipped despite penalties. Further, the fire suppression rules took over a year to be enacted, and even then the airlines were given three years to comply. No major overhaul of airline safety resulted from this crash, though policy changes did occur.

But did ValuJet deserve the blame heaped upon it? All major participants in the case—other than company officials—identified the company as one of the major culprits in the deaths of more than a hundred people. The company had a string of prior safety problems that the FAA had either overlooked or had been slow to investigate. That plus the company's rapid expansion and questionable maintenance practices made them the likely focus of blame. But was this accurate?

An alternative view is articulated in the written record of the House Aviation Subcommittee hearing. At the request of ValuJet, the MIT professor Arnold Barnett, who had studied accident rates for over two decades, offered his views on the incident. He used the statistical argument: aviation's safety record compared with that of other transportation modes. In the case of ValuJet, before the crash the airline had carried 9.7 million passengers with no passenger injuries.

Further, Barnett questioned the FAA's use of the term *accident* in compiling its data on airline safety. The term can mean many things, from a flight attendant breaking an ankle during air turbulence to people dying in a crash. Therefore, passenger risk is not really reflected in FAA accident reports. In the crash in question, no airline personnel made any mistakes in the operation of the plane; an oxygen generator accident could have occurred on any airline. In short, ValuJet was unfairly criticized for an accident that had nothing to do with the operation of the plane.[58] The only other person to raise this point during the hearing was ValuJet's president; no members of the committee considered the matter.[59]

Ultimately, ValuJet could not survive. Perception was everything, and few rushed to the airline's defense.

Conclusion

The ValuJet crash highlights the success and the weakness of the aviation system of the 1990s. The economy airline benefited consumers through low prices, and its rapid growth was a plus for a presidential administration promoting low-cost airlines. But the crash revealed the inadequacies in FAA oversight. Ultimately, however, the ValuJet crash did not have a major effect on the operations of the airline industry (short of specific safety reforms that the NTSB had first proposed in 1988), although it did attract significant attention from stakeholders in aviation safety.

The main findings of this chapter include the following:

—Successful, low-cost airline start-ups tend to be subject to more intense media scrutiny when one of their planes crashes and a link can be made between cost cutting and safety.

—Government officials who endorse the safety record of an airline after a crash are put on the defensive when lapses in record-keeping and oversight are subsequently shown to exist.

—The postcrash scenario highlights the tensions between the FAA and the NTSB.

—Congressional oversight after a crash is often limited to short, high-profile committee investigations in which legislators challenge and involved parties defend.

CHAPTER 6

The Crash of TWA Flight 800

> We're looking at a criminal act. We're looking at somebody who
> either put a bomb on it or shot a missile, a surface-to-air missile.
> —*Senator Orrin Hatch*

> The Safety Board concludes that the in-flight breakup of TWA
> flight 800 was not initiated by a bomb or a missile strike.
> —*National Transportation Safety Board,* Aircraft Accident
> Report . . . TWA Flight 800

Before the events of September 11, 2001, there was TWA flight 800. The Boeing 747 fell into Long Island Sound in 1996, killing more than 200 passengers and crew and becoming the year's top news story.

Typically, plane crashes do not capture public and press attention for a sustained period of time. TWA flight 800 was different, becoming the subject of more than 40 percent of *New York Times* stories on specific plane accidents in the 1990s. The prospect of terrorism, the dearth of evidence for any particular cause, and the zeal of political entrepreneurs kept the event alive in both the media and the halls of government.

A mysterious crash two years prior, of USAir flight 427 in Pennsylvania, did not receive nearly the same attention because it was missing the key elements of an active political entrepreneur and the possibility of terrorism and government conspiracy. The crash of USAir flight 427 was a technical matter to be resolved by the National Transportation Safety Board (NTSB) and the Federal Aviation Administration (FAA). The TWA crash, though it was the object of the most expensive plane crash investigation in history, was routine from a safety perspective. The recommendations regarding terrorism made by the Gore Commission, created after the TWA crash and in the wake of other terror acts, gathered dust until the events of September 11 spurred interest in them.

In this chapter the events surrounding the crash of TWA flight 800 are examined. A central theme of our analysis is that high-profile plane crashes often divert attention and resources away from other air safety issues and do not necessarily lead to improvements in safety. Media coverage and government attention do not guarantee greater safety in the skies, and no crash in the 1990s attained such media scrutiny.

The Crash

At 8:31 p.m. on July 17, 1996, the Boeing 747 operating as Trans World Airlines (TWA) flight 800, en route from JFK International Airport to Charles DeGaulle International Airport in Paris, began a deadly descent into Long Island Sound after exploding in midair and literally breaking in half. All 230 passengers and crew perished as a result of either the explosion or the impact from hitting the water.

Immediately after the crash, the press and public officials began speculating on the cause of the disaster. The most prevalent theory in the days immediately following the accident was that a bomb or a missile brought down the Boeing 747. In other words, it was an act of terrorism. This connection, made without significant evidence, was reinforced by the temporal proximity of the summer Olympics, set to begin on July 19, and the subsequent bombing at the Olympics on July 27. Contributing to the terror hypothesis was the 747's reputation for being "impregnable."[1] This primed individuals—from the mass public to the highest government officials—to suspect terrorism. Senator Orrin Hatch (R-Utah) told reporters that he was sure that at a minimum sabotage and maybe terrorism was to blame.[2] The other two theories were that mechanical failure was to blame or that friendly fire, in the form of a surface-to-air missile, downed the plane.

An investigation began immediately, with the Federal Bureau of Investigation (FBI) and the NTSB working in tandem. The latter was the lead agency in charge of the investigation, although it would defer to the FBI if criminal activity were established. James Kallstrom was the FBI's representative on the case, while the NTSB entourage was led by Vice Chairman Robert Francis. They probed all possible scenarios, eventually concluding the plane was felled by an explosion in the center fuel tank. Sabotage was ruled out as a determinant, though the precise cause was unclear. The NTSB did not issue its final report until August 23, 2000, more than four years after the crash. In the interim, all branches of the government became involved, and interagency squabbling took center stage during key points in the investigation. Policy recommendations proposed by Congress, a presidential commission, and the NTSB mostly languished.

The Immediate Aftermath

The initial focus after the crash of TWA flight 800 was threefold: recovering the plane and bodies, assisting victims' families, and determining what caused the crash. Media attention was intense on all fronts. Stories about the victims were plentiful initially, with headlines like "Amid Plane's Rubble Lie Shattered Hopes and Dreams," but dissipated after about two weeks.[3] The victims' families remained in the news due to their complaints regarding their treatment by TWA, the release of passenger information, and the handling of recovered remains. Families were concerned about not receiving proper financial compensation since the crash took place in international waters under the auspices of the Death on the High Seas Act. This law greatly limits payments to victims even if negligence by the airline is established in court. Their complaints led to new rules regarding the way passengers are treated after a tragedy and the size of financial remuneration. Ultimately these were the most substantive policy changes to come out of the crash, and neither related directly to aviation safety.

Meanwhile, political actors began offering their sympathies and promised to keep close watch on the investigation. President Clinton crafted a typical presidential response to a tragedy: the display of sympathy and the symbolic action statement.

> First, on behalf of the American people, I want to say to the families of the passengers of Flight 800, we are well aware that only the passage of time, the love of your family, and faith in God can ease your pain. But America stands with you. Our thoughts, our prayers, have been with you through the night, and they will be with you in the days to come. . . .
>
> Our government is doing everything we can to continue the search for survivors and to find out the causes of this accident. Chief of Staff Leon Panetta has just met in the White House Situation Room with all the agencies involved and has finished briefing me on our response. I have asked him to insure that our response will continue to be prompt, effective, and comprehensive.[4]

The terms "Chief of Staff" and "White House Situation Room" symbolically brought the office of the presidency into the resolution of the disaster, and the direct presidential request ("I have asked him") provided the impression of active involvement, despite the reality that the administration could do little so soon after a crash. When the president visited with the families of the victims the following week, *ABC World News Tonight* aired the following comments from members of the families: "It was a good feeling. It shows that the president really cares about us." "He was just very reassuring as a human being."[5] The president probably did feel genuine concern and sympathy while visiting with family members, but just as important, he offered reassurance. After families' complaints about their treatment by the airline, the president dispatched James Lee Witt, the director of the Federal Emergency Management Agency (FEMA), to serve as the "president's eyes and ears" during the investigation.[6]

Given that the immediate suspicion after the crash was that a bomb took down TWA flight 800, regulators had to create the appearance that this risk would be lessened. The FAA administrator David Hinson stated vaguely, "The FAA's security program will be modified as needed to ensure the safety of the traveling public."[7] Security was tightened following the crash, with additional baggage checks performed at selected airports across the country, including Dulles International, Reagan National, JFK International, and Hartsfield International in Atlanta. Of course, these measures were largely symbolic, since a terrorist could still smuggle a bomb aboard a plane at a smaller airport. On July 25 President Clinton ordered increased baggage and cargo inspections, checks of cabin and cargo holds on international flights, and more thorough questioning of passengers.[8]

After the initial saturation coverage, news accounts began to focus nearly exclusively on the recovery effort and its contribution to the investigation. A cause had still not been determined, and the long, slow salvaging process provided the press with new stories every day. The investigation itself was covered nearly every day from the day of the crash to the beginning of September. The lengthy process of gathering the wreckage was fodder for daily news stories, and the causal search generated political theater.

Was It a Bomb, a Missile, or a Malfunction?

The search for the cause is usually a technical matter that attracts limited press attention, unless there is some unusual element involved. Three scenarios dominated coverage immediately after the TWA crash: a mechanical malfunction, a bomb placed aboard the aircraft, and a surface-to-air missile fired at the plane by either hostile or friendly fire. Under title 49 of the *U.S. Code* the NTSB was the lead agency in charge of a crash investigation. But if a criminal act is found to be involved, control may be ceded to the FBI. In the TWA flight 800 investigation the FBI seemed to usurp that authority. There was tension between the two agencies during the investigation and a shared view that the other was uncooperative and not forthcoming with information. Their missions clashed: The NTSB presents as much information to the public as possible, while the FBI keeps evidence secret if its release would jeopardize an ongoing investigation.

The FBI's Kallstrom quickly became a media favorite. At a press conference soon after the tragedy, he barely disguised his view that terrorism was the likely cause and that the focus should shift to finding the criminals: "If it is a terrorist event, we then have the challenge to find out who the perpetrators were, who the cowards were that did this, as [we] do in all these other investigations. And I guarantee you that the resources of the FBI, all of federal law enforcement, and the great law enforcement team we have at every level will be used on that investigation."[9] Earlier in the press conference, he stated, "We're not here to take over the investigation yet." There was little doubt that the FBI wanted control of the case, and he was the take-charge individual keeping the bureau and the terror theory in the forefront even after the assertion was widely discredited.[10] In part as a consequence of the turf battles that occurred after this crash, Congress in 2000 passed legislation that gave the attorney general the authority to make the FBI the lead investigative agency after a crash if the "circumstances reasonably indicate that the accident may have been caused by an intentional criminal act."[11]

Government representatives refused at any point to state that terrorism was the cause of the crash, but they did little to discourage reporters from such an inference, as evidenced by news articles. The *New York Times,* the *Washington Post,* and other elite newspapers portrayed the investigators as checking out several leads but as leaning heavily toward the bomb theory. The press thrives on quickly resolved, clear-cut stories yet is in dire need of information in the event of a long investigation. This may clash with an investigative timetable.

Serving as an agenda setter for other news outlets, the *New York Times* provides the best example of this information search. A few days into the investigation, a quick resolution was evidently not imminent, and the *Times* required new material to sustain the story. The bomb theory was being emphasized in its news stories. Though reporters would dutifully mention that two other theories were still under review, new information was often framed in terms of the terror angle. This view was not initially discouraged by Kallstrom and Francis, who intimated that the crash was likely caused by a criminal act. Even after they publicly backed away from this suggestion (though not ruling it out), the *Times* maintained this stance.

Two stories that ran in July were framed by the terror theory but followed this suggestion with a caveat.

> The crash remains classified as an accident, but law enforcement officials in the United States and other countries are continuing to pursue various theories of terrorist involvement. . . . But both safety and FBI officials say that, since they have only scant physical evidence so far from the plane itself, it remains an open question whether the explosion was caused by catastrophic mechanical failure or foul play. And much of the available evidence is not definitive.[12]
>
> With the crucial evidence—the shattered wreckage—lying, unlocated, under 120 feet of water, federal investigators still could not officially declare what they deeply believe: that the explosion was the result of a criminal act. . . ."We did not move the ball in terms of finding the wreckage," Mr. Kallstrom added. But his agents had questioned "thousands" of people and had made progress in compiling leads for each of the three following possibilities: "There was a bomb on the plane; the plane was hit with a rocket; or there was a mechanical, electrical, or some malfunction on the plane that caused the plane to explode," Mr. Kallstrom said.[13]

Perhaps even more telling is the way in which the *Times* covered news that did not suggest a bomb. A July 24 story, under the headline "No Evidence of Explosive So Far in Crash Inquiry," led with this sentence: "Investigators examining the small amount of wreckage recovered so far from the crash of Trans World Airlines Flight 800 said yesterday that they had not yet found any concrete evidence that the plane was destroyed by an explosive device."[14]

The *Times* coverage can be contrasted to that of the *Washington Post*. When a trace of an explosive chemical found in the plane's wreckage was reported on August 24, 1996, the *Times* headline stated, "Prime Evidence Found that Device Exploded in Cabin of Flight 800," while the *Washington Post* headlined its story, "Explosive Traces in Wreckage of Flight 800 'Inconclusive,' Officials Want More Evidence before Criminal Finding."[15]

This coverage to some degree reflected the organizational perspective of the FBI. In congressional hearings, witnesses testified that Kallstrom wanted only individuals who were "on board" with the bomb theory to remain on the investigation. William Tobin, the former FBI chief metallurgist, testified at a Senate hearing that there was "group think" involved in the investigation and that the bureau was wedded to the bomb-missile theory. From this standpoint there needed to be evidence to the contrary before the bomb theory would be ruled out, and the bureau ignored the views of scientific experts. This perspective can be seen in the following statement from Tobin:

> I was ordered to, in a rather frenzied manner, to go conduct an exhaustive search in contact with my NTSB liaison . . . to find a certain overhead bin that was characterized as in pristine condition. But it was in a very emotional, very frenzied manner, so I inquired as to why I was looking for this particular pristine overhead bin on the port side of the aircraft, that was from the left-hand side of the aircraft. I was told that that was proof that NTSB was, quote, "squirreling away evidence" and stashing evidence, which again flies in the face of my interpretation of whose aircraft this was.
>
> But, so I inquired as to why the pristine overhead bin was of such significance. I was told that that was demonstrative proof that they were squirreling away evidence. That the recovery had been captured on a videotape from the USS *Grapple* or the USS *Grasp* which—one of the recovery ships. And on the videotape it showed this overhead bin being raised or set on the deck.
>
> And I said, well I'm still missing some critical information, why is this important, why is this critical? To which I was advised that it had a suitcase, a badly charred and damaged suitcase inside the overhead bin. And my response at that point was, well I'm still missing some critical information. Why are we looking for this, quote, "pristine overhead bin"? Are you suggesting that there was a bomb in the suitcase that went off? Yes. Well that went off instantaneously, brought down the 747, with no reporting on the FDR or CVR, flight data recorder or the cockpit voice recorder, and didn't put a scratch on the overhead bin. And I was told, yes, we want that overhead bin, and I was continued—told to go find that overhead bin.[16]

Probably the biggest embarrassment for the FBI occurred when bomb residue was found on the plane and Tobin warned that this was not definitive proof. Kallstrom was convinced that this was a bomb, and he would most likely have released a statement to that effect, but Tobin had testified that he warned Kallstrom that he would publicly disavow that theory. Kallstrom instead simply reported the information, stopping short of saying it was a bomb.

It turned out that the bomb residue was left after a training session for bomb-sniffing dogs, which had been held on the plane on June 10. According to others on the case, the FBI continued its intransigence when the Bureau of Alcohol, Tobacco, and Firearms (ATF) wanted to release a report in January 1997 stating that a bomb was not the cause. Kallstrom thought this was premature, saying in a letter to the NTSB, "I believe it is unfortunate that ATF, for reasons that are unknown to me, chose to prepare a report expressing an opinion regarding the cause of this tragedy before the investigation has been completed. It is an extraordinary violation of investigative protocol."[17] Some may defend Kallstrom and the FBI by noting the culture of the agency, which viewed the task as checking out every possible lead, every possible hint that a criminal act occurred. The bureau would be criticized if something was missed and criminal activity was later discovered.

The FBI's persistence had an effect on the way the government handled the crash by putting aviation security and terrorism back on the agenda. Conspiracy theories proffered by former presidential press secretary Pierre Salinger and others focused on friendly fire or an enemy missile downing the plane. The notion of a government cover-up kept the terror angle alive, and such theories are still widely circulated. In November 18, 1997, after spending $20 million, the FBI issued a report claiming that no evidence of a bomb was found. But in the meantime, a focus had been placed on airline security.[18] Independent of the bureau's involvement, the NTSB went about its work, searching for the cause.

Of all the parties to the investigation, Boeing faced the highest stakes. Once terrorism was ruled out, attention turned toward some malfunction of the aircraft, so blame deflection would not be a viable strategy. Instead, the company in May 1997 asked airlines to inspect center fuel tanks on 747s.[19] It continued to issue alerts regarding the 747 as circumstances warranted. However, the *Washington Post* in 1999 revealed that the company had failed to turn over a report suggesting that the center fuel tank on a similar military plane could overheat.[20] Once the focus fell squarely on the aircraft, Boeing had few viable strategies other than determining the cause.

The White House Commission:
Lots of Talk, Little Action

The bomb theory brought aviation security to preeminent agenda status. President Clinton created the White House Commission on Aviation Safety and Security, led by Vice President Al Gore. The commission was given forty-five days to create recommendations increasing flight safety. The Gore Commission released its initial recommendations on September 6, 1996, with presidential acceptance three days later. The final report was sent to the president on February 12, 1997.[21] The report was not without controversy. Especially questionable was the plan to use passenger profiles to determine which travelers to scrutinize most closely. The aviation safety proposals were almost immediately redefined as an issue of civil liberties, so the subsequent connection to TWA flight 800 was tenuous at best.

One year after the final report was released, only fifteen of fifty-seven recommendations had been enacted.[22] Many bordered on the trivial. For instance, one instructed the FAA that "nonquantifiable safety and security benefits should be included in the analysis of proposals," to which the agency assented.[23] Given that cost-benefit analysis by definition requires numerical calculations, implementation would seem impossible. The primary contribution of the commission was not to make air traffic safer but to create the perception that action was forthcoming. A year later, when a status report was issued, terrorism was not a primary concern, and attention to commission recommendations waned.

Victoria Cummock, a commission member whose husband was killed when Pan Am flight 103 was downed, expressed her initial enthusiasm and subsequent disdain for the process on the television program *Dateline NBC*. She inadvertently captured the essence of a commission's ultimate contribution to the political process: "I was elated. My gosh, this is going to be a serious look at what we need to do to ensure the flying public flies safely and securely." The reporter, Chris Hansen, then intoned:

> Cummock now says the entire process was flawed from the start. That by the time all of the commissioners were appointed, their preliminary security recommendations were already due on the president's desk. The result, Cummock says, the recommendations had to be written for the commissioners by government staffers. . . . And five months later when the final report was finished, Cummock charges that the section dealing with aviation security offered little more than recycled recommendations from previous commissions, recommendations that were never fully implemented after Pan Am 103.[24]

Often the creation of a committee to study a prominent problem is symbolic placation, a delaying tactic, and a way to make it appear that decisionmakers are addressing a problem "without actually doing anything."[25] The commission created after the bombing of Pan Am flight 103 over Lockerbie, Scotland, also submitted recommendations, most of which were not enacted due to strong opposition.[26] A primary purpose of commissions is to create the appearance of activity; afterward, elites can wrangle over the feasibility of the recommendations. Further, since commissions are often composed of political insiders, radical suggestions are not likely to emerge.[27] A comment by Neil Livingstone, identified by NBC as a "top counterterrorism expert," sums up the commission's role: "I think it was designed largely to reassure the public that the government was doing something."[28]

Some of the Gore Commission's recommendations include the following:

—The federal government should consider aviation security as a national security issue and provide substantial funding for capital improvements.

—The FAA should establish federally mandated standards for security enhancements. These enhancements should include standards for use of explosive detection system (EDS) machines, training programs for security personnel, automated bag-match technology, development of profiling programs (manual and automated), and use of explosive detection canine teams.

—The FAA should work with airlines and airport consortia to ensure that all passengers are positively identified and subjected to security procedures before they board aircraft.

—The FAA should work with industry to develop a national program to increase the professionalism of the aviation security work force, including screening personnel.

—Access to airport-controlled areas must be secured, and the physical security of aircraft must be ensured.

—Screening companies should be certified and screeners' performance improved.

—Full bag-passenger matching should be implemented.[29]

In a 1999 book, *Aviation Terrorism and Security,* Brian Jenkins writes about the commission,

> The absence of consensus on the nature and magnitude of the terror threat continues to be one of the principal obstacles to maintaining an effective aviation security program. The terror threat in the United

States is real . . . but it is diverse, amorphous, and difficult to depict in terms that allow precise calculation of security measures or that convince determined skeptics that such measures are even necessary. . . . One, of course, would like to have seen less politics, less resistance, more secure funding, faster progress in achieving the security goals laid out by the Commission. Fortunately, we have not yet suffered another airline tragedy that would accelerate the process.[30]

This statement foreshadows subsequent developments, and the above recommendations should look familiar to readers who have followed the events of September 11, as many of the changes implemented after the attacks (see chapter 7) were also proposed by the Gore Commission.

It's Showtime: TWA Congressional Hearings

TWA flight 800 provided an opportunity for elected officials to take positions on issues, gain exposure, and question investigators. While ordinarily one hearing is held after a crash, several were staged after this mishap (see table 6-1). Some hearings were informational, others investigatory. They represented an opportunity for elected officials to demonstrate that they were keeping tabs on the investigation and on airline security and provided information and an opportunity to discuss potential reforms to the system.

Charles Grassley (R-Iowa), one of the Senate's FBI adversaries, used his subcommittee chairmanship to take the bureau to task:

Now, this is a story about how the world's preeminent law enforcement agency, at least in terms of image and expectations, sometimes acted like it didn't even have a clue. I believe that each and every FBI agent employee who showed up on the scene of that tragic crash did the best job they could and had the best motives. . . . There was a basic problem, however. In my view it was one of leadership. FBI leadership in the case of the TWA flight 800 was a disaster. The FBI says that its investigation in this case is a model for the future. The FBI believes that even now. I say that because of their testimony they submitted for this hearing. If the FBI still believes that after this hearing, then I think the American people should be very alarmed about whether or not the FBI gets the message. Because this investigation, which by statute was supposed to be run by the NTSB, but

Table 6-1   *Major Congressional Hearings on TWA Flight 800*[a]

Date	Committee (subcommittee)	Topic
9/25/96	Senate Commerce, Science, and Transportation	Aid to families of air crash victims
8/1/96	Senate Select Intelligence	Terrorism threats (general)
8/1/96	Senate Commerce, Science, and Transportation	Aviation security challenges
9/11/96	House Transportation and Infrastructure (Aviation)	Aviation security and antiterrorism efforts
9/19/96	House Science	Technological solutions to improve aviation security
4/9/97	Senate Commerce, Science, and Transportation	Aviation accident investigations
3/5/97	Senate Commerce, Science, and Transportation (Aviation)	Gore Commission findings
7/10/97	House Transportation and Infrastructure (Aviation)	Investigation update
5/14/98	House Transportation and Infrastructure (Aviation)	Aviation security
5/10/99	Senate Judiciary (Administrative Oversight and Courts)	FBI handling of crash investigation

a. Table does not include hearings regarding specific legislation.

which was commandeered by the FBI, is a model of failure, not success. And anyone who doubts that is not confronting reality.[31]

At an August 1996 hearing following soon after the tragedy, Senator Ernest Hollings (D-S.C.), a longtime opponent of the industry, called for the federalization of airport security: "So, it's a terrorism threat and . . . I think it's a national security issue. I don't think we can wait around now. I think we ought to take over that responsibility," referring to airline security.[32] In another instance, Representative James Traficant (D-Ohio) conducted an inquiry into the event and presented a report to the House Transportation and Infrastructure Committee Subcommittee on Aviation in 1998.[33] Nothing of consequence emerged from these hearings except for further insight into the internal workings of the crash investigation.

The NTSB's Initial Finding: No Finding

The FBI closed its criminal probe into TWA flight 800 on November 18, 1997, but was ready to reopen the investigation if necessary. Meanwhile, the NTSB presented its evidence in public hearings in December of the same year. An explosion in the center fuel tank, the NTSB said, caused the crash, but what brought about the blast was unknown. A week-long series of hearings received extensive attention by the press, with the *New York Times* and the *Washington Post* covering most of the hearings and the nightly television news shows providing sporadic coverage. The NTSB issued a symbolic promise: "We are by no means finished. Our work will continue, and we will spare no effort to determine the cause of the crash of TWA 800." But the hearings represented partial closure.[34]

Up to this point, the investigation was not effective in finding a cause and a solution. The proximate cause was relatively clear: The fuel tank exploded due to a spark. But questions remained: What caused the spark? Could it be prevented? Could it be that the explosion was indeed random? The failure to answer these queries during the hearing indicates that the investigation was not a complete success, at least not yet. By then, terrorism had been ruled out, and the issue became defined as a technical concern. More 747s had not exploded, so the immediacy of the problem lessened. The debate was couched in complicated language, and press attention waned. The issue had lost most of its intensity.

Regardless, safety experts used the hearings to show that, despite the failure to find a clear cause, safer planes would result. Hal Thomas, a technical engineer at Honeywell, said, "What we really have is an accident where we may not know the cause, but it has forced us—everybody in the industry—to sit back and really evaluate all our fundamental premises for designing airplanes, and in the long run, even without knowing the cause of TWA 800, the end result will be much safer airplanes."[35]

At that point, the NTSB continued its investigation and eventually made further recommendations regarding the safety of fuel tanks. The uncertainty surrounding the case gave an advantage to those who would minimize new antiterror proposals or fuel tank regulations. Without a clear-cut cause, interests could argue that costly regulations could not sensibly be implemented. If there is no identifiable problem, why fix it? As of mid-2002, the NTSB's goal of changing the way fuel tanks are handled remained on its "most wanted" list of recommendations.[36] The FAA, given this notification more than five years before, refused to mandate nonflammable fuel due to high costs.

Journalistic interest reappeared during the second anniversary of the crash. A new theory was propounded by a Harvard English and American literature professor, Elaine Scarry, who argued that electromagnetic interference (EMI) from nearby navy vessels caused wires to produce a spark that started the fire in the central fuel tank.[37] NTSB representatives conceded that, under certain levels, EMI from external sources would be sufficient to down an airliner but said that there was not enough present at the time of flight 800's demise to justify such a conclusion in that case.[38]

The NTSB Report: Imperfect Closure

On August 23, 2000, more than four years after the crash of TWA flight 800, the NTSB issued its final report, with this conclusion:

> The National Transportation Safety Board determines that the probable cause of the TWA flight 800 accident was an explosion of the center wing fuel tank (CWT), resulting from ignition of the flammable fuel/air mixture in the tank. The source of ignition energy for the explosion could not be determined with certainty, but, of the sources evaluated by the investigation, the most likely was a short circuit outside of the CWT that allowed excessive voltage to enter it through electrical wiring associated with the fuel quantity indication system.
>
> Contributing factors to the accident were the design and certification concept that fuel tank explosions could be prevented solely by precluding all ignition sources and the design and certification of the Boeing 747 with heat sources located beneath the CWT with no means to reduce the heat transferred into the CWT or to render the fuel vapor in the tank nonflammable.[39]

Policy Change

There was little in the way of significant policy change as a consequence of TWA flight 800. In October 1996 the Federal Aviation Reauthorization Act of 1996 included some aviation security provisions, such as background checks for screeners and instructions to the FAA to do further research on bomb detection equipment; these provisions were either ignored or poorly funded.[40] The status quo was unaffected until September 11, 2001. Part of this legislation also included the Aviation Disaster Family Assistance Act of 1996, giving the NTSB authority to deal with families after the crash as well as with passenger manifests.

In April 2000 the Aviation Investment and Reform Act was enacted, reforming the Death on the High Seas Act, which limited how much families of victims could collect.[41] Congress had held hearings in 1997 addressing the issue of family compensation for airline crash victims, but several years passed before legislation was enacted. A provision made it retroactive to July 16, 1996, covering TWA flight 800. As discussed earlier, Congress also passed legislation clarifying NTSB and FBI involvement in postcrash investigations.

In the regulatory arena, the NTSB argued that since the "spark" allowing ignition of the fuel-air mixture could never be known, the solution was to eliminate all possible ignition sources or make the fuel nonflammable. In June 2001 the FAA issued a final rule, nearly five years after the crash, that would minimize flammable vapors and eliminate the risk of a spark igniting the tank.[42] The NTSB said that the rule did not go far enough in eliminating the risk of such vapors. In August 2001 a report provided to the FAA noted that all methods to render fuel nonflammable were too costly and did not satisfy cost-benefit analysis.[43] In the same month, the FAA improved inspections of wiring, a possible cause for the explosion of flight 800 as well as the crash of a Swissair flight in 1998. The agency had previously requested inspections of 747s after the TWA crash. A USA Today investigation suggested that the FAA knew of wiring problems on aircraft before these two crashes but chose not to act.[44]

In late 2002 the FAA announced that it had made progress in the development of an inerting system but further analysis was required.[45] Whether the FAA will take further action remains an open question; but regardless, the fuel tank issue is an illustration of FAA delay in implementing NTSB recommendations. The crash demonstrates the tensions facing the FAA when engaging in rule making. In response to the FAA report, Jim Hurd, one of the task force members who had lost a son on the TWA flight, said, "The report basically says it's acceptable to have a fuel tank explosion every four years. . . . It was my duty to be the conscience for the group. When they say it's acceptable to have another fuel tank explosion, I say, 'Is it really acceptable?'"[46]

A precise cause of the explosion could not be determined, but the families of the victims needed to blame someone to receive restitution for damages and establish closure. The clear choices were Boeing and TWA. The institutionalized form of blaming—the lawsuit—was undertaken by some families. The first lawsuits against Boeing and TWA were filed in Federal District Court in Brooklyn on October 21, 1996. Since then, many have been settled.[47]

Analysis

This crash received the most coverage of any in the 1990s (see box 6-1). It clearly shifted the focus in aviation safety, with the investigation directing attention to terrorism and later to fuel tank safety. However, little progress was made on either front. Media coverage of the investigation waxed and waned depending on the day's events. Terrorism became a public issue, temporarily, after the crash, due to the possibility that a bomb or missile brought down flight 800, but support for additional security measures could not be sustained once terrorism was ruled out. Only the confirmed terror act of September 11, 2001, sparked any action on airline security.

Some safety experts involved in TWA flight 800 believe that the mystery surrounding the crash has led to safer planes generally, because of all the research done on fuel tanks.[48] Of course investigators use crashes to learn about potential dangers in the skies. But this seems at odds with a rational, systematic approach to safety and reinforces the idea that airline safety is at present a reactive enterprise. The case of flight 800 also illustrates the overriding belief in the aviation community that crashes must be "solved" and that there is no element of randomness. This tenacity is reflected in the years and millions of dollars spent investigating TWA flight 800.

Conclusion

The TWA flight 800 investigation cost Boeing, the FBI, and the NTSB at least $87 million.[49] The disaster produced few policy changes, focused on unrelated causes, and received more press coverage than any crash in the 1990s. Calling the FAA a tombstone agency is imprecise: Death is no guarantee that the agency will act; nor, to be fair, should it be. This case demonstrates that, in the absence of death, FAA action on safety issues will be painfully slow. With fatalities, action on safety issues will still be long and laborious.

The following themes are highlighted in this chapter:

—The possibility of terrorism or friendly fire kept attention on the TWA case but also led to a focus on aviation security. Once the issue was no longer terrorism, the push for security died.

—The impetus for greater airline safety was quashed by the inability of the NTSB to determine the precise cause. This allowed the FAA to enact weak standards with reference to cost-benefit analysis.

Box 6-1   New York Times *Coverage of TWA Flight 800,*
1996–2000

1996: 297 stories (51 front page)
  July: 123 stories (25 front page)
  August: 88 stories (14 front page)
  September: 30 stories (4 front page)
  October: 18 stories (2 front page)
  November: 18 stories (3 front page)
  December: 20 stories (3 front page)
1997: 64 stories (10 front page)
1998: 11 stories (1 front page)
1999: 19 stories (1 front page)
2000: 6 stories (1 front page)
  Total: 397 stories (64 front page)

Source: Authors' calculations based on *New York Times Index,* various years.

—The TWA case illustrates the way in which crashes divert resources without necessarily leading to increased safety.

—Causal uncertainty allows those who wish to contain an issue to keep regulations from being implemented.

—High levels of media scrutiny and government attention are no guarantee of safety reform. Paradoxically, this may lead to the diversion of limited resources and government attention to areas highlighted by the accident, thereby preventing other aspects of aviation safety from receiving proper scrutiny.

CHAPTER 7

Safety versus Security in the Wake of September 11

The objective of terrorism is to influence U.S. foreign policy in the most cowardly fashion, by random destruction of innocent American lives. . . . We do have the collective national will to act against terrorists. The American people demand it, the administration has moved, and the Congress now has an opportunity to act on a broad basis with this very effective and decisive piece of legislation that is pending before us.

—*Congressional Record, vol. 135, no. 121*

There are dramatic events in every culture that are remembered for years after they occur. In the United States the list over the past four decades includes assassinations, the Challenger explosion, and the Nixon resignation. While terror acts had been a part of everyday existence in settings throughout the world, most Americans did not experience them close to home—the notable exceptions being the World Trade Center and Oklahoma City bombings. When terrorists planned and carried out the commandeering of four separate airliners leaving from Eastern cities heading toward the West Coast with the intention of destroying major symbolic icons, September 11 was added to that list.

Initial perceptions were of the form "the world has changed forever" or "America will never be the same." These claims are somewhat overblown. While about 3,000 people lost their lives in the terror attacks, as we write this chapter America has largely returned to business as usual, albeit with a heightened sense of security.

The attacks and their subsequent fallout moved many issues down on the government agenda, but this was a temporary rather than a lasting effect. There was, however, a marked effect on the aviation industry. Security procedures in the airports and on planes came into question. All aspects of the security process were reexamined, severely affecting airline travel: Initially the domestic airspace was shut down for the first time in aviation history. Subsequently, travel resumed on a limited basis and gradually moved toward a complete resumption of service. Many flights were cancelled, and some Americans were reluctant to fly. Several carriers (with Southwest being a notable exception) faced serious financial problems and lobbied the government for bailouts.

Many policy changes in aviation security were unprecedented in their scope and in the speed at which they were enacted, but none of the issues was new to the political agenda. The quotation introducing this chapter could have been from a congressional debate immediately following the September 11 attacks, but in fact it is from a 1989 House debate on a bill authorizing "$279 million to tighten airport security and purchase new bomb detection devices." The bill, H.R. 1659, passed 392 to 31 in the House but died in the Senate.[1] The impetus for the 1989 bill was undoubtedly the terror bombing of a Pan Am flight over Lockerbie, Scotland, in 1988. In the end, a watered-down measure was enacted into law. This is an oft-repeated pattern: "The bombing of Pan Am Flight 103. The mysterious crash of TWA Flight 800. The World Trade Center. Each tragedy was followed by cries for reform. But in the 13 years since a bomb exploded on Pan Am Flight 103 over Lockerbie, Scotland, almost nothing has happened."[2]

Typically, journalistic accounts of the airline industry focus on the industry's clout in Washington as the reason that security reforms are rare. This widely held view is incomplete, as reform is difficult for three other reasons: Most security measures are costly but are of undetermined effectiveness; technology for security is in its infancy and is extremely expensive; and the domestic airline system is far more complicated than in countries such as Israel, which some view as the ideal model in airline security. For these reasons, airlines have an advantage in lobbying over security issues.

Economists refer to products or services that are nonrivalrous and nondepletable as public goods. Once a public good is provided, nobody can be prevented from using it and one person's use does not affect the amount available to others. An example is clean air. Aviation security, defined as a natural security matter, also fits into this category. Yet before September 11 the airlines controlled much of their own security. Their optimal level of security may be lower than the societal optimum, because they can purchase insurance and seek government bailouts in the event of a breach. This is not evidence of airline misfeasance but rather the rational calculation expected in a market economy.

Until September 11 airline security had not typically been defined as a national security matter. Previously the airline industry was responsible for protecting aircraft, crews, and passengers. Airlines could resist regulations occasionally proposed after crashes by pointing out the flaws in the proposals. They were advantaged by the lag time between the occurrence of a crash and the availability of new technologies. This led to slow change in the industry. By the time the industry could develop effective equipment, the call for reform had quieted and was replaced by other issues on the agenda.

The sheer visual and psychological impact of September 11 guaranteed that several changes to aviation security would be enacted. Here we consider the motivations of the parties involved with airline security and discuss the issue's evolution. A key is the shifting policy focus away from safety and toward security due to September 11.

The Public, the Industry, and the Government: How the Players View Airline Security

The aviation security system received its greatest scrutiny after the attacks. Many observers were alarmed at the vulnerability of the nation's airports. Substantial security gaps allowed easy access to the aviation infrastructure, from the terminal to the tarmac. Adequate airline security requires three essential ingredients: vigilant oversight, adequate funding, and careful planning. Security is labor and capital intensive and is ineffective when hastily implemented. The private actors most affected by airline security are the flying public and the airlines. Congress, the Federal Aviation Administration (FAA), and on occasion commissions are the government bodies that deal with airline security. Each has different interests and resources, creating a political environment that makes reform extremely difficult.

The Flying Public: Low Interest, Low Resources

The industry requires the support of paying passengers. People fly because it is the fastest mode of transportation between most cities. Convenience and cost are the major attractions of air travel. Many passengers will not want to wait in lines, answer a lot of questions, be subject to searches, and so forth. Much has been written about air rage, a phenomenon in which passengers are abusive toward airline employees, often due to frayed nerves caused by extended delays. This issue even generated its own website (www.skyrage.org). Airline travel is stressful, with crowded airports and tight connections. Simply put, the public wants to minimize hassles.

Safety and security enter the picture intermittently. Most people do not think about safety or security unless there is a crash. Normally passenger loads on the affected airline drop for a short period after such an incident but then resume to their prior levels. While September 11 has made passengers more receptive to security issues, speed and convenience will once again dominate in the near future. Norman Mineta, the Department of Transportation secretary, underscored the importance of convenience when he pledged that waits at airport screening lines would be no longer than ten minutes and proposed the motto, "No weapons, no waiting."[3]

The Airline Industry: High Interest, High Resources

Before September 11 nearly all security costs were borne by the airlines, which wanted to keep these costs to a minimum. Other major costs are fixed (aging airliners, union contracts, and airport rentals), but security was one cost that could be controlled. Lobbying is a major airline activity. According to the Center for Responsive Politics, in 2000 the airlines spent over $16 million and the industry overall $46 million on lobbying.[4] These expenditures solidify legislative support when issues reach the government agenda. Meanwhile, airline pilots and flight attendants depend on the industry for their safety and their livelihood.

The Federal Aviation Administration

The FAA operated for many years under the dual mandate of promoting as well as regulating airline traffic. The promotion mandate has now been eliminated. However, the agency has worked closely with the airline industry over the years, stressing voluntary compliance. A cooperative, subgovernmental relationship has developed, with the FAA avoiding meaningful regulation to improve security unless an egregious fault has been found.

Congress

The main congressional actors have been members of the aviation subcommittees of the transportation committees of the two houses, as well as of the transportation subcommittees of the appropriations committees. Generally speaking, two types of legislator serve on these committees. One type has an airline company (for example, James Oberstar [D-Minn.] and Northwest Airlines) or airport (William Lipinski [D-Ill.] and Midway Airport) as a regional or constituent interest. These legislators are primarily concerned with protecting these stakeholders. The second type is from less urban areas and seeks additional service from the major airlines. Neither group is concerned primarily with additional regulation unless a major problem appears. Legislative attentiveness is generally dependent upon a loss of, or threat to, life.

Federal Bureau of Investigation and the National Transportation Safety Board

The Federal Bureau of Investigation (FBI) is the lead agency in crash investigations involving criminal acts. Because of its expertise in dealing with crashes, the National Transportation Safety Board (NTSB) is often asked to assist the FBI in various aspects of the inquiry. Tension arises between the agencies when there is uncertainty over the cause of the crash, as evidenced by the TWA flight 800 investigation.

Commissions

Occasionally, independent commissions enter the process for short periods of time. Politicians can create fact-finding groups, empanelled for the objective of examining certain aspects of airline safety or security to find shortcomings correctable through regulation. These are advisory bodies whose power and attention diminish once recommendations are made, and their suggestions are rarely implemented. Commissions often become issue burial grounds.

Airlines have an interest in security for financial reasons, with considerable resources devoted to the issue's regulatory aspects. Meanwhile, key congressional and FAA officials have little interest in imposing new regulations on the industry. Short of a triggering event, advances in this area are infrequent. This argument is supported empirically by the last three decades of airline security law.

Airline Security before September 11: An Oxymoron?

Far from being a rationally planned and organized system, airline security—like many policy areas—emerged in piecemeal fashion. Change required a formative event capturing public attention that galvanized officials to act. Efforts at improving security never occurred in a vacuum but were pushed by triggering events. When lives were threatened or lost, the industry responded to that specific problem; a holistic approach to security was nonexistent. Attention to security was totally reactive and never proactive. Airline security breaches and the corrective measures taken to address them are listed below.

—In 1971 a passenger aboard a flight over the state of Washington demanded and was paid a ransom and parachuted from the plane. In consequence, a latch was installed on the passenger doors of all aircraft to prevent them from being opened during flight.

—In 1972 another airline was hijacked and a ransom demanded. As a result, passengers and their carry-on luggage were subject to screening.

—In 1985 a hijacking on the ground in the Athens, Greece, airport, lasting seventeen days, was supported by the airline's cleaning staff, who placed weapons on the plane. In consequence airline employees were made subject to background checks.

—In 1986 explosives were found in the luggage of an innocent passenger. Thereafter, passengers were asked whether they had packed their bags themselves.

—In the mid-1980s several bombing incidents led to bag searches for international flights and a system of matching bags with passengers.

—The 1988 Pan Am crash in Scotland, caused by plastic explosives in a radio in a checked bag led to a switch to more sophisticated CT scanners.

—In the 1990s only TWA flight 800 prompted some movement on security, but most of the recommendations made by the Gore Commission after that crash were never implemented until after September 11.[5]

The most substantial changes during the 1980s resulted from the pivotal crash of Pan Am flight 103 over Lockerbie, Scotland, in December 1988. While any loss of life in a plane crash is tragic, some crashes have more potential for policy impact than others. Libyan terrorists boarded that flight in Malta and checked baggage though to New York. They disembarked at the next stop but had placed plastic explosives, hidden inside a radio, in their luggage. The bomb exploded while the flight was in progress.

The Pan Am bombing led to the formation of a presidential commission to investigate possible changes. A mixture of suggestions and requirements resulted in sixty-four requests included in the 1990 Aviation Security Act.[6] Most of these provisions were never carried out, and the subsequent decade produced no major improvements. The law addressed concerns in four major areas:[7]

—Explosive detection devices. The FAA was directed to develop explosive detection devices for domestic airports by November 1993. When that date arrived, the FAA had certified only one system, InVision Technologies CTX 5000. Three airports used it by 1994. Its cost was prohibitive ($1 million each), and error rates were high. The General Accounting Office (GAO) estimated that $2 billion would be required for airport installation.

—Background checks. The law mandated that the FAA issue regulations demanding criminal record checks for the previous ten years for all airline employees and job applicants as well as requiring fingerprinting. Only in 1996 did the agency require background checks, and these covered only the preceding five years.

—Training for screeners. The law recommended that the FAA raise training standards for security personnel, but the FAA imposed only minimal requirements when it finally acted in 1993. Screeners were required to receive eight hours of classroom instruction and four hours of hands-on training.

—Bag matching. The act recommended that all bags be matched with passengers. That was done on international flights but not on domestic flights. Finally in 1995 the FAA recommended such actions for domestic flights. When the airlines resisted, the agency retreated.

While some safety measures had been enacted in the 1970s and 1980s, the real chance for reform and upgrading protection of airliners from terror incursions followed the Pan Am disaster. Yet only one major piece of federal legislation in the early 1990s appeared, which was a combination of suggested and required actions. The FAA either took no action or waited several years to act. When it did act, the response was much more limited than the law appeared to require.

Why did Lockerbie produce so little change? The standard response is airline opposition to any measures involving considerable time and money. This is a potent argument, as the industry currently has more than twenty full-time lobbyists—many of them former White House aides and transportation officials—to argue its case on Capitol Hill.[8] In 1990 the airlines hired former FBI and CIA director William Webster to head its lobbying team.[9] Paul Hudson, executive director of the Aviation Consumer Action Project, a nonprofit oversight group, put it well: "I can't think of one thing that [the airlines] have proposed to enhance security, and I can think of many things they have done to inhibit it. When things occur that indicate a need for corrective action, [the proposals] are defused and delayed and watered down, to where the resulting measures have no effect."[10] In addition, the FAA has never taken a confrontational position with the airlines but has tried to gain voluntary compliance. When none was forthcoming, a minimalist response was adopted.

But this is only part of the story. Besides the FAA and the airline industry, there are two other key players: Congress and the flying public. Congress, while it took corrective steps in 1990, never engaged in oversight or follow-up legislation when it became clear that the FAA would take only minimal action.

The main stakeholder is the traveling public. Additional security measures meant delays or additional costs the airlines would pass on to the customer. But customers did not have security on the top of their list of aviation concerns, only wanting to get to their destination as quickly as possible. Given the increasing popularity of air travel, there was already congestion in the airports. As a consequence, before the events of September 11, airport and airline access was relatively easy and uneventful.

Consider the following hypothetical case of a traveler departing from a major commercial airport. He drives to a parking lot near the airport with a friend, who will accompany him to the boarding area to see the departure. At the ticket counter, his bags are checked without inspection, and two to three bags of varying size are lugged onto the plane. When the passenger is given his boarding pass, he is asked two perfunctory questions: Did your bags ever leave your sight? Did anyone ask you to carry something aboard the plane? In proceeding to the gate, the passenger and his friend pass though a security check consisting of a metal detector. During this security check, a screener uses an X-ray machine to examine the passenger's carry-on bags for guns, bombs, bomb-assembly items, long knives, and other potential weapons.

The passenger and his friend wait at the gate for the boarding announcement. When his row is called, the passenger walks onto the airliner and to his seat. Problems that might have drawn his attention would have been a delay in his flight or a cancellation of his flight, concerns that would be exacerbated during busy periods such as holidays. After September 11, this scenario would change radically.

Before September 11 government officials were aware of airport security problems. Agents routinely sneaked handguns and mock bombs through checkpoints. In May 2000 the GAO (as part of a larger study on security breaches at federal agencies and airports) reported the ease of airport access by someone using fake identification:

> At the two airports visited, agents used tickets that had been issued in their undercover names for commercial flights. These agents declared themselves as armed law enforcement officers, displayed their spurious badges and identification, and were issued "law enforcement" boarding passes by the airline representative at the ticket counter. The agents then presented themselves at the security checkpoints and were waved around the magnetometers. Neither the agents nor their valises were screened.[11]

In June 2000 the GAO issued a report referring to problems with security screeners and noting that planes could be targets for terror attacks.[12] In an ironic twist, news reports indicate that al-Qaida terrorists used the May 2000 GAO report to study how best to circumvent airport security.[13]

The Challenge of Aviation Security: Politics versus Protection

While security issues received very little attention from the media and most politicians before the September 11 attacks, the scenario changed dramatically afterward. Security issues appeared in the media on a regular basis, with a continuous stream of examples about shortcomings in the security apparatus. Illustrations included individuals passing through security checkpoints with no inspections or passing inspection with weapons in their bags or on their persons, either intentionally or unintentionally. Americans were alarmed to find out just how vulnerable airports were to individuals with malign motives. Security violations were found to be commonplace and the issue of airline security multifaceted. What is often overlooked is the monumental challenge that airline security poses. There are several problem areas:

—Nonpassengers. Should nontravelers in the airport be treated the same as passengers, or should their freedom of movement be restricted? Should they be permitted into waiting areas beyond security checkpoints? How likely is it that they are security risks?

—Vehicles. Transportation to the airport is mainly by private cars, which are capable of carrying bombs. Where should cars be allowed to park at the airport? And for how long?

—Passengers. In general, the assumption is that all passengers are potential carriers of explosive materials or weapons. Passengers pass through a metal detector sensitive to certain types of metal, and they can be scanned with a hand-held wand and asked to deposit articles in a container (keys, watch, and so on) and rechecked. In extreme cases they can be strip searched. Background checks are also possible. Passengers' names can be subject to computer checks of known terrorists or criminals and passengers themselves subject to questioning about their trip: its purpose, who is to meet them, the length of trip, and so forth. Among the grounds for such further checks are the purchase of a one-way ticket, the last-minute purchase of the ticket, paying cash for the ticket, and having no baggage.

—Baggage. Carry-on bags can be limited in number and subject to an inspection by an X-ray machine or a screener, during which the bag is checked for explosives residue. Checked bags present a greater challenge. They can be screened by an X-ray machine, subject to a hand search, or even sniffed by dogs trained to detect certain explosive materials. The final problem is to make sure that both passengers and their bags depart together. A possible security danger is that people check baggage with explosives and then do not board the plane. Another risk is that passengers depart the plane at a stop before their destination.

—Airport screeners. Airport screeners are the main line of defense against untoward activity. In the wake of September 11, concerns were raised about their training, knowledge, and background. Interestingly, by all accounts they performed their jobs properly on the day of the attacks. The rules implemented by the FAA—and not challenged by Congress—allowed the terrorists to use the planes as weapons. The FAA and Congress blamed the screeners, a politically weak group, to deflect blame.

—X-ray machines. How sophisticated are the machines that all passengers must pass though? Are they sufficiently sensitive to threats that can be in the form of liquids, mechanical parts, powders, fuses, and the like? These machines vary in their capacity to detect dangerous paraphernalia. In addition, they are only as effective as the individuals operating them. Since September 11 airports in several cities were shut down temporarily after passengers passed through unplugged X-ray machines or screeners were literally asleep on the job.

—Airplane on the ground. A major point of danger is the airliner while it is on the ground. The plane is vulnerable while the flight crews are being changed. Who has access to the plane during this time, and what activities are they engaged in? When the next group of passengers enter the airplane cabin, to what extent do the flight crews visually check them to determine if anyone is acting suspiciously? This check can even assume the form of profiling, in which flight crews are sensitive to certain demographic characteristics.

—Airplane in flight. Once the plane is in the air, the concern is the unruly passenger who threatens the lives of other passengers or attempts to take over the aircraft. What procedures are in place to deal with these situations? A vulnerable spot is the cockpit door. Once the plane is in flight the door must be closed and locked until landing. Is the door properly constructed or reinforced to withstand the efforts of someone attempting to dislodge or open it so he can get into the cockpit?

—Airport workers. Airport workers have unfettered access to all areas of the airport and airplanes. As a consequence, careful background checks may be necessary to ensure that workers will not pose a threat to security.

All of the above situations are potential flash points, where lax security procedures can mean an airline crash and loss of life. The media and Congress were quick to find blame targets after September 11. Such responses capture the public's attention and are politically popular, but they miss an important point. Airport security is only as strong as its weakest link. Errors are inevitable, but the key is to minimize risk while keeping planes in the air profitably.

All airport security measures are costly; too much security will mean that airline travel will no longer be economically feasible. A key principle of engineering is redundancy. Major systems on a plane have a backup in the event that the primary system fails. This would also be the ideal for security, but it is an expensive proposition and may not be economically tractable. Imagine a world with bag matching on every flight, scanners for all checked luggage, individual questioning of all passengers by trained officers, and police officers on every flight. This may work in a small transportation system but, by all accounts, would be unaffordable in a large system.

In addition, technology to detect explosives is in its infancy, in part because there has been little demand for it until now. To provide adequate security, technology must keep up with those who would defeat it. Without a steady stream of business, the incentive for research and development does not exist. False alarm rates on machines are significant, and the GAO has expressed concern that relying on screeners to resolve false alarms may lead the system to break down:

> These devices ultimately depend upon human beings to resolve alarms.
> This activity can range from closer inspection of a computer image

and a judgment call, to a hand search of the item in question. The ultimate detection of explosives depends on extra steps being taken by security personnel—a correct judgment by them—to determine whether an explosive is present. Because many of the devices' alarms signify only the potential for explosives being present, the true detection of explosives requires human intervention. The higher the false alarm rate, the greater is the system's need to rely on human judgment. As we noted in our previous reports, this reliance could be a weak link in the explosives detection process. In addition, relying on human judgments has implications for the selection and training of operators for new equipment.[14]

The key for aviation security is to develop a system that deploys resources in the optimal manner.[15] For instance, this might entail random screening of checked baggage and random questioning of passengers by specially trained personnel. However, risk management is not politically palatable; to say that some random percentage of bags will be screened, to save on the costs of machines and allow resources for other areas of security, may have adverse political consequences. Aviation security will tend to produce rules that focus on total enforcement of a rule that may do nothing, whereas a more strategic approach may be far more successful. This has been true of the aftermath of nearly all terror incidents, including September 11 (see below). While we do not argue for a particular type of aviation security, an approach that focuses on one threat but ignores others is clearly insufficient.

The Immediate Response to September 11

In addition to affecting the rhythm of air travel, the events of September 11 changed the perception of aviation terrorism. Typically, terrorists were viewed as hijackers (who would demand that the plane fly to another destination) or bombers (who would attempt to destroy the plane in flight). The extensive planning and determination required to arrange that four separate flights would crash into buildings within a short time span demonstrates that hijacking can put more at risk than the lives of the passengers. Airline security had rarely been viewed as a national security issue; September 11 changed that.

After the airline security net was so effectively breached, the immediate response was to shut all airports and to reopen them slowly over a period of days. (Reagan National Airport, with its close proximity to Washington, D.C., remained closed for several weeks; it reopened with additional requirements regarding flight plans in and out of the airport.) Within days National Guard troops were mobilized at all of the nation's 429 commercial airports. In addition, airport security officers and local police patrolled traffic corridors, symbolizing that security was to be handled differently from this point forward. Only passengers and authorized personnel were allowed past security checkpoints. There was talk of expanding the federal sky marshals program, whereby plainclothes officers board flights randomly to intercept potential trouble.

Within a few days of the attacks, the FAA issued orders tightening existing security measures at the airport:

—Restricting parking around airports and limiting curbside bag check-in.

—Limiting passengers to one carry-on bag plus a personal item.

—Requiring that passengers have a photo identification to show along with their boarding pass.

—Refusing to allow aboard knives of any length, box cutters, ice picks, metal nail files, bats, golf clubs, ski poles, hockey sticks, and other items.

—Adding to the screening of passengers at the gate.[16]

Within eleven days of the terror attacks, Congress passed a $15 billion bill designed to help the ailing domestic airline industry. The money came in the form of both cash grants and low-interest loans. The legislation was designed to help the industry weather the economic downturn following the catastrophic events, as airline traffic fell and airports closed.

On November 16, after hearings and partisan wrangling over control of the new security system, legislators passed the Aviation and Transportation Security Act. The act completely transformed the entire security picture at airports and on flights. The House voted 410 to 9 in favor, while the Senate endorsed it by a voice vote. President Bush signed the bill into law two days later, at Reagan National Airport. Now, he said, "security comes first," and "for the first time, airport security will become a direct federal responsibility."[17] The terror attack redefined airport security as a national security matter and also framed it as a public good to be provided by government.

The major features of the law are as follows:[18]

—The undersecretary of a new division of the Department of Transportation (DOT), the Transportation Security Administration (TSA), whose job is to ensure security in all modes of transportation, was given the authority to "issue, rescind, and revise all regulations" necessary to carry out the functions of the job.[19]

—Airport screeners were to become federal employees within one year; as such, they were to be given more training and to be subject to stiffer background checks.

—Private security screening programs were to be tested at five airports in varying risk categories one year after the legislation was implemented. In three years airports could opt out of the federal system and use private security companies.

—Cockpit doors were to be strengthened and locked during flights.

—The federal sky marshals program was to be revived.

—Airlines had sixty days to increase inspection of checked bags, with a system in place by the end of 2002 to detect all explosives.

—To pay for these upgrades in security, passengers were to be charged an additional $2.50 a flight segment and up to $10 for a round trip.

—The TSA undersecretary was authorized to implement a "trusted passenger program," to expedite the security screening of frequent flyers and others.

Implementation of the Aviation and Transportation Security Act

The law was groundbreaking in terms of the way it changed airline travel, even if its ultimate effect on airline security is uncertain. Before September 11 speed was of paramount importance, but now it was to be balanced by a concern for security. The FAA administrator Jane Garvey emphasized this change: "Just as Pearl Harbor was the dividing line for an isolationist nation, September 11 was a dividing line for a free and open society—that may have valued convenience more than security."[20] Each aspect of air travel, starting with airport access, was altered with a new agency in charge of aviation security.

Screening Passengers and Their Bags

The most extreme security measure was the strip search, a procedure rarely used before the attacks. In a widely covered case, the senior member of the House, John Dingell (D-Mich.), was forced to remove all of his clothing at Reagan National Airport because his artificial hip set off a security alarm. DOT Secretary Mineta subsequently called him to apologize.[21] In addition, passengers are now more likely to be called aside for additional wandings, required to show identification several times before boarding an aircraft, and subject to random searches.

Before September 11 carry-on baggage was checked by X-ray machines for explosives before the passenger reached the boarding area. Manual searches or machine screening for plastic explosives in carry-on baggage were used infrequently. The new legislation demanded much more aggressive screening. Airlines had sixty days to start screening all checked baggage with one of four methods: X-ray machines, hand searches, bomb-sniffing dogs, and bag matching. The DOT was given the authority to determine which means were acceptable and to allow others at its discretion. The first three were soon found not to be feasible on a large-scale basis. There were not enough X-ray machines and dogs to do extensive searches, and hand searches en masse would require an expanded workforce.

Bag matching, used in most international airports for several years and for all international flights leaving the United States, had not previously been used on domestic flights due to cost and delays. Bag matching does not deter suicide bombers, nor does it detect explosives. The DOT initially allowed the airlines to meet the requirements of the law by authorizing bag matching only on the first leg of a flight. But bag matching on originating flights does not make air travel safer, since terrorists can easily board a plane with a bomb in their stowed baggage, disembark at the end of their first leg, and then detonate the bomb by remote control during the next leg of the flight. The DOT action was a compromise to prevent what could have been stunning delays if bag matching were required. Bag matching was, anyway, a temporary, stopgap measure.

Under the law the TSA was to ensure that "explosive detection systems are deployed as soon as possible to ensure that all United States airports . . . have sufficient explosive detection systems to screen all checked baggage no later than December 31, 2002, and that as soon as such systems are in place at an airport, all checked baggage at the airport is screened by those systems."[22] With estimates of 3.8 million checked bags a day, or 1.4 billion a year, this specification presents a daunting task for the airlines and the security industry.[23] Further, the CT scanners currently in use cost $1 million each, and some airports will have to be reconfigured to accommodate the new machines, which each require 600 square feet of space.[24] Not surprisingly, the December 31, 2002, deadline was not met and was extended by Congress under the Homeland Security Act.

The Screeners

In the fall of 2001, 28,000 people were employed to screen baggage by contractors for the airlines.[25] These employees inspected all carry-on baggage with X-ray machines and watched as passengers passed through metal detectors. If one set off the alarm, that person would be subject to manual scanning, and suspicious bags were opened and examined.

Investigators found serious problems with all aspects of airport screening. The airlines paid for the screeners and wanted to spend as little as possible. The result was low pay, similar to wages at airport parking garages or concessions. Training was minimal, as the FAA required only twelve hours of in-class training, and background checks were often improperly conducted. The largest private company handling airport security was Argenbright, which had screening contracts for airports in Boston, Washington, and Newark, where on September 11 four teams of hijackers passed through security carrying small knives and box cutters. Argenbright was simply a scapegoat, since in each of the situations the company was not at fault. The weapons used by the hijackers (small knives, box cutters) were not prohibited items before that day. This has been forgotten in the frenzy over increased security.

Still, Argenbright and other security companies had made enough mistakes that major problems were uncovered once they were under intense scrutiny. Argenbright officials admitted that forged documents permitted employees with criminal records to be hired. District managers altered employee work records (they were subsequently fined and sentenced). High school diplomas were not required, and many screeners did not have American citizenship. Further, many employees skipped all or part of the training and testing. An investigation by the DOT inspector general (IG) after September 11 found that, at Dulles International Airport, seven of twenty screeners randomly given the skills test failed; that test is supposed to be administered to all new employees. The IG also filed suit against Argenbright for violating probation regarding its failure to properly train employees at Philadelphia International Airport.[26]

After the hijackings, Argenbright scrambled to improve its image. First, the president and founder, Frank Argenbright, retired and was replaced by a new owner. The company promised to increase the screeners' wages to between $9 and $13 an hour. Two screeners were to be hired for every X-ray machine. Further, all employee records were to be checked for criminal records. The training program would be expanded to forty hours, with stricter supervision.[27]

Despite all these moves, security companies were still plagued by embarrassing incidents, such as passengers with weapons breaching security. Media exposés showing successful attempts to bypass security did not improve the companies' reputations. Given these problems, there was no surprise when Congress ended private screening within two months after the terror attacks. The new law required screeners to become federal employees within one year. This posed an enormous logistical challenge and would cost billions of dollars. The initial contract, for more than $100 million, for hiring and testing screeners was awarded to NCS Pearson Inc. in March 2002.[28] A similar contract was awarded to Lockheed Martin for training the new workforce.[29] Federal screeners were in place by November 2002.

The Airliner and Its Flight

Who is responsible for the security of the plane between flights? Before September 11 only airline and airport employees were to board or approach the plane. Since security was lax, however, unauthorized personnel were often able to break this rule. After the crashes the FAA ordered airlines to search between flights for items that might be useful to potential hijackers. Some regional airlines used flight attendants to undertake this task. However, the flight attendants' union opposed this rule, arguing that flight attendants did not have the time or training to conduct such searches.[30] In addition, it argued, the flight crew already carefully screened all travelers as they boarded the plane.

Unruly passengers have always threatened the security of aircraft. Throughout the 1990s the primary responsibility for dealing with them rested with the FAA. A study by *USA Today* finds that such passengers were rarely fined and that security precautions were never upgraded despite occasional incidents in the air. In 1996 the FAA made a zero-tolerance pledge with respect to such incidents. In about two-thirds of the cases handled over the 1990s, however, the FAA failed to collect fines.[31] Former agency officials said such inaction was justified because the perpetrators were minor irritants and not threats to airline security. Air rage, however, took on a new meaning after September 11, and the FAA then wanted to transfer responsibility for such outbursts to the TSA.[32]

One of the principal concerns of airline security in flight is the door separating passengers and pilots. Once the plane is loaded and ready to take off, according to the rules, the cockpit door must be shut from take-off until the plane lands at the destination gate. Before September 11 these doors were meant simply to separate the pilots and the rest of the cabin, not to establish a secure area. After the September 11 events the FAA initially required all of the 6,000 U.S. airliners to have bars and deadbolts on their cockpit doors. In January 2002 new rules required further fortification by April 9, 2003: Cockpit doors were to be resistant to small-arms fire, bombs, grenades, and physical attempts to enter the cabin.[33]

There was a debate about whether pilots should be allowed to carry guns on board.[34] United Airlines wanted to allow stun guns in the cockpit. Pilots discussed use of tactics such as sudden movements of the plane in the air to throw the hijackers off balance. Flight personnel talked about taking self-defense courses. No formal guidelines existed in the preattack world other than compliance with hijacker demands, but in January 2002 the FAA proposed new rules for flight crew safety. These were kept secret, but the FAA administrator Jane Garvey said that the flight crew would be trained to thwart the objectives of terrorists.[35]

Aviation security was a watchword but not a behavioral imperative before September 11. These events created a new environment (see table 7-1). But although security procedures in airports and on planes have dramatically increased, some experts argue that such procedures are primarily symbolic, are designed to reassure the traveling public, and do not actually deter terrorists. This argument suggests that the motivation of federal officials was blame avoidance and the reassurance of potential fliers.

For instance, flight crews have been upset about the searches they must undergo. Their frustration comes from a belief that heightened security measures are primarily a public relations exercise. One pilot, speaking for many, said, "Most pilots realize the security program is a feel-good program for the public. We're putting on this show for the passengers and cameras."[36] Others cite the concern with inappropriate targets. Robert Crandall, the former president of American Airlines, said, "But what we're doing now, selecting people at random for pat-down searches, picking out congressmen and eighty-year-old women, that's just foolishness."[37] Others suggest that more emphasis should be placed on detecting explosives rather than weapons, since once cockpit doors are fortified, a weapon would not be as potent as an explosive. In other words, a vigorous debate

Table 7-1   *Airline Security before and Immediately after September 11, 2001*

Area of concern	Before September 11	After September 11
Airport access	Parking close to airport; minimal monitoring	Greater distance for parking; increased monitoring
Terminal	Minimal police presence	National Guard troops initially; significant police presence afterward
Nonpassengers	Gate access	No access beyond checkpoint in most cases
Passenger screening	Whole-body metal detector; infrequent wanding	Whole-body metal detector; frequent wanding; random personal checks
Passenger checks	Photo ID; computer-assisted passenger prescreening program (CAPPS); screening questions	Photo ID; CAPPS; screening questions; random checks
Carry-on baggage	X-ray and bomb residue screening, with occasional hand checks	X-ray and bomb residue screening, with frequent and random hand checks
Checked baggage	Minimal screening	Every bag screened by 1 of 4 methods: bag matching (the modal means), x-ray machines, hand searching, and bomb-sniffing dogs
Prohibited items	Few restrictions on small knives, box cutters, and other potential weapons	Restrictions for a certain period on all of these, as well as certain personal items, like nail clippers
Security screeners	No criminal background checks; U.S. citizenship not required; no serious testing or training; low wages	Criminal background checks; U.S. citizenship required; increased in-class and hands-on training; serious testing; increased wages
Between-flight security	No search	Passenger searches
In-flight security	Easily penetrable cabin door; crew trained to comply with hijacker; passengers compliant	Fortified cabin door; crew and passengers resist attacks; increased training

has ensued over what airport security should look like in the wake of September 11.

Some argue that nothing short of importing the El Al model used by the Israeli airline will work. This airline's security procedure has the following elements:

—Inspection of every bag for bombs and weapons.

—Armed security agents on every flight.

—Close questioning of every passenger about travel plans.

—Profiling of passengers.

For several reasons this model may not fit the American system. First, it would increase costs and require either a significant reduction in flights or further delays, angering passengers and possibly reducing revenue (the U.S. domestic system is much larger than the Israeli operation).

Second, profiling is highly controversial and has been interpreted as discriminatory against certain ethnic groups. While there is evidence that ethnic profiling would lead to more efficient airline security, the political repercussions of such profiling would raise even greater problems. The tactic might be more palatable if it were combined with other high-risk features. Still, civil rights groups would need to be assured that profiling would protect civil liberties. Alternatives include a "trusted traveler" card, whereby individuals could voluntarily agree to background checks in exchange for getting through security more quickly. All of these proposals are attempts at more effectively identifying high-risk passengers. The crux of an efficient security system is the ability to effectively screen passengers, and this requires the identification of dangerous individuals.

The initial response to September 11 was speedy implementation and enforcement of limited rules that failed to reflect a holistic approach to security. Complete bag matching on originating flights would not prevent another Lockerbie and was implemented because it was feasible and minimized delays. Nail clippers on board an aircraft were not permitted for a time, while plastic explosives could potentially be carried on board undetected. The law stated that, if possible, all checked bags should be screened with bomb-detecting equipment by the end of 2002. However, the technology was prone to failure, and there were not enough machines or enough workers to staff the machines.

Airline security is not a new issue, and many experts offered alternative ways to set up a system. At least initially, political symbolism triumphed over rational planning. For instance, passenger profiling is certainly one option for streamlining procedures, but its controversial nature precludes its adoption. Changes in aviation security are significant in terms of spending and implementation, but their long-term effectiveness remains an open question. An initial short-run examination by the DOT indicates that the effectiveness of security has not improved since September 11.[38]

The TSA will play a pivotal role in determining the success of airline security. The agency experienced growing pains in its first year, with estimates of a staff of 70,000, more than twice the initial prediction of 30,000. Projections for fiscal year 2002 appropriations nearly tripled, from $2.2 billion to $6.8 billion.[39] The increased costs for the TSA were due to congressional deadlines, including the December 31, 2002, target to deploy explosives detection systems. That transition to a new system would not be painless or costless, but in a hearing before the House Appropriations Committee Subcommittee on Transportation, members of Congress criticized the TSA for cost overruns. David Obey (D-Wis.) asked, "Does the agency really take this committee to be a bunch of chumps, or do you simply expect that we are going to supinely provide blank checks?"[40] Subcommittee chairman Harold Rogers (R-Ky.) stated that Congress "will not tolerate dictatorial attitudes at TSA."[41] In many ways the agency fell victim to the unreasonable requirements set by Congress as well as the natural tendency for an agency to maximize its budget. The unenviable task of creating an agency while simultaneously implementing major policy reforms creates unrealistic expectations. Still, all involved realize that security involves a significant investment of resources, with quick implementation often costing much but accomplishing little.

One of TSA's next challenges will be its move from the Department of Transportation to the newly created Homeland Security Department. The creation of this new department is daunting, as it will bring under its umbrella organizations—new and old—from existing departments. This means that organizational cultures will have to be blended. How TSA will fit in with this new regime is an open question.

Safety versus Security: How September 11 Reframed the Debate

Before September 11 the operative term in debates about protecting the lives of airline passengers was *safety*. The enemies of safety were poor airliner construction and lax maintenance. The response was usually reactive: When an airline crash occurred and a mechanism was found to be working improperly, a recommendation was made by the NTSB to remedy the problem. This required possible action by the airline manufacturer in making future planes safer or by airport maintenance officials (including pilots) in being more vigilant in checking certain potential mechanical problems on the airliner itself. Frequently, weather problems or pilot error contributed to the mix.

After September 11 the word *safety* either was deemphasized or disappeared from the debate to be replaced by another symbol: *security*. Here, the aircraft's construction, functioning, and maintenance were given lower priority; the new enemy was terrorists and their weapons. For example, after the crash of American Airlines flight 587 over New York on November 12, 2001—barely two months after the events of September 11—terrorism was an initial concern. Once mechanical failure and pilot error came to the fore as likely causes, the crash received less attention.

After September 11 security moved safety down on the aviation agenda. As argued earlier, plane crashes can divert resources away from safety issues that have not yet resulted in an accident. Similarly, aviation security can divert resources away from crash prevention. Groups ranging from the Air Transport Association to the FAA to the NTSB to the Coalition of Airline Pilots have expressed concern that safety issues have been thrust aside in favor of security issues.[42] A fixed level of resources for aviation regulation implies that more money for security means less money for safety. Only increased spending can avoid such a trade-off.

Americans tolerate a certain (low) number of plane crashes as a price for airline travel. An individual plane crash requires some unusual feature to receive extensive attention. On the contrary, the flying public is completely unwilling to accept acts of terror. To the extent that elected officials and regulators take costly symbolic actions to deal with security in these cases, aviation safety will take a back seat for a period of time. This demonstrates once again the reactive nature of airline regulation.

Conclusion

The reaction to the events of September 11 reinforces several of the themes of this book. Triggering events shift regulatory priorities, and regulatory response in aviation is reactive rather than proactive. In this case, the shift in priorities was from safety to security, rather than within these particular domains. This shift adds another dimension to the battle over aviation regulation, a battle that will be waged long into the future.

Several key points are made in this chapter:

—Before September 11 the aviation industry focused on mechanical safety; aviation security was not on the agenda. The terror attacks reframed the debate and diverted resources away from aviation safety and toward aviation security.

—After September 11 the issue of aviation security was redefined as an issue of national security. The airlines had economic incentives to pay little attention to security, but the government would now be in control of security.

—To deflect blame from their oversight failures, elected officials and bureaucrats declared that they were trying to improve an airline security system that was in disarray. But it is important to note that on September 11 no airline or security screening employee violated any FAA or government regulation.

—Whether the new measures stemming from the Aviation and Transportation Security Act will be effective is an open question, as many of the actions taken thus far are symbolic. Efforts to improve airline security go to extremes but do not necessarily increase security. A holistic and carefully planned approach is needed, but reactive regulation is by definition a response to specific events. The two may be incompatible.

—There are no easy answers to airline security questions. The new era will feature political wrangling, trial and error, and more airline accidents. Unlike the past, when a hijacking or a bombing would bring temporary attention to an issue, the events of September 11 transformed the concern and guaranteed its presence on the permanent government agenda, alongside education, the economy, and national defense, at least for the foreseeable future.

Overall, the events of September 11 changed the image of the airport forever. Before it was seen primarily as a transportation terminal offering the fastest means of moving from one location to another. The terminals accommodated increasing numbers of flights in increasingly crowded skies. The principal problems used to lie with the weather, mechanical problems, and cancelled flights. The terminal is now perceived primarily in security terms, featuring armed guards and checkpoints.

Our view is that the optimal system for aviation security is very different from one dependent on political reaction. After September 11 elected officials needed to reassure the flying public that air travel was safe. Dramatic actions were needed to accomplish that goal, regardless of their effectiveness, but as long as regulation is reactive, piecemeal policymaking will be the norm, and a carefully planned security system will remain elusive.

CHAPTER 8

Safety and Symbolism in Aviation Politics

There are many ways to get from point A to point B in the United States: driving, riding a bus, taking a train, or flying in an airplane. We focus on airline travel because it is an important part of the economy and distinct from other modes of travel in a number of ways. Compared to its competitors on distances of a few hundred miles or more, flying involves faster speeds, less travel time, and a greater loss of control (from having literally no exit option). A flight can be convenient—or terrifying.

Crashes focus attention on the fallibility in any transportation system. From 1991 through 2000 transportation fatality rates were highest for cars, followed by trains, buses, and planes.[1] Yet hundreds can die when a single airliner falters. The story is guaranteed to make the front page of most newspapers and to be featured prominently for several days. This industry reflects an interesting duality. It is the most reliable of all the transportation modes in death avoidance. Yet a crash involving many fatalities achieves maximum media attention and causes concern for the public at large.

Normally commercial aviation safety receives sporadic attention from the media and Congress. When mishaps occur, however, the press focuses on the event, often portraying some aspect of the industry in a negative manner. If the airliner had prior mechanical problems or the airline had problematic reviews, then those items will come out in the official postcrash investigation. To determine the actual pattern of events, all crashes in the 1990s were examined with special attention to three crashes. Table 8-1

Table 8-1   *Three Major Plane Crashes, Summary*

Item	USAir, 1994	ValuJet, 1996	TWA, 1996
Fatalities[a]	132	110	230
Type of plane	Boeing 737	McDonnell Douglas DC-9	Boeing 747
Cause	Rudder malfunction	Fire in cargo hold	Center fuel tank explosion
Speed of investigation	Slow	Fast	Slow
Result	Uncertainty	Certain cause	Uncertainty
Nonaviation actors	Gore	Schiavo, Gore	Kallstrom, Salinger, Scarry, Gore
Media targets	USAir, Boeing, FAA, NTSB	ValuJet, SabreTech, FAA	TWA, Boeing, FBI
Presidential involvement	None	None	Formed commission
Congressional involvement	None	House hearing; FAA dual mandate eliminated	Senate and House hearings; NTSB-FAA relationship clarified; stronger victim rights
Company response	New personnel; review of procedures	New name; new personnel; tighter maintenance standards, ground workers retrained; fewer outside contractors	Tighter security procedures
Manufacturer response	Focus on rudder	Minimal	Focus on fuel tanks and wiring
New regulations	Rudder modifications; pilot training	Temporary airline shutdown; fire suppression equipment; oxidizing materials banned from aircraft	Some changes to flammability of fuel tanks; wiring inspections

a. There were no survivors of any of these crashes.

summarizes the major components of those three cases, demonstrating several linkages among plane crashes, media coverage, and transportation policy.

Results of the Analysis

Some of the following results are based on the quantitative evidence presented in chapter 3 and others on case analysis.

—Media coverage increases as the scope of the tragedy increases, and long-term media interest requires a narrative to drive the plot.

—Media interest is encouraged by the involvement of previously invisible government officials with no formal background in aviation matters.

—Continuing media interest depends on identifying targets of blame.

—Media narratives require symbolic heroes.

—After a crash, media interest and policy relevance sometimes clash.

—Congressional and presidential involvement in airline crashes is either symbolic or limited.

—Airline responses to a crash focus on public relations, personnel moves, more vigilance, increased training, and improved training methods.

—Aircraft manufacturers focus on testing and minor changes in design.

—The regulatory response of the Federal Aviation Administration (FAA) to crashes is limited and slow.

—Crashes are neither necessary nor sufficient for changes in public policy. In general, airline crashes divert resources from other aspects of aviation safety unrelated to a crash, which may represent misallocated resources. Crashes can shift the focus of regulators and elected officials, so they do affect the policy debate.

Media Coverage and the Scope of the Tragedy

Body counts can dominate a story for the first few days after a crash. If only a few are killed, minimal coverage results, because the accident resembles a car wreck or a bus crash. The sheer enormity of the tragedy is seemingly lessened.[2] If hundreds perish, the story will get saturation coverage for many days after a crash. After that, however, something more is needed.

Each of the three crashes investigated in this volume developed a story line that kept journalists interested long after the event itself. In the case of USAir, a mystery emerged. What caused the crash and the one in Colorado Springs that preceded it? Here the image of government investigators always finding a cause was challenged, and the continuing inquiry generated periodic interest over a five-year period. The technical nature of the investigation meant that constant coverage could not be sustained. This is consistent with the mixed support in chapter 3 for the claim that greater causal uncertainty increases media coverage.

ValuJet was the nation's rising airline star until one of its planes fell into a Florida swamp. Soon the plot involved negligence. The FAA and

ValuJet officials had engaged in sloppy record-keeping, failed to communicate among units, and ignored problematic in-flight performance. When this precrash pattern was investigated, doubts were raised about ValuJet, leading to the grounding of the airline.

The TWA crash was initially linked to terrorism. The notion that others deliberately took the plane to the depths of the ocean raised issues that had never been explored seriously in prior domestic crashes. Media coverage set the standard for future crash analysis. The subsequent move from terrorism to a mysterious mechanical malfunction generated continued press interest.

Media Coverage and the Involvement of Public Figures

The extreme statements of nonaviation officials directly affected two of the crashes. Mary Schiavo, a former prosecutor who became inspector general for the Department of Transportation (DOT), made inflammatory statements about the performance of ValuJet, commercial aviation, and the competence of the FAA. Within days of the crash she wrote a widely read magazine article about the dangers of aviation and appeared on television network news programs to declare that ValuJet was an unsafe airline, that the oversight body was not performing its function, and that it was in fact a "tombstone agency." Such charges guaranteed continued media coverage. James Kallstrom injected the terror element into the TWA crash. Even a former presidential press secretary asserted that the TWA plane was downed by friendly fire.

These suggestions required the response of officials from the U.S. Navy, the Defense Department, and the Federal Bureau of Investigation (FBI). Al Gore's involvement in airline safety also received significant attention.

Media Coverage and Targets of Blame

In each of the three cases studied, culprits emerged as the focus of media analysis, especially the airlines, plane manufacturers or aviation companies, and relevant government agencies. The airline always came in for criticism, though the case of TWA involved the way it treated passengers' families rather than its culpability in the crash. USAir and ValuJet were depicted as responsible for their crashes. Economic issues were also stressed in the cases of USAir and ValuJet but for opposite reasons. In the USAir case, its financial woes were linked to a need to scrimp on safety. In the

SAFETY AND SYMBOLISM 147

other instance, ValuJet was said to be too focused on expansion and grew too quickly. In the USAir and TWA crashes, Boeing built the planes, and press reports focused on prior problems with the aircraft in question. The manufacturer had either ignored or downplayed problems with flight performance. Press accounts stressed they had prior warnings but did not act.

The oversight agency (FAA) was a media focus in two of the cases (USAir, ValuJet). Here there were frequent stories about inadequate supervision and a failure to communicate between regional and national headquarters about problems and delays in bringing about necessary changes. The FAA always faces the risk of blame. After a crash, it is in a no-win situation, defending an industry under difficult conditions. First, crash scene "visuals" engage the public. Then the media focus turns to the anguish of the victims' families. Further, everyone wants answers as to what happened. The FAA is in the position of being the government defender of the industry.

The FAA has only two possible responses. The first is the statistical defense of flight as the safest transportation mode. The other is to postpone action until the National Transportation Safety Board (NTSB) investigation is complete, which takes months if not years. In the interim, FAA officials hope that their prior oversight of the airline and plane manufacturers will not reveal negligence. Otherwise, negative publicity will befall the agency. The only positive outcome is if the probable cause (such as weather) does not cast the FAA as a culprit and therefore a target for the media.

Media Coverage and Symbolic Heroes

If airline companies, aircraft manufacturers, and the FAA are targets of blame, whom can the media use as positive role models? Often it is the employees of another government agency, the NTSB, which is generally portrayed in a positive light. Unlike FAA officials, these employees are not depicted as inefficient bureaucrats protecting powerful economic interests. After the three crashes the picture that emerged was of investigators methodically combing through the crash debris and being careful not to speculate prematurely about the cause of the crash. While reports mentioned the inability of the NTSB to deliver a precise causal agent, the board was not cast in a negative light. Why?

Media stories focused on the fact that NTSB recommendations in various areas of flight safety had been ignored or watered down by the FAA.

The NTSB was cast as an organization devoted to safety (part of its title) but frustrated in its ability to accomplish its mission. One analyst notes that "to the public and the news media, NTSB investigators were crusaders for safety who could do no wrong. They were the guys in the white hats who found everybody else's mistakes."[3] The head of the NTSB in this period was Jim Hall, who was adept in using the media to portray his agency as a frustrated reformer fighting against entrenched interests.

Media Interest and Policy Relevance

The media help to set the government's agenda, so priorities may be reshuffled. For example, an accident killing 200 people gives no more information a priori regarding the safety of an aircraft than one killing a few. But as seen in chapter 3, the number of deaths is positively related to the amount of coverage a crash receives, with such occurrences typically receiving significant scrutiny from the government.

Congressional and Presidential Responses

There was no legislative response to the USAir crash. After the ValuJet crash, hearings were held and problems were evaluated, but the only new law related to this crash was on eliminating the aviation promotion function of the FAA. (Some FAA reforms were also enacted as part of a 1996 FAA reauthorization bill but were not tied closely with ValuJet.) The congressional response to the TWA crash brought on a number of committee investigations and a lot of rhetoric but little action, save for clarifying the NTSB's and FBI's roles in an investigation and changing the way victims' families were treated after a crash.

A presidential advisory commission was created after the ValuJet and TWA crashes, which produced a variety of recommendations, but many had been raised by the NTSB earlier and ignored.

Responses of Airlines and Aircraft Manufacturers

After a crash, airlines often initiate advertising campaigns to reassure the flying public that all is well. ValuJet and USAir changed personnel, improved inspection procedures, improved pilot training, and rewrote their manuals. ValuJet even changed its name.

In the ValuJet crash the focus was not on the plane's safety. In the other two cases, Boeing aircraft were involved. Boeing tested the planes extensively to determine the possible causes of the crashes and to improve certain mechanisms, both slow and time-consuming efforts. In part the manufacturer defended its aircraft as safe independent of the crashes.

The FAA Response

The FAA generally implements around 80 percent of NTSB recommendations. This figure, however, belies the fact that the FAA sometimes takes years, even decades, to require airlines to fully implement a safety initiative. After each of the three crashes examined in this book, the NTSB suggested corrective actions to the FAA.

After the USAir crash, the FAA proposed minor (and then major) changes to the aircraft's rudder, but action was delayed for two or three years to give the airlines further time to make minor modifications. The FAA finally required a new rudder system design, but the new mechanism would not be replaced on older planes until 2008, by some estimates. After the ValuJet crash, carriers were banned from carrying oxygen generators in cargo holds, although some airlines continued the practice. All cargo holds were then required to have fire-suppression systems installed, but years passed before that recommendation was implemented. In the aftermath of the TWA crash, the FAA required some inspections and improvements to the fuel tanks of 747s but has delayed action on requiring the inerting of fuel tanks—a proposal first made in the early 1970s—while it continues to study the issue. FAA representative Thomas McSweeny defended the agency's temporizing:

> When the FAA makes a decision and then later changes its mind, I don't think it's a matter of saying we got in wrong the first time. I think it's a matter of saying the facts changed, and it's a matter of saying that the FAA is open minded enough to change its mind when in fact there are good reasons to do it, rather than continue blindly down the same path because we made a decision in the past that doesn't appear right now to be the right decision.[4]

Lengthy decisionmaking processes are not automatically grounds for criticism. The FAA has more constituencies than the NTSB and would be blamed if implementation requirements harmed the industry or proved to be unwarranted. Since the agency implements most NTSB suggestions eventually, one explanation might be that the agency simply needs the time to discuss possible actions with all stakeholders. Another explanation is that delays save money.

The Effect of Crashes on Policy

Plane crashes have a powerful agenda-setting ability. Even if a particular air safety policy is a low priority, a plane crash moves it up immediately. The NTSB views a crash as a window of opportunity to push for safety reforms, and the FAA realizes that the problem brought to light by the crash must be addressed, even if those actions are purely symbolic. Media attention contributes to this. The attacks of September 11 represent another shift—from safety to security (a theme discussed later in the chapter).

The view that the FAA is a tombstone agency is not quite right. Yes, it does devote more attention to a given policy area after a crash. But the agency engages in rule making separate and apart from plane crashes, and meanwhile it certainly does not implement some major recommendations proposed by the NTSB in the wake of a crash. It is more accurate to claim that regulation in major areas of air safety is reactive regulation. That is, if major changes occur, they will be after a crash, but a crash does not guarantee reform.

Crucial Players and Plane Crashes

After a plane crashes, several actors are crucially involved. In the private sector are the airline and the plane's manufacturer. In the public sector are the NTSB, the FAA, and congressional committees charged with oversight in this area.

The Private Sector

After a crash, airline companies, plane manufacturers, and even parts manufacturers face three problems.

The first is the question of legal liability: To what extent were their actions a cause of the crash? The answer to this will in part determine the amount of money allocated to victims in ensuing legal settlements. The second issue is cost: To what extent will funding have to be allocated to changing or improving the quality of the plane and safety procedures? Corrective action can cost hundreds of millions of dollars. The third issue is image: To what extent will these groups be thought of as sloppy, inefficient, negligent? Could this affect the number of future travelers?

All of these issues ultimately involve money and a negative impact on the company's profit statement. Each must devise strategies to keep these economic losses at a minimum.

The Public Sector

The NTSB is the focal point of accident investigations. Its two objectives are to find the cause of the plane crash and to suggest changes that will decrease the likelihood of the same problem arising in the future. But there are tensions and conflicts within the board. The scope of many accident investigations is daunting, and the board must investigate every plane, train, and boat mishap. With a limited budget and an overworked staff, the NTSB must rely on others to help with its investigation. This "party system" allows the airline, the airliner manufacturer, the pilots' union, the FAA, and other relevant groups to participate in the investigation.

Critics argue that the NTSB is therefore beholden to the interests of these other parties and that their participation prevents a fair and impartial verdict being reached. The party system also has its supporters. Pluralism creates an environment in which varied interests, working to protect their own reputations, guard against inappropriate accusations. In a sense, each acts as a control on the passions of others. In this view, the NTSB acts as the arbiter of the group. Implausible theories can be quickly ruled out in the competition among affected interests. An NTSB investigator has observed, "Competing interests help keep one special interest from taking over."[5]

The party system produces minimal conflict when consensus exists regarding the cause of the crash. However, when disagreements arise or there is uncertainty, as in the case of the USAir and TWA crashes, opinions are drafted and continuously altered as disputes continue and tests are rerun. The threat of legal and economic liability looms large; the party deemed most responsible for the crash faces lawsuits involving millions of dollars. The investigators must sort out these issues and present their conclusions to the five-person NTSB board for a formal vote as to what happened. Investigations that ultimately provide no definitive answers appear to be failures, given the exceptional record of the NTSB in determining the cause of crashes.

The FAA has the authority to implement safety reforms. It is a large organization, with 50,000 employees and a multibillion-dollar budget. In normal times, the FAA has low media visibility and minimal legislative oversight. A plane crash, however, changes the situation, raising the agency's visibility and the specter of accusations of inadequate regulation of the airline industry. At this juncture, the agency faces a dilemma: Is it a captured agency, reflecting the interests of those it regulates?

Even the casual observer can see signs suggesting capture. For example, the agency is slow to recommend changes that will cost airlines or manufacturers money. A predictable pattern unfolds. First the recommendations (often made by the NTSB) must be studied. Then the affected parties are given considerable time to make the changes, ranging from months to years. Further, the public statements of the agency often appear to support airlines and give short shrift to NTSB concerns.

Part of the problem for the FAA stems from its dual mandate of promotion and regulation, and although this mandate was formally eliminated after the ValuJet crash, basic patterns at the FAA have not changed. Reasonable people can argue about whether the FAA does enough to regulate airline safety, but its performance is a clear reflection of the political environment in which it operates.

The principal groups performing bureaucratic oversight are the relevant congressional committees. Their primary concerns are expanding transportation modes in their districts and protecting economic interests (transportation companies within their districts). Investigative efforts in this realm require three elements: loss of life, media interest, and signs of administrative mismanagement. Crashes provide the loss-of-life ingredient, but media interest is short-lived without a larger theme. Administrative mismanagement can provide that larger theme, and if signs of it are found, a congressional inquiry may be forthcoming. Absent this, the committees' focus will be on other transportation issues, such as consumer problems. Further, the events of September 11 have shifted the focus of legislative committees to the issue of security and terrorism in air travel.

The Politics of Aviation Safety

The making of public policy often involves disputes over which actors can best achieve a certain objective. These objectives are often captured or summarized by a word or image that conveys to the average citizen everything that is desirable in that particular policy bailiwick. These symbols do not have specific meanings, which permits a variety of attributed associations. The political battles revolve around which party is best able to achieve a particular symbolic end. Disputes are thus framed in such positive terms that no one questions their desirability. Examples include *jobs, work, clean air, clean water, learning,* and *helping children.* Occasionally issues become battlegrounds between opposing symbols. In the area of abortion and euthanasia, the fight is between *life* and *choice.* In battles between states and the federal government, the symbolic division is between *local control* and *uniform standards.*

The symbolic terms in transportation include *cost, accessibility, speed,* and *comfort.* The overarching symbol used by all parties as a measuring stick for success is *safety.* This is particularly true in the aviation sector, as a particular policy success is measured by the extent to which safety is achieved. *Safety* is the mantra of all those involved in the area of aviation: legislators, bureaucrats, aircraft manufacturers, and airline officials and employees. The term *safety* is never challenged, as no one wants unsafe planes. There is never any debate about the desirability of the objective.

Flying can be a terrifying enterprise for many people. The individual gives up all control of movement to others in a conveyance flying hundreds of miles an hour in a crowded sky, sometimes in adverse weather. Cars provide choices: The driver can get off the road at certain points; planes cannot. An airline thus uses a symbol like *safety* to assure the flying public that its fears are unfounded. When a plane crashes, the term *safety* has particular symbolic potency and meaning. Usually lives have been lost and others have been seriously injured. A debate develops over who or what caused the plane to crash, and all relevant parties wrap themselves in the symbolic garb of safety advocates.

But the question can be asked: What is *safety?* Looking it up in the dictionary is not helpful when dealing with a symbol. Symbols have connotative meanings, implied and associative. In the aftermath of a plane crash participants use the term in different contexts. They appear to be talking to each other but are often talking past one another. The media evaluate all parties by the standard of whether they are "promoting safety." The same is true for politicians, business people, onlookers, and the flying public. Consider the words of Mary Schiavo:

> The FAA has no definition of *safety*—no official definition, that is. *Safety* is not defined in the Federal Aviation Act of 1958. It is not

specified in the FAA regulations. It is not explained in the agency's guidelines. So FAA officials can't say what safety is. . . . And without a sanctioned definition of *safety,* there can be no safety yardstick, no safety standard. So the FAA cannot—will not—say what constitutes a safety problem, when safety is compromised, or what makes aviation safe. . . . Deciding that safety is at risk, or should be improved, is an informal, fluid quest.[6]

What is the symbolic antonym for *safety?* Here there is no agreement, but the one term to be avoided is *accident.* Some accidents are inevitable in any transportation mode, but the term makes everyone uncomfortable. While accidents can never be ruled out of any complex environment, the implicit objective is to eliminate them all.

Another term rarely used by those in the aviation business is *unsafe.* The safety continuum does not range from *safe* to *unsafe* in spoken or written usage. Instead the term *safe* is used in the superlative form: *safer* as opposed to simply *safe.* In January 1997, when Boeing decided to improve the rudder systems on all 737s, a company official said that the adjustment "will serve to make a safe airplane even safer." At the FAA the official position was that Boeing was "simply making it better."[7]

For conflict to occur, there must be disagreement over some aspect of a policy. Since all participants agree that a safe aviation system is a worthy policy objective, disputes can be understood as differences over the meaning of "safe." At least six definitions are currently in use by parties in the aviation business. These definitions drive the debate. Each is considered here, with illustrations drawn from the USAir, ValuJet, and TWA crashes.

Definition 1: Safety Defined as the Statistical Probability of Dying in a Plane Crash

What is the likelihood that any particular plane flight will crash? How does the fatality rate involved in flying compare with other activities? This safety definition used by the FAA, airlines, and manufacturers is a fairly simple and straightforward assessment involving a passenger's risk of death. It is a statistical calculation based on the number of people killed in airline mishaps per number of passenger miles or number of flights. This definition is used whenever the industry is under media scrutiny, particularly in postcrash periods.

Leading officials use this definition particularly when comparing flying to other transportation modes. Here the evidence is clear. Compared with

car and train travel, aviation is safer—and has been for several decades. In fact, being a passenger in a commercial airliner is one of the safest activities available to the public. From 1991 through 2000 average passenger deaths for every 100 million passenger miles were as follows:
—Automobiles, 0.88.
—Trains, 0.08.
—Buses, 0.03.
—Airlines, 0.02.[8]

The leading scholar on aviation safety statistics is Arnold Barnett, a professor of management operations and research at the Massachusetts Institute of Technology. For more than two decades he has documented the relative safety of commercial aviation, often testifying before congressional committees when such matters are raised. His message is always the same: Commercial aviation is the safest transportation mode, and a recent failure does not change that assessment.[9] Barnett uses a measure of safety that assesses the probability of dying on a randomly selected flight. This statistic does not account for the length of the flight, since most accidents occur at takeoff or landing. For instance, between two choices of flights between San Francisco and Atlanta (a direct flight or two flights that involve a connection at an interim point), the risk of death is higher in the latter, even though the distance traveled is roughly identical.

What about a comparison of death rates with activities other than transportation? One frequently cited statistic is that a person has as much chance of dying in a plane accident as winning a state lottery jackpot.[10] Further, people have a greater chance of dying in work-related accidents than in a plane mishap. What about truly difficult or dangerous situations? The chances of dying in a plane crash in 1998 were much less than in any of the following conditions: excessive heat, excessive cold, snakebites, bee stings, lightning, suicide, drowning, firearms, or falls.[11] Plane travel, by comparison, is one of the safest public activities.

This definition can be used by analysts in a slightly different context. What about the risk of flying with an airline with a record of multiple crashes in a short period of time? The focus often is not the relative frequency but the absolute number of crashes. After the USAir crash outside of Pittsburgh in 1994, the numbers looked grim. The airline had five crashes in as many years; of the previous seven major crashes, four were USAir planes; and its planes were the last three commercial domestic airliners to have crashed. Was USAir unsafe?

USAir was subject to great media scrutiny. Probability models were used to see if its planes were more likely to crash than those of other airlines. Statistical experts reported that the chance of the airline's planes being at greater risk in flight compared to other airlines was minimal.[12] Two researchers analyzed USAir's safety record of 1987–96 compared with other carriers, asking the following question: Suppose that all airlines were equally safe; then what is the chance that the worst airline in a "lottery" of crashes would have fared as badly as or worse than USAir? The answer is one in nine, which does not meet the standard statistical threshold for accepting a finding.[13] Given that flight deaths are rare to begin with, even focusing on a carrier with multiple mishaps does not change the picture of safety in the skies, according to this definition.

As a consequence, for those who accept this safety criterion, there is no premium on taking any immediate corrective action following a crash. Clearly, planes are not unsafe. Plane travel has the statistical edge particularly when compared to automobile travel. In this instance, statistics are used as a wedge against further reform. Cost-benefit analysis, usually required by law, takes into account whether the expected lives saved from a reform are worth its additional cost, and such analysis drives many regulatory decisions.

Definition 2: Safety Defined as No One Being Killed in a Crash

An alternative measure is much simpler. How many people were killed flying commercial aircraft? Here the emphasis is not on a comparative but on an absolute consideration. If people die, then flying is unsafe. If none die, then flying is safe. This is a demanding definition. While some years (1993, 1998, 2002) have been victim free for major U.S. carriers, most years have had at least one plane crash death.

This measure is usually not used by those in the aviation business or in government but is implicit in the media reporting of a crash. Here the emphasis is on the body count, eyewitness accounts, and the grieving families of the victims. These images conjure up the idea of error, failure, and an unnecessary loss of life. The images are part of the media reports for days and provide a powerful visual definition of safety or the lack thereof. Occasionally transportation officials use this definition as a measure of safety, but they usually have not spent their lives in the aviation business. (An example is Secretary of Transportation Federico Peña, appointed as head of the agency by President Clinton in 1993. His prior experience was as mayor of Denver.)

By this definition, 1994 was the worst year for commercial aviation since 1988. Five airplanes crashed in that period, with hundreds of lives lost and public confidence shaken. Peña thought a dramatic action was needed to win the public's trust and convened a safety conference in January 1995, inviting nearly a thousand experts from the public and private sectors to discuss problems in commercial aviation. Participants were expected to develop a list of suggestions that, if implemented, would make commercial aviation safer. In his keynote speech, Peña raised the safety bar and called for a criterion of zero accidents. "We have to get out of the mind-set of saying, 'No matter how hard we try, we will have accidents,' and into 'We will not have accidents.'"[14]

While such a definition can temporarily calm the fears of the mass public, it is difficult to achieve. Any accident, by this definition, means that the whole system is unsafe. And aviation cannot remain accident free for a long period of time, given the number of daily flights. This definition will usually come back to haunt the endorser. Further crashes will require similar symbolic efforts. After his problematic handling of the ValuJet crash, Peña subsequently moved from DOT to head the Department of Energy.

Definition 3: Safety Defined as the Absence of Unsolved Crashes

In the previous definition, any fatal mishap or a company with multiple crashes is deemed unsafe. Definition 3 accepts the inevitability of crashes, but its focus is on the postaccident scenario. Safety depends on determining the cause of all accidents. This definition involves primarily one group of aviation experts, the NTSB. If a cause is not determined, then another tragedy may occur for the same reason. Investigations can take years and lose the media's attention. However, the key is the NTSB's aircraft accident report, which provides the definitive determination of the cause. If the report is not forthcoming, a sense of unease is cast over the entire industry.

There is a second element in seeking answers for mishaps. Even worse than not solving a crash is having a previously unsolved case that bears close resemblance to a currently unsolved case. NTSB investigators faced this situation in the USAir crash. This definition was implied by a journalist who wrote, "The unforgivable sin in aviation is not killing a planeload of passengers—it is killing two planeloads because of the same cause."[15]

This problem, while infrequent, casts a pall over the investigators. After the NTSB initially failed to determine the cause of a USAir crash in Colorado, a reporter concluded, "It was an embarrassing admission of defeat. 'Undetermined reasons.' Those were painful words, an acknowledgment that the NTSB wasn't up to the job."[16] While the investigation of the USAir flight 427 crash dragged on, an FAA official said, "Unexplained accidents are something that just cry for somebody to explain them. In this business, it's just not acceptable as far as I'm concerned."[17] Similar concerns existed after the TWA crash.

The NTSB is required by law to determine the "probable cause" of a crash.[18] Only three crashes are still designated "undetermined."[19] Rudder malfunction is identified as the probable cause in both USAir crashes. But the source of the rudder malfunction remains subject to speculation. The final cause of the TWA crash is similar, with a focus on the center fuel tank explosion, but the ignition source is unknown. Since the actual cause has never been determined in any of the three investigations, they could be seen as failures.

This safety definition is demanding for those involved, allowing for no failures or uncertainties on the part of investigators. No matter how long the time period, causes must be found and the public must be given a satisfactory answer.

Definition 4: Safety Defined as the In-Flight Performance of Planes and Airlines

Both the FAA and the NTSB collect data on flight performance, making a distinction between accidents and incidents. The term *accident* in data collection has a much broader definition than one might expect, referring not only to people killed or injured during a flight but also to serious damage to the plane. The NTSB defines an *accident* as "an occurrence associated with the operation of an aircraft which takes place between the time any person boards the aircraft with the intention of flight and all such persons have disembarked, and in which any person suffers death or serious injury, or in which the aircraft receives substantial damage." An *incident* is defined as "an occurrence other than an accident, associated with the operation of an aircraft, which affects or could affect the safety of operations."[20]

Barnett notes that, by the NTSB definition, accidents include a flight attendant breaking an ankle while "standing in a galley during unexpected turbulence. . . . A substantial number of 'accidents' include difficulties that the airline could not have foreseen or [that] portend little threat of a major crash."[21] Thus the accident data include both deaths and minor in-flight injuries.

The assumption here is that planes or airlines with a significant number of flight interruptions, either "accidents" or "incidents," are not safe. All these occurrences are recorded by the FAA and the NTSB and can be publicized during the investigation of a company's performance after a crash. For example, between the start of ValuJet's operation in 1993 and its Everglades crash in 1996, the airline had more "accidents" and "incidents" per 100,000 flights than any other U.S. commercial jet carrier. Schiavo based her statement that ValuJet was unsafe in part on these statistics.[22]

Media investigations of plane crashes often use the accident-incident definition of safety. Frequent press accounts of past problems often plague the airline, which may in fact have lost no passengers in such occurrences. Although officials downplay such occurrences as predictive of future crashes, they raise a red flag for the press. Media coverage of ValuJet lasted for weeks because the airline had had a number of incidents in previous months, indicating—by this definition—that it was an unsafe airline.

When the NTSB identifies a causal agent, officials argue that problems downing one airliner should be eliminated in similar aircraft. Whenever a new plane crash can be attributed to a previous recommendation that had been ignored, the NTSB will point this out as evidence of poor regulation on the part of the FAA. The assumption is that if a plane crashes and the cause is discovered, then it was not a completely negative event. Corrective measures can then be taken, and the problem will not recur. Failure to accomplish this indicates that the system has failed.

Definition 5: Safety Defined as the Ground Performance of Planes and Airlines

Planes typically spend more time on the ground than in the sky. While aircraft remain out of flight sequence, their maintenance and the perfor-

mance of personnel are monitored by the FAA and the airline. Is maintenance performed so as to make sure the aircraft are flightworthy? Are the
pilots properly trained in all aspects of flight?

After the crash of USAir flight 427, the airline's flight operations, pilot
training, and maintenance records were examined. On a number of occasions USAir flights were found to have left the gate without sufficient fuel.
Press reports also revealed sloppy record-keeping and maintenance procedures. Even the airline's procedural manuals raised concerns.[23] Thus the
company was characterized as unsafe because of lax oversight of ground
operations.

Definition 5 is often the province of the media, which look at on-ground
performance factors as a key to safety. When the *New York Times* investigation of USAir's prior record first broke, most major newspapers carried a version of it.[24] A similar argument played out in the ValuJet case.
After the event, media stories focused on the laxity of the FAA and the
airline. The articles used terms like "beset by safety problems" and "shortcomings in safety matters." What led to these charges? As it turned out,
the last FAA structural inspection of the airline's planes was two years
prior, and it had not inspected its manuals, procedures, or mechanical
shops at all. USAir itself had not kept complete training records for maintenance workers and had no internal audit program.[25]

Thus incomplete record-keeping and surveillance made the airline "unsafe." However, FAA officials never used that term when referring to this
particular definition. They would use terms like "an accounting problem,
an audit problem, not a substance problem," or "we have an audit problem, not a safety problem. Safety was not compromised."[26] When officials
finally took the unusual step of shutting down the airline one month after
the crash, they made no reference to whether the planes were safe or unsafe. Instead the terms that were used were "failure to establish airworthiness," "multiple shortcomings in supervision of maintenance contractors,"
and "serious deficiencies."[27]

Definition 6: Safety Defined as Invulnerability to Terrorism

The focus of definition 6 is on intentional actions to down the airliner. For
instance, a bomb can be placed on a bag aboard a plane in the cargo hold
or passenger area. An individual could ignite an explosive during the flight.
The plane could be taken over by armed individuals en route. Possibly
even a missile could be fired at the plane. None of these relate to sloppy

record-keeping or incident reports. A plane resembles an area of armed combat, and passengers assume the roles of innocent civilians.

This definition involves a new group of officials and removes the "usual suspects" from a defining role. Instead, law enforcement agencies own this definition. With domestic flights, the FBI takes the primary role in determining the causal agent. Early on, domestic crashes did not raise the possibility of terror attacks. All that changed with the TWA crash. Once FBI agent James Kallstrom and others indicated that terrorism was a prime suspect, that dimension became part of the public and media mind-set for all subsequent crashes. The (later debunked) report by former presidential press secretary Pierre Salinger that a navy missile had accidentally downed the TWA jet added fuel to the theory of outside involvement. This frame was reinforced by the events of September 11. Now when a crash occurs, this is the first definition that comes to mind for many.

Progress on Aviation Safety and Problem Definition

In issue disputes, there is a presumption that a meaningful dialogue can take place. However, when protagonists use key words with no single meaning, confusion reigns. These conflicts come to light when media interest is engaged. In the absence of air crashes (at least until September 11), coverage of aviation safety matters is minimal. However, once a crash occurs and lives are lost, a predictable sequence of events unfolds.

Most protagonists move quickly to one of two positions. Airplane executives, aircraft manufacturers, transportation officials, and statisticians use definition 1. This position transcends any individual crash, as all other issues become secondary. While there may be individual problems with a particular airline, the skies are safe. Their message: Continue to fly.

The media take the adversarial position, with an immediate response focusing on loss of life, or definition 2. Pictures of crash debris are shown; body recovery is visually recorded. The large number of people dead means a safety problem. Once the bodies have been recovered and the rubble investigated, this initial definitional conflict recedes in importance. In fact the crash will lose media attention unless another disagreement over definitions begins.

Airline officials use definition 1 throughout the course of the investigation. However, there is one crack in their rhetorical armor. The NTSB is the one agency pushing for corrective actions from manufacturers, airlines, and the FAA. To further this aim the NTSB also uses definitions 4 and 5. If attention is focused on previous negligence, action is more likely. The NTSB holds news briefings and is the chief source of media information about what is transpiring. The press needs to know which cause possibilities are being pursued, and the NTSB needs a public advocate to push for more stringent enforcement of existing rules and for the promulgation of new ones.

There is one difference between the media's and the NTSB's use of definitions 4 and 5. The media adopt an investigatory stance to find out what really happened in the face of lapses in oversight efforts. If the public becomes anxious as a consequence, then that is a sign of good reporting. However, NTSB officials must be more careful. While the emphasis on oversight errors by the FAA and airlines cast the board in a positive light and help make changes in current regulations possible, this stance can be overdone. The NTSB does not want the public to avoid flying. Its officials are therefore caught in a definitional bind. They believe in definition 1, like other officials. However, they want their investigations to have an impact and thus resort to reminders that their prior warnings, if acted upon, might have prevented the crash. But too much emphasis on this theme can unnecessarily alarm the public and politicians.

Media interest depends on moving from definition 2 to one focusing on unsafe conditions. In cases with lasting media interest, most journalists move to definitions 4 and 5. Past procedures and behavior are causally linked to safety, using FAA statistics or reports of problems with the plane and the airline. The use of definition 3 complicates the safety issue. While government officials will still defend definition 1, the latter is troublesome for the NTSB, whose reputation is dependent on an unblemished record.

So after a crash, journalists often attack the FAA and the airline for lax procedures and a sloppy flying record. These officials respond by citing overall statistical patterns and deemphasizing definitions 4 and 5. In the three cases studied in this volume, only when the number of occurrences under definitions 4 and 5 were numerous and a congressional hearing was looming did FAA officials shut down an airline. The blame game lasts until the media exhaust their focus on administrative lapses and on records showing sloppiness during flight or on the ground and until one or another of the oversight agencies wins the definitional battle. Bureaucrats are battered, and companies are presented as uncaring profiteers. Attempts to prevent change (by the FAA and the airlines) are couched in the fact that airline travel is extremely safe and that additional changes may not add much to the already excellent safety record of airlines. Proponents of change (the NTSB) focus on the elimination of any causal agent linked with passenger loss of life.

The three cases we studied varied in definitional conflicts after the first few days. The USAir crash was dominated by the mystery theme, which was quickly reinforced by the unsolved crash in Colorado Springs. Almost five years passed before the NTSB issued an explanatory report. The five-year-long uncertainty kept the story alive at different time periods. A secondary definitional difference pitted the statistical definition of safety versus USAir's record in other flights, in ground oversight, and in the rudder system on 737s. Further, NTSB officials also noted prior lapses in safety enforcement by the FAA. The absence of action in two areas was highlighted. The board pushed for the inspection of all 737s for possible rudder malfunctions as well as more sophisticated flight data recorders on these aircraft.

In the case of ValuJet, the safety battle was between statistical probabilities of death and air and ground oversight. After the rapid discovery of the cause, the media had a field day uncovering reports that showed that the FAA had found problems with ValuJet's performance and did not act. NTSB officials found major problems with a subcontractor's handling of dangerous cargo and poor fire suppression equipment on many aircraft. For six years before the crash, NTSB officials had pressured the FAA to require fire suppression systems on all aircraft, but airlines and the agency resisted such requests due to cost. Media reports focused on ValuJet's efforts at expanding business and its failure to exercise proper oversight of its operations. These elements drove the story for several months.

The TWA case presented an entirely different dispute. This became a matter of jurisdictional rivalry between the FBI and the NTSB. Once an FBI agent raised the terror angle, the media latched onto the story. Subsequent official withdrawal of the terror angle did not remove it from media interest as further reports of friendly fire expanded the focus of the crash. A secondary consideration was uncertainty. When the NTSB report was finally issued, no specific causal agents were found. The board concluded that the center fuel tank exploded but did not know precisely what caused the blast. Even though the initial causal element was never determined with certainty, the NTSB felt that the possibility of a center fuel tank explosion should be eliminated and pushed for making that occurrence impossible in the future.

Each of the postcrash scenarios involved a public airing of long-standing conflicts among adversarial groups. All used language and sym-

Table 8-2   *Definitions of Safety Used by Adversarial Groups, Three Plane Crashes*[a]

Period	FAA, airlines, and manufacturers	NTSB	Media
Immediate aftermath	Definition 1	. . .	Definition 2
USAir			
Major conflict	Definition 1	Definition 3	Definition 3
Secondary conflict	Definition 1	Definitions 4 and 5	Definitions 4 and 5
ValuJet			
Major conflict	Definition 1	Definitions 4 and 5	Definitions 4 and 5
TWA			
Major conflict	Definition 1	Definition 6	Definition 6
Secondary conflict	Definition 1	Definition 3	Definition 3

a. Definitions are described in text.

bols to buttress their positions. The postcrash exchanges were made by people not so much speaking to one another as reiterating prior arguments altered to the particular circumstances of the case. Table 8-2 summarizes these findings.

The preeminence of safety as the principal symbol overarching all transportation issues has been challenged by the events of September 11, 2001. The term *security* has now taken precedence. *Safety* refers to statistical probabilities of death and the conditions of the plane and its personnel before an accident. *Security* conjures up the idea of intentional behavior. A focus on security shifts the spotlight from mechanical problems or record-keeping to profiling passengers and preventing passengers judged to be dangerous from boarding a plane. In the immediate aftermath of a plane crash the focus is on definition 1, or safety defined as the statistical probability of dying in a plane crash. But that focus quickly gives way to the chances of terrorism. Only when that issue is resolved in the negative will the definition shift to the others outlined above. The TWA crash brought terrorism into the range of possibility. The events of September 11 brought it center stage.

Consider the crash of an American Airlines Airbus on November 12, 2001. The *New York Times* report the following day combines deaths with terrorism: "260 on Jet Die in Queens Crash; 6 to 9 Missing as 12 Homes Burn; U.S. Doubts Link to Terrorism."[28] The article ruled out a terror link at the outset, but still the story was initially defined that way. On another level, though, flight 587 reminded everyone that planes would still fall from the sky after September 11 for reasons unrelated to terrorism. The emphasis on sabotage in postcrash speculation is one of the major changes in aviation stemming from the events of September 11.

Recommendations

In many reviews of actor performance in substantive areas, the emphasis tends to be on the following questions: Should more money be expended by the relevant government agencies? Are more personnel required? How can bureaucrats become more efficient and effective? Although these are relevant concerns in the area of aviation policy, they are not spotlighted here. Our emphasis is on directing existing resources toward altering the stakeholder mix in a postcrash environment. We believe that notions of safety should reflect overall crash risks and structural problems in the system rather than be dominated by specific crashes or high-profile events; this is reflected in our four recommendations.

Since actors impose a variety of meanings on the term *safety,* our recommendations are tied to specific definitions. Otherwise our proposals exist without context. In most postcrash scenarios, the first three definitions of *safety* come into play until the NTSB determines why the plane went down. Reliance on statistical measures and intense media coverage of tragedies is difficult to alter. Our recommendations concentrate on what features of the final three definitions can be modified to mitigate problems in the policy process. Here the concern is the battle for agenda control. What types of issue will occupy officials and the media?

Government Agency Agendas

The agendas of government agencies charged with aviation safety must not be dominated by crashes or tilted toward security concerns. In the process of responding to such occurrences, agencies' resources can be overtaxed, producing other regulatory problems. In this way, airline safety policy is reactive. To the extent that plane crashes are in many respects random events, airline safety regulation may be random as well.

Crashes may detract from other ongoing, less high-profile problems. The issue of runway incursions, or "close calls" on the ground, is a significant concern but will not receive serious attention until a major runway collision occurs. Similarly, the air traffic control system in the United States is embarrassingly outdated.[29] By contrast, these industrywide issues have received a fraction of the attention that low-cost airlines received after the

ValuJet crash, despite the fact that many agreed that ValuJet's crash was not indicative of the entire industry or even of that airline's overall safety.

The catastrophe of September 11 dramatically shifted the attention on aviation from safety to security. Since multiple agencies with different responsibilities now monitor aviation, the DOT, the Department of Homeland Security, Congress, and the president must ensure that the proper balance is struck between aviation safety and security. In a promising note, during her Senate confirmation hearing in September 2002, Marion Blakey (the FAA administrator as of December 2002) indicated that airline safety would be her top priority and that she would leave security to other agencies.[30]

A New Safety Agency

A new safety agency needs to be created to assume some of the FAA's current responsibilities. There is a necessary tension between the NTSB and the FAA. The former proposes and the latter disposes. However, the FAA often ignores NTSB recommendations for years—sometimes decades—before implementing them. A few years ago the FAA mandate was moved from promotion and oversight to just the latter, but this was a symbolic gesture. In 1994 and 1996 reforms in the FAA's organizational structure were implemented, including instituting a fixed five-year term for the administrator and making the agency more independent of the DOT. However, the DOT secretary, serving at the pleasure of the president, has de facto ultimate control. In the summer of 2002 Congress considered legislation that would require the DOT secretary to issue an annual report addressing its responses to significant NTSB recommendations.[31]

Still, the inclinations of the FAA have not changed: It continues to work closely and cooperatively with airline companies and manufacturers. When airline security was being reconfigured, the Transportation Security Administration was created. What about an equivalent Airline Safety Agency? Safety regulation could be given to the new agency, with the FAA left to handle other industry issues. There is precedent for the creation of an independent safety agency to handle the implementation of recommendations. The FAA (and its safety predecessors the Civil Aeronautics Board and the Civil Aeronautics Authority) were originally independent agencies whose heads did not serve at the pleasure of the president.[32]

The new agency would still need to balance the views of different interests—just as the NTSB does in its investigations—but it may feel less pressure to react to day-to-day events as the FAA does. There have been proposals to make the FAA an independent agency (a proposal even passed the House in the mid-1990s). A new agency would be preferable to an independent FAA, as it would not carry past symbolic and economic history. The FAA could retain control over airports and air traffic control, which are both linked to safety but are not safety issues per se. It would also supervise aspects of general aviation. Admittedly its responsibilities would be reduced, but it would not cease to exist.

Of course, interest protection drives agency creation as well as the regulatory process. As political scientist Terry Moe argues, impacted groups will battle over the creation and structure of a new government unit because the stakes are high. Once an agency is created, changing it is extremely difficult; compromise is often required, and there is uncertainty over how the agency will evolve and who will be in charge. This often results in agencies designed to address uncertainty and reflect compromise rather than to actually engage in effective regulation. As Moe puts it, "In the politics of structural choice, the inevitability of compromise means that agencies will be burdened with structures fully intended to cause their failure."[33] With that caveat, we suggest that the time has come to consider a new government unit to handle safety. Safety and security are closely related; if one is reconfigured, why not the other?

Congressional Responsibilities

Congress should set realistic target dates and identify funding sources in legislation designed to improve airline safety and security. In general, congressional oversight of airline safety has been infrequent, and rhetoric exceeds action. Legislation has been riddled with loopholes allowing congressional members to claim credit for improving safety or security while giving bureaucratic units unrealistic target dates to expedite new procedures. Such is true of the terror legislation passed after September 11. More realistic target dates are necessary in setting up new bureaucratic units to deal with complicated problems.

Care should be taken with respect to who pays for new regulatory procedures. Passengers benefit from a system with few crashes, so safety improvements should be partially funded by airline ticket taxes. However, security measures should be supported by general revenues, since attacks in the skies are a matter of national defense. Terrorists target an entire country, not specific plane passengers. If plane tickets are taxed further to provide for improved security measures, price-sensitive Americans will be dissuaded from returning to the skies, and air travelers would be subsidizing national defense. In mid-2002 a plan to increase the security surcharge was defeated. The next step ought to be a reduction or repeal of the tax.

Clear Definitions

The language used to define postcrash issues must be simplified and clarified. All occupations have their own terminology and jargon that permit their members to communicate but that mystify outsiders. A careful selection of words enables its user to define conflictual issues in the best possible light and to neutralize potential opponents. Such a practice taken to the extreme limits participation to the few. This is particularly true in the aviation sector. Aircraft are complex machines involving a myriad of interacting parts. The terminology associated with aviation issues is exceedingly complex. Opaque terminology gives control over issues to those who can understand the language and keeps outsiders, including the public and the media, at a distance.

Obviously an entirely new aviation vocabulary cannot be created. However, some issues raised during crash investigations could be simplified to give the public and the media a greater understanding of the process. Aviation statistics need to be clarified. While the FAA produces numbers and categories, their relevance is difficult to fathom. For example, *accident* is a general term including events not related to the performance of the plane. Statistical categories need to be made comprehensible to the layperson. The distinction between the terms *probable cause* and *actual cause* could be better explained. The NTSB uses the term *probable cause* in its accident reports regardless of the precision with which it can identify the causal agent. A distinction needs to be made between crashes with a clear causal agent and those for which an exact cause cannot be identified.

Conclusion

An airline crash brings two competing human responses into play. The first is fear. Images of plane and human remains scattered about evoke concerns among all who view them. Could it happen again? Is flying safe? The second response, acceptance of the ultimate safety of flying, uses the force of logic. The media stress the first response, while officials focus on the second. Fear, however, usually trumps logic as a prime reaction to disaster situations.

The postcrash investigation involves both company officials and public officials, who converge on the crash scene to determine the cause of the crash. It is a scenario that is bound to end in disagreement over notions of economics, legalities, status, prestige, and public perception. Battles over what *safety* means and how crashes affect notions of safe skies will continue as long as planes take off. We hope this book provides a framework for understanding these conflicts and how the symbolic use of the term *safety* protects and promotes competing interests.

Crashes, Probable Cause, and Policy Change

Avianca, January 25, 1990. Cause: human error (ran out of fuel). Policy change: stricter requirements for foreign carriers.

Northwest Airlines, December 3, 1990. Cause: human error (collision). Policy change: exit rows widened, nighttime ban on waiting on runway before takeoff.

USAir/Skywest, February 1, 1991. Cause: human error (collision). Policy change: exit rows widened; nighttime ban on waiting on runway before takeoff.

United Airlines, March 3, 1991. Cause: mechanical problem (rudders). Policy change: new rudder design; pilot training.

Atlantic Southeast Airlines, April 5, 1991. Cause: mechanical problem. Policy change: inspection of worn propeller parts.

L'Express Airlines, July 10, 1991. Cause: pilot error (wind shear and bad weather). Policy change: none.

Continental Express, September 11, 1991. Cause: human error (maintenance, missing screws). Policy change: flight crew notification of prior maintenance.

CommutAir, January 3, 1992. Cause: human error. Policy change: none.

USAir, March 22, 1992. Cause: human error (poor deicing procedures). Policy change: new deicing procedures.

GP Express, June 8, 1992. Cause: human error (poor pilot training). Policy change: more operating experience for pilots.

Express Airlines (Northwest), December 1, 1993. Cause: human error. Policy change: stricter rules for commuter planes.

Atlantic Coast/United Express, January 7, 1994. Cause: human error. Policy change: stricter rules for commuter planes, replacement of seatbelts.

USAir, July 2, 1994. Cause: human error (wind shear). Policy change: redesigned wind-shear detection system, installation of baby seats (pending).

USAir, September 8, 1994. Cause: mechanical. Policy change: redesign of rudder control system, pilot training.

American Eagle, October 31, 1994. Cause: human error (ice on wings). Policy change: ATR model planes grounded in bad weather, stricter rules for commuter planes, new deicing procedures.

Flagship Airlines (American Eagle), December 13, 1994. Cause: human error (poor pilot training). Policy change: pilot safety records monitored and made public, stricter rules for commuter planes.

Atlantic Southeast (Delta Connection), August 21, 1995. Cause: mechanical. Policy change: none.

American Airlines, December 20, 1995. Cause: human error (crash into mountain). Policy change: lowered reliance on automation (voluntary), new early warning detection systems (voluntary), and enhanced ground proximity warning system.

ValuJet, May 11, 1996. Cause: human error (subcontractor). Policy change: dual FAA mandate eliminated, hazardous material regulations tightened, smoke detectors and fire suppression equipment in cargo holds (voluntary initially, then formal), chemical oxygen canisters banned.

Delta Airlines, July 6, 1996. Cause: mechanical. Policy change: none.

TWA, July 17, 1996. Cause: mechanical. Policy change: some White House Commission recommendations, Aviation Disaster Family Assistance Act of 1996, terror guidelines, inspection of wiring, Aviation Investment and Reform Act (reform of Death on High Seas Act), fuel tank proposals partially implemented, FBI primacy in investigations if attorney general determines a criminal act is involved.

Great Lakes Aviation (United Express), November 19, 1996. Cause: human error. Policy change: none.

Comair, January 9, 1997. Cause: wing ice. Policy change: wing ice policies.

Korean Air, August 6, 1997. Cause: human error (fatigue; controlled flight into terrain). Policy change: enforcement of fatigue rules.

Swissair, September 2, 1998. Cause: mechanical (wiring) (no final report yet). Policy change: inspection of wiring and insulation, Aviation Investment and Reform Act (reform of Death on High Seas Act).

American Airlines, June 1, 1999. Cause: human error (fatigue, bad weather, pilot error). Policy change: enforcement of fatigue regulations.

EgyptAir, October 31, 1999. Cause: pilot error (suicide). Policy change: Aviation Investment and Reform Act (reform of Death on High Seas Act).

Notes

Chapter One

1. "Driver Killed in Laporte Crash," *South Bend Tribune*, July 17, 1996, p. B2.

2. "Police Identify Trucker Killed in Crash," *Columbus Dispatch*, July 17, 1996, p. 7B.

3. Tim O'Neill, "Victims to Be Buried Together; Crash on I-44 Killed Sisters, Their Children," *St. Louis Post-Dispatch*, July 17, 1996, p. 3B.

4. This figure includes all individuals killed as a result of a motor vehicle accident (including pedestrians and other nonoccupants). The week began at midnight on July 13 and ended at 11:59 p.m. on July 20. National Highway Traffic Safety Administration, fatality analysis reporting system (FARS) database.

5. "TWA Explosion, U.S. Election, Olympic Bomb Voted Top Stories of 1996," Associated Press, December 26, 1996, p.m.-cycle wire story.

6. Barry Glassner, *The Culture of Fear: Why Americans Are Afraid of the Wrong Things* (Basic Books, 1999); Usha Lee McFarling, "The Crash of Flight 261: Plane Crashes Stoke Psyche's Deepest Fears," *Los Angeles Times*, February 4, 2000, p. A1.

7. See www.airlines.org/public/industry/23.asp (May 2, 2001).

8. Bureau of Transportation Statistics, *Airport Activity Statistics of Certificated Air Carriers*, various years.

9. Kenneth M. Mead, "Flight Delays and Cancellations, Federal Aviation Administration," statement prepared for the Committee on Appropriations, Subcommittee on Transportation and Related Agencies, U.S. House of Representatives, March 15, 2001.

10. Eleanor Singer and Phyllis M. Endreny, *Reporting on Risk* (Russell Sage, 1993), p. 104.

11. "AIAA, History of Flight, 1910s" (www.flight100.org/history/1910s.html[August 14, 2001]).

12. Among the many histories of commercial aviation is T. A. Heppenheimer, *Turbulent Skies* (Wiley, 1995).

13. P.L. 95-504.

14. Robert W. Poole Jr. and Viggo Butler, "Airline Deregulation: The Unfinished Revolution," *Regulation,* vol. 22 (1999), pp. 44–51.

15. This has led some savvy travelers to purchase lower-price tickets to destinations that require a stopover in their hub city. Then they simply get off at the hub city. This is called hidden-city ticketing, a violation of airline rules.

16. It initially serviced Houston, Dallas, and San Antonio. See Southwest Airlines fact sheet (www.southwest.com/about_swa/press/factsheet.html[May 1, 2002]).

17. Steven A. Morrison and Clifford Winston, *The Evolution of the Airline Industry* (Brookings, 1995).

18. See www.airlines.org/public/industry/display1.asp?id=8 (August 14, 2001).

19. For example, see Nancy L. Rose, "Fear of Flying? Economic Analyses of Airline Safety," *Journal of Economic Perspectives,* vol. 6, no. 2 (1992), pp. 75–94; Clinton V. Oster Jr., John S. Strong, and C. Kurt Zorn, *Why Airplanes Crash* (Oxford University Press, 1992). For a different perspective, see Arnold Barnett and Mary K. Higgins, "Airline Safety: The Last Decade," *Management Science,* vol. 35 (1989), pp. 1–21.

20. Rose, "Fear of Flying?"

21. Ibid.

22. Leonard L. Nethercutt and Stephen W. Pruitt, "Touched by Tragedy: Capital Market Lessons from the Crash of ValuJet Flight 592," *Economics Letters,* vol. 56 (1997), pp. 351–58.

23. Whether air travel would be even safer in a regulated marketplace is a separate question.

24. The FAA announced a "safer skies" initiative in April 1998, which had as one of its goals an 80 percent reduction in the aviation accident rate by 2007.

25. The Department of Transportation values a human life at $2.7 million. See Sylvia Adcock, "One Lonely Voice: Aviation Panel Member Challenges Report to FAA," *Newsday,* July 22, 1998, p. A3.

26. Tammy O. Tengs and others, "Five-Hundred Lifesaving Interventions and Their Cost-Effectiveness," *Risk Analysis,* vol. 15 (1995), pp. 369–90.

27. One can find a list of the NTSB's "most-wanted safety improvements" on its web page, which also states, however, that all aviation suggestions require action by the FAA. See www.ntsb.gov/Recs/mostwanted/aviation_issues.htm.

28. Rose, "Fear of Flying?"

29. Charles Perrow, *Normal Accidents* (Basic Books, 1984), p. 167.

30. "Managing for Safety: A Briefing for Airline Senior Management," Icarus Committee Briefing 5, Flight Safety Foundation, Alexandria, Va., May 1998.

31. Bernard C. Cohen, *The Press and Foreign Policy* (Princeton University Press, 1963), p. 13; emphasis in original.

32. Roger Lowenstein, "Into Thin Air," *New York Times Magazine,* February 17, 2002, pp. 40–45.

33. Air Transport Association, "Economic Trends and Challenges for the U.S. Airline Industry," Washington, April 2002.

34. Air Transport Association, "State of the U.S. Airline Industry, 2002–2003," Washington, November 25, 2002; "Annual Traffic and Capacity" (www. airlines.org/public/industry/display1.asp?nid=1032).

35. Air Transport Association, "State of the U.S. Airline Industry."

36. "Can This Airline Be Saved?" (www.forbes.com/2001/11/06/ 1106united.html[May 1, 2002]).

37. Air Transport Association, "State of the U.S. Airline Industry."

38. Lowenstein, "Into Thin Air."

39. Gaye Tuchman, *Making News* (Free Press, 1978), p. 23.

40. Robert M. Entman, *Democracy without Citizens: Media and the Decay of American Politics* (Oxford University Press, 1989).

41. Frank Baumgartner and Bryan D. Jones, *Agendas and Instability in American Politics* (University of Chicago Press, 1993).

42. Christopher Bosso, "Setting the Agenda: Mass Media and the Discovery of Famine in Ethiopia," in Michael Margolis and Gary Mauser, eds., *Manipulating Public Opinion* (Pacific Grove, Calif.: Brooks-Cole, 1989).

43. Remarks by Jim Hall before the Aviation Safety Alliance Media Seminar, Washington, April 6, 2000.

44. E. L. Quarantelli, "A Study of Disasters and Mass Communication," in Lynne Masel Walters, Lee Wilkins, and Tim Walters, eds., *Bad Tidings: Communication and Catastrophe* (Hillsdale, N.J.: Erlbaum, 1989), p. 1.

45. Dorothy Nelkin, *Selling Science: How the Press Conveys Science and Technology* (Freeman, 1995), p. 167.

46. Conrad Smith, *Media and Apocalypse* (Westport, Conn.: Greenwood, 1992).

47. Ibid., p. 56.

48. For example, see Robert Davis and Christina Piño-Marina, "Bodies and Clues Sought in 757 Crash," *USA Today,* February 8, 1996, p. 1A.

49. For example, see Don Phillips, "Jet's Everglades Crash Site Yields Few Clues to Tragedy," *New York Times,* May 13, 1996, p. A1; Mike Williams, "The Crash of Flight 592: The Site," *Atlanta Journal and Constitution,* May 12, 1996, p. 10A.

50. Glassner, *The Culture of Fear.*

51. CBS News, telephone poll released July 1996.

52. Kaiser Family Foundation, telephone poll released September 16, 1998.

53. Gallup, telephone poll released November 23, 1999.

54. Paul Slovic, Baruch Fischhoff, and Sarah Lichtenstein, "Facts and Fears: Understanding Perceived Risk," in Richard C. Schwing and Walter A. Albers, eds., *Societal Risk Assessment: How Safe Is Safe Enough?* (Plenum, 1980).

55. John Allen Paulos, "After a Crash, Fear Overtakes Logic," *New York Times,* November 2, 1999, p. A31.

56. Thomas A. Birkland, *After Disaster* (Georgetown University Press, 1997), p. 32.

57. Cynthia C. Lebow and others, *Safety in the Skies: Personnel and Parties in NTSB Aviation Accident Investigations* (Santa Monica, Calif.: RAND, 1999), p. 3.

58. One study shows that news sources overemphasize certain causes of death, such as drug use, car accidents, and toxic agents. See Karen Frost and others, "Relative Risk in the News Media: A Quantification of Misrepresentation," *American Journal of Public Health,* vol. 87 (1997), pp. 842–45.

59. Arnold Barnett, "Air Safety: End of the Golden Age?" *Chance,* vol. 3 (1990), pp. 8–12.

Chapter Two

1. The fourteen-month figure is drawn from Thomas Mann and Norman Ornstein, "After the Campaign, What?" *Brookings Review,* vol. 18 (2000), pp. 44–48.

2. Budget and employment figures are from U.S. Department of Transportation, *2003 Budget in Brief.* These figures do not include the United States Coast Guard and the Transportation Security Administration, which are now a part of the newly created Department of Homeland Security.

3. See www.dot.gov/mission.htm (May 3, 2002).

4. As noted, the United States Coast Guard and the Transportation Security Administration, formerly of the Department of Transportation, are now a part of the newly created Department of Homeland Security.

5. Admittedly, Secretary of Transportation Norman Mineta became the focus of extensive media attention after the events of September 11.

6. Don Phillips, "Mineta Brings Pro-transit Views, Pragmatic Outlooks," *Washington Post,* January 4, 2001, p. A19.

7. Laurence Zuckerman, "Clinton Is Calling for More Scrutiny of Major Airlines," *New York Times,* January 16, 2001, pp. A1, C6.

8. Mary Schiavo, *Flying Blind, Flying Safe* (Avon Books, 1997).

9. P.L. 104-264.

10. Glenn Johnson, "Cellucci Could Still Win a Post," *Boston Globe,* January 3, 2001, p. A1.

11. Matthew Brelis, "Earning Her Wings," *Boston Globe Magazine,* September 6, 1998, p. 12.

12. Ibid.

13. "New Alaska Crash Probe Exposes Old FAA Failings," *USA Today,* December 19, 2000, p. 14A.

14. General Accounting Office, "Air Traffic Control: Status of FAA's Modernization Program," RCED-99-25, December 3, 1998, p. 15.

15. Ronald White, "Jane Garvey," *Los Angeles Times,* April 3, 2000, p. M3.

16. Harris Interactive, telephone poll released October 18, 2000.

17. Alan Levin, "FAA Safety Report's Timing Incenses Airline Officials," *USA Today,* December 11, 2000, p. 26A.

18. Ibid.

19. Gary Stoller, "Just How Safe Is That Jet?" *USA Today,* March 13, 2000, p. B1.

20. Ibid.

21. Ibid.

22. Don Phillips, "Mineta Opposes Privatizing FAA Functions," *Washington Post,* March 14, 2001, p. E3.

23. Trend data from Cynthia C. Lebow and others, *Safety in the Skies: Personnel and Parties in NTSB Aviation Accident Investigations* (Santa Monica, Calif.: RAND, 1999); recent data from *Budget of the U.S. Government, Fiscal Year 2003,* appendix.

24. Matthew Wald, "RAND to Assess How Federal Safety Board Runs Crash Inquiries," *New York Times,* July 17, 1998, p. A16.

25. Jonathan Salant, "NTSB Lessons of an Accident Often Go Unlearned," *USA Today,* May 28, 2001, p. A7.

26. "Aviation Issues" (www.ntsb.gov/recs/mostwanted/aviation_issues.htm [May 3, 2002]).

27. Salant, "NTSB Lessons of an Accident Often Go Unlearned."

28. See NTSB recommendations A-96-174 and A-96-175.

29. Salant, "NTSB Lessons of an Accident Often Go Unlearned."

30. White House Commission on Aviation Safety and Security, "Final Report to President Clinton," February 12, 1997.

31. Tammy O. Tengs and others, "Five-Hundred Lifesaving Interventions and Their Cost-Effectiveness," *Risk Analysis,* vol. 15 (1995), pp. 369–90.

32. Paul Mann, "Safety Politicized: FAA versus NTSB," *Aviation Week and Space Technology,* November 4, 1996, pp. 56–65.

33. Lebow and others, *Safety in the Skies.*

34. Ibid., p. 46.

35. Ibid.

36. Matthew Wald, "Transportation Safety Board Hurt by 'Serious Overload,' Study Finds," *New York Times,* December 10, 1999, p. A25.

37. Remarks by Jim Hall before the Aviation Safety Alliance Media Seminar, Washington, April 6, 2000.

38. Lebow and others, *Safety in the Skies.*

39. In part, this is because delays and congestion virtually disappeared due to the sharp reduction in flights.

40. Michael Barone and Grant Ujifusa, *The Almanac of American Politics, 1999* (Washington: National Journal).

41. Ibid.

42. Norman Mineta served in this position in 1995 but resigned in October of that year and is now the head of the DOT.

43. Barone and Ujifusa, *The Almanac of American Politics, 1995; 1997; 1999.*

44. Alan Levin, "Lawmakers Plead for 'Critical' Funds for FAA," *USA Today,* November 2, 2001, p. 3A.

45. Barone and Ujifusa, *The Almanac of American Politics, 1999.*

46. Ibid.

47. Ibid.

48. Although the principal responsibility of the Senate Environment and Public Works Committee is public works in the form of water projects and highway construction, and it can enter the airline arena through its concern with noise and air pollution, it is not a major player in airline regulation.

49. Zuckerman, "Clinton Is Calling for More Scrutiny of Major Airlines."

50. Mathew D. McCubbins and Thomas Schwartz, "Congressional Oversight Overlooked: Police Patrols versus Fire Alarms," *American Journal of Political Science*, vol. 28 (1984), pp. 165–79.

51. Thomas Benton, "Hill Ready to Wrest Control in America's Frustrated Skies," *CQ Weekly Report*, June 23, 2001, pp. 1488–92.

52. Barone and Ujifusa, *The Almanac of American Politics, 1997*.

53. Bureau of Transportation Statistics, *Airport Activity Statistics of Certificated Air Carriers, 2001*.

54. Robert A. Doughty, "United Airlines: Prepared for the Worst," in Jack Gottschalk, ed., *Crisis Response* (Detroit: Gale, 1993).

55. Sally J. Ray, *Strategic Communication in Crisis Management: Lessons from the Airline Industry* (Quorum Books, 1999).

56. Thomas A. Birkland and Radhika Nath, "Business and Political Dimensions in Disaster Management," *Journal of Public Policy*, vol. 20, no. 3 (2000), pp. 275–303.

57. Severin Borenstein and Martin B. Zimmerman, "Market Incentives for Safe Commercial Airline Operation," *American Economic Review*, vol. 78 (1988), pp. 913–35.

58. Leonard L. Nethercutt and Stephen W. Pruitt, "Touched by Tragedy: Capital Market Lessons from the Crash of ValuJet Flight 592," *Economics Letters*, vol. 56 (1997), pp. 351–58.

59. Geoff Jones and Aram Gesar, *Commercial Aircraft* (New York: Pyramid Media Group, 2001).

60. "Boeing in Brief" (www.boeing.com/companyoffices/aboutus/brief.html[May 7, 2002]).

61. Blake Morrison, "Crash Lawyers Like Boeing Move," *USA Today*, May 16, 2001, p. A1.

62. Jones and Gesar, *Commercial Aircraft*.

63. Bob Davis and Bill Nichols, "Leadership Slow to Come to the FAA," *USA Today*, April 23, 1997, p. 8A.

64. Alan Levin, David Field, and Marilyn Adams, "Flight Delays Hidden, Report Says," *USA Today*, July 25, 2000, p. 3A.

65. Phillips, "Mineta Brings Pro-transit Views, Pragmatic Outlooks."

66. Matthew Wald, "Growing Old at Air Traffic Control," *New York Times*, April 3, 2001, p. A16.

67. For an example of blame shifting, see Bill Adair, *The Mystery of Flight 427: Inside a Crash Investigation* (Smithsonian Institution Press, 2002).

68. Bob Arnot, "Boarding Pass?" *Dateline NBC*, September 15, 1997.

69. See www.1800airsafe.com for a description of the benefits afforded to members.

70. Ricardo Alonso-Zaldivar, "Little-Known Law Helps Loved Ones of Air Crash Victims Cope," *Los Angeles Times,* December 12, 2000, p. A5.

71. "Souls on board" is the phrase used in the industry to refer to the number of passengers on a distressed plane.

72. Lebow and others, *Safety in the Skies.*

73. Fred Bayles, "Crashes Becoming Too Mysterious to Solve," *USA Today,* August 21, 2000, p. A4.

74. This example is taken from Clinton V. Oster Jr., John S. Strong, and C. Kurt Zorn, *Why Airplanes Crash* (Oxford University Press, 1992).

75. Charles Perrow, *Normal Accidents* (Basic Books, 1984).

76. Ibid., p. 134.

77. P.L. 106-424.

78. Ray, *Strategic Communication in Crisis Management.*

79. *Congressional Record,* daily ed., September 13, 1994, p. S12752.

80. 104 S. Res. 280, 1996.

81. Nearly all cases are resolved without going to trial. Blake Morrison, "Tragedy's Bottom Line," *USA Today,* January 5, 2000.

82. Blake Morrison, "Crash Lawyers Like Boeing Move," *USA Today,* May 16, 2001, p. A1.

83. Frank Baumgartner and Bryan D. Jones, *Agendas and Instability in American Politics* (University of Chicago Press, 1993).

Chapter Three

1. Associated Press, "Northwest to Pay $7.1 Million to Stranded Passengers," January 9, 2001.

2. Michael Grunwald, "As 'Soft Money' Flew in, a McCain Crusade Faded," *Washington Post,* October 20, 1999, p. A1.

3. Dianne Feinstein, press release, July 13, 2001.

4. Cynthia C. Lebow and others, *Safety in the Skies: Personnel and Parties in NTSB Aviation Accident Investigations* (Santa Monica, Calif.: RAND, 1999).

5. Paul Slovic, Baruch Fischhoff, and Sarah Lichtenstein, "Rating the Risks," *Environment,* vol. 2, no. 3 (1979), p. 14.

6. Paul Slovic, Baruch Fischhoff, and Sarah Lichtenstein, "Facts and Fears: Understanding Perceived Risk," in Richard C. Schwing and Walter A. Albers, eds., *Societal Risk Assessment: How Safe Is Safe Enough?* (Plenum, 1980).

7. Bureau of Transportation Statistics, *Airport Activity Statistics of Certificated Air Carriers,* various years.

8. *FAA Aerospace Forecasts, Fiscal Years 2002–2013,* table 11.

9. Arnold Barnett, Michael Abraham, and Victor Schimmel, "Airline Safety: Some Empirical Findings," *Management Science,* vol. 25 (1979), pp. 1045–56; Arnold Barnett and Mary K. Higgins, "Airline Safety: The Last Decade," *Management Science,* vol. 35 (1989), pp. 1–21.

10. For statistics-oriented readers, the Q-value is the probability of dying on a randomly selected flight. It is calculated as the sum of the probabilities of dying, given that you are on a plane that crashed, divided by the total number of flights.

11. This calculation refers only to major domestic airlines. Therefore, commuter airlines before March 20, 1997—the date that they were classified as major domestic carriers—and foreign carriers are excluded.

12. James Reason, *Managing the Risks of Organizational Accidents* (Aldershot, U.K.: Ashgate, 1997).

13. Adam Bryant, "Flying Is as Safe as Swiss Cheese," *New York Times,* August 4, 1996, sec. 4, p. 3.

14. Interview with Don Libera, NTSB deputy chief financial officer, February 27, 2002.

15. Barry Glassner argues that the FAA "has mandated scores of safety requirements over the years, only a small proportion of which were in response to pressures following particular accidents." He challenges the view that the FAA is a tombstone agency. See his *The Culture of Fear: Why Americans Are Afraid of the Wrong Things* (Basic Books, 1999), p. 187.

16. There is no uniform standard for valuing life, and there are disputes regarding how life should be valued. Further, cost-benefit analysis is not binding when it conflicts with an agency's legislative mandate. See W. Kip Viscusi, "Equivalent Frames of Reference for Judging Risk Regulation Policies," *NYU Environmental Law Journal,* vol. 3 (1995), pp. 431–68, for a discussion of the economic theory for valuing life and the way this can be used to improve the regulatory process. The Environmental Protection Agency, among others, has been inconsistent in valuing life. A GAO report, "Air Pollution: Information Contained in EPA's Regulatory Impact Analyses Can Be Made Clearer" (April 1997), notes that the EPA provides varying figures for the value of life and offers no rationale for its choices.

17. We obtained all recommendations made by the board after every crash in the 1990s. Portions of these data were provided to us by the NTSB. We also used the FAA's National Aviation Safety Data Analysis Center to gather information (www.nasdac.faa.gov).

18. Harry Stoffer and Bill Heltzel, "Billions versus Body Counts: How the FAA Balances Cost against Safety of Airlines," *Pittsburgh Post-Gazette,* December 4, 1994, p. A1.

19. General Accounting Office, "Aviation Safety: FAA Generally Agrees with but Is Slow in Implementing Safety Recommendations," September 1996.

20. Ibid., p. 5.

21. BBC, "TWA Flight 800," video, 1997.

22. The FAA created a working group to study the matter. See NTSB recommendations A-96-174 and A-96-175.

23. FAA, "Fact Sheet: FAA Requirements on Pilot Flight Time and Rest," June 4, 1999.

24. FAA, "Notice of Enforcement Policy: Flight Crewmember Flight Time Limitations and Rest Requirements," May 14, 2001.

25. Jim Hall, remarks before Child Passenger Safety in Aviation meeting, December 15, 1999.

26. David Stout, "FAA Orders Toddler Seats on Airliners," *New York Times,* December 16, 1999, p. A17; Alan Levin, "FAA Pushing Child Restraints," *USA Today,* December 16, 1999, p. 1A.

27. "Child Restraint Systems," *Federal Register,* vol. 66, no. 232 (2001), p. 61961. An advanced notice of proposed rule making, which allows feedback before the initial writing of a rule, was issued in 1998.

28. The airline was grounded on June 17, 1996. See FAA, "Fact Sheet: FAA Oversight of ValuJet," August 14, 1997.

29. Douglass Cater, *The Fourth Branch of Government* (Boston: Houghton Mifflin, 1959).

30. Analyzing only crashes that receive extensive attention or result in significant policy change would be what statisticians refer to as selecting on the dependent variable.

31. Thomas A. Birkland, *After Disaster* (Georgetown University Press, 1997), p. 31.

32. Conrad Smith, *Media and Apocalypse* (Westport, Conn.: Greenwood, 1992), pp. 127–29.

33. Todd Curtis, "Airline Accidents and Media Bias" (www.airsafe.com/nyt_bias.htm [May 1,2002]).

34. In the first specification, all crashes except for Swissair, for which a final report was not issued as of May 2002, are included. However, TWA flight 800 is an outlier, since it received far and away more attention than any other crash. Therefore, to test the sensitivity of the analysis to that crash, we ran the regression a second time, this time leaving out TWA flight 800. The causal uncertainty variable performed terribly once TWA flight 800 was left out of the equation and was not significant even with that flight in the equation. In addition, since TWA flight 800 represented a major puzzle for investigators, leaving this observation out of the regression may make causal uncertainty look less important than it is. Also, because the number of observations is very small, slight perturbations in the data can have a large effect. All told, we cannot reach any firm conclusions about this hypothesis. The hypothesis regarding proximity to a major metropolitan area is statistically significant in the regression with the TWA flight but not in the regression without it. It is substantively significant in both specifications.

35. It is difficult for scholars to directly link crashes to policy. New policies we identified based on crashes include stricter rules for commuter aircraft, changes in exit rows, and keeping better track of pilot performance.

36. Kalpana Srinivasan, "Nation's 78 Largest Airports to Undergo Security Checks," Associated Press, March 11, 1999.

37. Robert Kolker, "Flier Beware," *New York Magazine,* August 13, 2001, pp. 30–37.

38. NTSB, *Aircraft Accident Report . . . Korean Air Flight 801,* adopted January 13, 2000.

39. Don Phillips, "Stricter Rules Proposed for Small Airlines; Commuter Crashes Spurred FAA Move," *Washington Post,* March 25, 1995, p. A1.

40. We rely on NTSB recommendations because they offer the most concrete link between a crash and policy. In the appendix we present what we consider major policy changes after crashes. We do not use this list in our test, however, because NTSB recommendations provide a measure of policy change (albeit not major policy change) that does not rely on subjective definitions.

41. Given that the FAA often says one thing and does another, the data we use may bias upward the percentage of recommendations that the FAA actually acts on. In addition, this test does not weight recommendations by importance. The NTSB often complains that the FAA fails to act on its *key* recommendations in a timely fashion.

42. Whether high-profile crashes produce policy changes of poorer quality or larger scope remains an open question.

Chapter Four

1. Angie Cannon, "FBI Revelations Raise Fears about Flying," Knight Ridder/ Tribune News Service, November 19, 1997.

2. This information is based on NTSB *Aircraft Accident Report . . . USAir Flight 427*, adopted March 24, 1999.

3. Richard Perez-Peña, "Airliner Crashes near Pittsburgh; All 131 on USAir Jet Are Killed," *New York Times*, September 9, 1994, p. A1.

4. John Cushman, "Transportation Officials Defend USAir's Record," *New York Times*, September 10, 1994, p. 1.

5. Perez-Peña, "Airliner Crashes near Pittsburgh."

6. Mark Belko, "Morgue Workers' Somber Job at an End," *Pittsburgh Post-Gazette*, October 8, 1994, p. A5.

7. PR newswire, "USAir Exploring Possibility of Acquiring Flight 427 Accident Site as Memorial," September 14, 1994. USAir never built the memorial; instead it bought three large tombstones at the closest cemetery, ten miles from the crash site. The inscriptions read, "In Loving Memory of Our Family Members and Friends Interred Here Who Died, September 8, 1994." Bill Adair, *The Mystery of Flight 427: Inside a Crash Investigation* (Smithsonian Institution Press, 2002), p. 125.

8. Tamar Lewin, "Crash of Flight 427: The Victims," *New York Times*, September 10, 1994, p. 9.

9. Cushman, "Transportation Officials Defend USAir's Record."

10. Ibid.

11. Perez-Peña, "Airliner Crashes near Pittsburgh."

12. This figure includes a 1989 USAir crash but excludes the 1992 crash of a CommutAir flight, which operated as a USAir Express flight.

13. Perez-Peña, "Airliner Crashes near Pittsburgh."

14. John Cushman, "Crash of Flight 427: The Investigation," *New York Times*, September 10, 1994, p. 1.

15. Adair, *The Mystery of Flight 427*.

16. *This Week with David Brinkley*, September 11, 1994.

17. CNN transcript, "USAir Assistant VP Discusses Crash of Flight 427," September 8, 1994.

18. NTSB, *Aircraft Accident Report . . . USAir Flight 427*, pp. 12–14.

19. John Cushman, "Crash Investigators Examine Condition of Right Engine," *New York Times*, September 13, p. A14.

20. Byron Acohido, "737 Part Could Misdirect Plane—Rudder Control on 2,200 Jets Has History of Problems," *Seattle Times,* September 28, 1994, p. A1.

21. Cushman, "Crash Investigators Examine Condition of Right Engine."

22. Adam Bryant, "USAir Crash Investigators Rule out More Causes," *New York Times,* September 16, 1994, p. A23.

23. John Cushman, "Crash Investigators Broaden Their Inquiry," *New York Times,* September 13, 1994, p. A14.

24. Bryant, "USAir Crash Investigators Rule out More Causes."

25. Ibid.

26. Cushman, "Crash Investigators Broaden Their Inquiry."

27. Douglas Frantz, "Pilot Offers Explanation for Odd Noise on USAir Jet," *New York Times,* November 23, 1994, p. A16.

28. NTSB, *Aircraft Accident Report . . .USAir Flight 427.*

29. Adam Bryant, "With Factors Ruled out, USAir Crash Emerges as a Puzzle," *New York Times,* September 18, 1994, p. 38.

30. Douglas Frantz and Ralph Blumenthal, "A Question of Safety: A Special Report," *New York Times,* November 13, 1994, p. 1.

31. Ibid.

32. Ibid.

33. Ibid.

34. Ibid.

35. Lornet Turnbull, "USAir's Man of Letters," *Pittsburgh Post-Gazette,* October 14, 1994, p. B12.

36. Ibid.

37. Frantz and Blumenthal, "A Question of Safety."

38. Sharon Voas, "USAir Hires Safety Auditor," *Pittsburgh Post-Gazette,* November 21, 1994, p. A1.

39. Advertisement, *New York Times,* November 21, 1994, p. A7.

40. Adair, *The Mystery of Flight 427,* p. 72.

41. Acohido, "737 Part Could Misdirect Plane."

42. Adair, *The Mystery of Flight 427.*

43. Ibid., pp. 112–14.

44. Ibid., pp. 168–69.

45. Byron Acohido, "Safety at Issue: The 737," *Seattle Times,* October 27, 1996, p. A1.

46. Ibid.

47. *Federal Register,* vol. 61, no. 227, pp. 59317–19.

48. Adair, *The Mystery of Flight 427,* p. 46.

49. Ibid., p. 104.

50. *Congressional Record,* September 13, 1994, S. 12752.

51. Peter DeFazio, letter to members of Congress on Boeing 737.

52. Matthew Wald, "70 Changes Urged to Ensure Airline Safety," *New York Times,* January 11, 1995, p. A12.

53. Lisa Burgess, "Aviation Experts Draw up Safety Recommendations," *Journal of Commerce,* January 12, 1995, p. 3B.

54. Hearing information drawn from official transcripts as well as *New York Times* accounts.

55. Matthew Wald, "Hydraulic Fluid Is Focus of USAir Crash Inquiry," *New York Times,* January 26, 1995, p. A12

56. Matthew Wald, "Two Downed 737's Make a Nightmare and a Mystery," *New York Times,* August 20, 1995, sec. 4, p. 4.

57. Hearing information drawn from official transcripts as well as *New York Times* accounts.

58. Michael Zielinski, FAA representative, testimony, NTSB hearing.

59. John Cox, USAir captain, testimony, NTSB hearing.

60. NTSB recommendations A-96-109, 110, 112, 118, 120.

61. Al Gore, "Remarks on Aviation Safety and Security," FDCH Political Transcripts, January 15, 1997.

62. Don Phillips, "FAA Orders Changes on Rudders of 737's Following 2 Crashes," *Washington Post,* January 16, 1997, p. A14.

63. NTSB, *Aircraft Accident Report . . . USAir Flight 427.*

64. Ibid., p. 296.

65. Adair, *The Mystery of Flight 427.*

66. NTSB, press release, SB 99-09, March 24, 1999.

67. Taken from NTSB, *Aircraft Accident Report . . . USAir Flight 427.*

68. Matthew Wald, "Rudder Flaw Cited in Boeing 737 Crashes," *New York Times,* March 24, 1999, p. A24.

69. Jonathan Silver and Lawrence Walsh, "NTSB Blames Rudder in USAir Crash," *Pittsburgh Post-Gazette,* March 25, 1999, p. A1.

70. Blake Morrison, "Tragedy's Bottom Line," *USA Today,* January 5, p. 1A.

71. CNN, "Boeing Holds News Conference on 737 Rudder Design Enhancements," September 14, 2000.

72. *Federal Register,* October 7, 2002, vol. 67, no. 194, pp. 62341–47.

73. *Federal Register,* November 18, 1999, vol. 64, no. 222, pp. 63139–57. As of December 2002 this rule had not been adopted.

74. Authors' calculations based on *New York Times Index,* various years.

75. Jim Hall, NTSB hearing on USAir Flight 427, January 23, 1995.

76. Wald, "Two Downed 737's Make a Nightmare and a Mystery."

77. Matthew Wald, "Clear Agreement Elusive on Fixing 737's Rudders," *New York Times,* February 24, 1997, p. B7.

78. Issues related to the crash were tacked onto a TWA-flight-800-inspired commission.

Chapter Five

1. Figures based on various ValuJet press releases.

2. Comparative profit statistics drawn from Rodney Ho, "Growing ValuJet's Earnings Still Soaring," *Atlanta Journal and Constitution,* February 7, 1996, p. 5D; income and profit data drawn from ValuJet press releases; stock information based on authors' analysis of ValuJet stock prices.

3. Lewis Jordan, the president of ValuJet, defended the salaries offered by the carrier, noting that the figures considered only base salary and ignored other incentives, like stock options, available to employees. In addition, he noted that ValuJet was a new company, so naturally salaries would tend to be lower due to lower seniority. Controlling for seniority, he argued, ValuJet's salaries were comparable with the major airlines. See testimony of Lewis Jordan before the Aviation Subcommittee, House Committee on Transportation and Infrastructure, June 25, 1996, for a further defense of ValuJet's business practices.

4. Andy Pasztor, Martha Brannigan, and Scott McCartney, "ValuJet's Penny-Pinching Comes under Scrutiny," *Wall Street Journal,* May 15, 1996, p. A2.

5. Adam Bryant, "The Crash in the Everglades: The Equipment, Fleet Was Old," *New York Times,* May 14, 1996, p. B7. Jordan defended the age of the fleet in congressional testimony, noting that other airlines' DC-9 fleets had average ages in the same range.

6. Asra Nomani and Michael Frisby, "Plane Crash May Force Clinton to Stop Talk about Cutting Air Travel Costs," *Wall Street Journal,* May 15, 1996, p. A2.

7. Ibid.

8. DOT, "New Low-Cost Airlines Benefit Consumers, DOT Study Finds," press release, DOT 79-96, April 23, 1996.

9. Elizabeth Marchak, "Budget Airline Slows Growth as Concerns on Safety Mount," *Cleveland Plain Dealer,* April 11, 1996, p. 1A.

10. Joan Biskupic and Don Phillips, "FAA Tracked Earlier Incidents during ValuJet's 2 1/2 Years of Operation," *Washington Post,* May 12, 1996, p. A22.

11. NTSB, *Aircraft Accident Report . . . ValuJet Airlines Flight 592,* adopted August 19, 1997.

12. Mireya Navarro, "Search Called off for Survivors of Crash in Everglades," *New York Times,* May 13, 1996, p. A1.

13. Robert McFadden, "109 Feared Dead as Jet Crashes in Everglades," May 12, 1996, *New York Times,* p. 1.

14. Navarro, "Search Called off for Survivors."

15. ABC *Nightline,* June 17, 1996, transcript.

16. Navarro, "Search Called off for Survivors."

17. Information on the crash is based on various news accounts as well as the *ValuJet Aircraft Accident Report* issued by the NTSB.

18. Matthew Wald, "Inquiry Turns to Chemicals in Jet's Cargo," *New York Times,* May 15, 1996, p. A1.

19. Matthew Wald, "Clerk's Mistake May Have Put Volatile Chemicals on Valujet Plane," *New York Times,* May 17, 1996, p. A1.

20. "DOT Issues Immediate Ban on Chemical Oxygen Generators as Cargo on Passenger Airlines," press release, DOT 112-96, May 23, 1996.

21. Bryant, "The Crash in the Everglades."

22. Adam Bryant, "Outspoken FAA Critic Quits Transportation Post," *New York Times,* July 9, 1996, p. A14.

23. Ibid.

24. Mary Schiavo, "Flying into Trouble," *Time,* March 31, 1997, pp. 52–61.

25. Mary Schiavo, "I Don't Like to Fly," *Newsweek,* May 20, 1996, p. 32.

26. Ibid.

27. Data from the following articles: "ValuJet's Job: Prove Low Cost Isn't Risky," *Wall Street Journal,* May 14, 1996, p. A3; Andy Pasztor, Martha Brannigan, and Scott McCartney, "ValuJet's Penny-Pinching Comes under Scrutiny," *Wall Street Journal,* May 15, 1996, p. A2; Matthew Wald, "FAA Asserts ValuJet Cargo Was Improper," *New York Times,* May 16, 1996, p. A1; Martha Brannigan and Asra Nomani, "New ValuJet Safety Checks Deal Financial Blow," *Wall Street Journal,* May 20, 1996, p. A3.

28. Matthew Wald, "FAA Cites Problems with Airline and Oversight," *New York Times,* May 18, 1996, p. 7.

29. See testimony of Lewis Jordan before the Aviation Subcommittee, House Committee on Transportation and Infrastructure, June 25, 1996.

30. Matthew Wald, "Crash Investigators Focus on How ValuJet and Contractors Handled Dangerous Cargo," *New York Times,* June 5, 1996, p. A14.

31. FAA statement on ValuJet, press release, APA 98-96, June 17, 1996.

32. Remarks prepared for delivery, Secretary of Transportation Federico Peña, FAA press conference, June 18, 1996.

33. Matthew Wald, "Aviation Agency Seeks to Shift Its Mission, Focusing on Safety," *New York Times,* June 19, 1996, p. A1.

34. Robert Pear, "Aviation Official Embroiled in Furor over ValuJet Crash Resigns," *New York Times,* June 19, 1996, p. A20.

35. Adam Bryant, "FAA Struggles as Airlines Turn to Subcontracts," *New York Times,* June 2, 1996, p. 1.

36. The following materials are taken from testimony and statements from participants in *Aviation Safety: Issues Raised by the Crash of ValuJet Flight 592,* Hearing before the Subcommittee on Aviation of the Committee on Transportation and Infrastructure, June 25 (GPO, 1996), pp. 9–272. Direct quotes are from Senator William Cohen (R-Maine), (p. 13); Jim Hall (p. 17); Steven Townes (pp. 221, 236, 260–61, 261); Lewis Jordan (pp. 226, 237); and Representative James Oberstar (D-Minn.), (p. 239). Indirect references are made to actions of William Cohen (pp. 9–14). Indirect references are made to statements from Mary Schiavo (pp. 18–23, 63–65, 208–13); David Hinson (pp. 23–25); James Oberstar (pp. 26–29; 50–62); several committee members (pp. 89, 96; 256, 271–72); David Hinson and Anthony Broderick (pp. 66–67, 97, 170, 172–73); Steven Townes (pp. 220–22); and Martin Bollinger (pp. 228–30).

37. Matthew Wald, "ValuJet and a Contractor Are Due to Face Each Other," *New York Times,* November 18, 1996, p. A12.

38. Matthew Wald, "ValuJet Fire May Have Been Roaring Inferno, Expert Says," *New York Times,* November 20, 1996, p. A23.

39. Ibid.

40. Ibid.

41. Matthew Wald, "Two Airlines Shipped Devices Cited in a Crash, Board Hears," *New York Times,* November 21, 1996, p. B14.

42. Martha Brannigan, "ValuJet Contractor Mishandled Canisters Linked to Florida Crash," *Wall Street Journal,* November 19, 1996, p. B4.

43. Matthew Wald, "Why FAA Ignored Contractor Hired by Valujet," *New York Times,* November 22, 1996, p. 10.

44. NTSB, *Aircraft Accident Report . . . ValuJet Airlines Flight 592,* executive summary, adopted August 19, 1997.

45. White House briefing, December 12, 1996.

46. Ibid.

47. Robert Davis, "Airlines Still Illegally Shipping Oxygen Generators, Officials Say," *USA Today,* August 20, 1997, p. 1A.

48. Gary Stoller, "Dangerous Cargo: Passengers in Peril," *USA Today,* April 27, 1998, p. 1B.

49. Scott Thurston, "FAA Formalizes Rule on Smoke Detectors," *Atlanta Journal and Constitution,* February 13, 1998, p. 8H.

50. David Hosansky, "Floor Action May Be Bumpy for Transportation Bill," *CQ Weekly Report,* July 20, 1996, p. 2042.

51. David Hosansky, "House, Senate Set to Clash over Air Travel Issues," *CQ Weekly Report,* August 24, 1996, p. 2390.

52. Matthew Wald, "Appeals Court Is Rejecting 8 Convictions in '96 Crash," *New York Times,* November 1, 2001, p. A20.

53. Tamar Charry, "Pan Am Takes to the Sky with a Familiar Approach; Valujet Opts for a New Tack," *New York Times,* October 10, 1996, p. D7.

54. Scott Thurston, "Jordan Promoted to ValuJet Chairman," Cox News Service, November 5, 1996.

55. Carrick Mollenkamp and Karen Fessler, "ValuJet Will Buy Airways for $66m and Shed Name," *Boston Globe,* July 11, 1997, p. C1.

56. Keith Alexander, "AirTran Hopes to Overcome History, Rivals," *USA Today,* April 6, 1998, p. B1.

57. Authors' calculations, based on *New York Times Index,* various years.

58. Statement of Arnold Barnett, *Aviation Safety: Issues Raised by the Crash of ValuJet Flight 592,* Hearing before the Subcommittee on Aviation of the Committee on Transportation and Infrastructure, June 25 (GPO, 1996).

59. Authors' analysis of the hearing record.

Chapter Six

1. Lorraine Adams and Ira Chinoy, "Fall of a Reliable Giant Rattles Pilots of 747s," *Washington Post,* July 29, 1996, p. A1.

2. CNN, "Source: FBI Finds Possible Bomb Residue on TWA Wreckage," July 20, 1996 (www.cnn.com/US/9607/20/twa.crash.probe[May 1, 2002]).

3. Serge F. Kovaleski and Angela Couloumbis, "Amid Plane's Rubble Lie Shattered Hopes and Dreams," *Washington Post,* July 20, 1996, p. A15.

4. "Remarks by President Clinton Concerning the TWA 747 Crash of Wednesday, July 17, 1996," Federal News Service, July 17, 1996.

5. Jim Wooten, "President Clinton Promises Stricter Security Measures," ABC *World News Tonight,* July 25, 1996.

6. Don Phillips, "Fuselage Section of Jet Found; 6 Bodies Recovered; Clinton Dispatches Director of FEMA," *Washington Post,* July 23, 1996, p. A1.

7. Alice Reid, "FAA Seeks to Soothe Passengers; Security Heightened at Some Airports," *Washington Post,* July 19, 1996, p. A24.

8. Roberto Suro and Don Phillips, "President Orders Airport Security to Be Tightened," *Washington Post,* July 26, 1996, p. A1.

9. James K. Kallstrom, "News Briefing on the Investigation into the Crash of TWA Flight 800," FDCH political transcripts, July 19, 1996.

10. In an odd twist, conspiracy theorists believe that the FBI and others covered up the existence of friendly fire or terrorism.

11. P.L. 106-424.

12. Matthew Purdy, "Search for Clues of Flight 800 Focuses on Ocean Floor," *New York Times,* July 21, 1996, p. A1.

13. John Kifner, "Air Crash Inquiry Fails Another Day to Find Wreckage," *New York Times,* July 22, 1996, p. A1.

14. Matthew Purdy, "No Evidence of Explosive So Far in Crash Inquiry," *New York Times,* July 24, 1996, p. A1.

15. Don Van Natta Jr., "Prime Evidence Found that Device Exploded in Cabin of Flight 800," *New York Times,* August 23, 1996, p. A1; Roberto Suro, "Explosive Traces in Wreckage of Flight 800 'Inconclusive,' Officials Want More Evidence before Criminal Finding," *Washington Post,* August 24, 1996, p. A3.

16. *Hearing of the Senate Judiciary Subcommittee on Administrative Oversight and the Courts, Administrative Oversight of the Investigation of TWA Flight 800,* May 10, 1999.

17. James K. Kallstrom, letter to NTSB, March 17, 1997 (abcnews.go.com/sections/us/DailyNews/letter990510.html).

18. Spending figure is from Michael Grunwald, "FBI Role in TWA Case Draws Senate Scrutiny," *Washington Post,* November 26, 1998, p. A1.

19. "Boeing Calls for Voluntary Fuel-Tank Inspections on 747s," Associated Press, May 23, 1997.

20. Michael Grunwald, "Boeing Delayed Fuel Tank Report; Problem Studied in 1980 Linked to '96 TWA Crash," *Washington Post,* October 30, 1999, p. A1.

21. White House Commission on Aviation Safety and Security, "Final Report to President Clinton," February 12, 1997.

22. White House Commission on Aviation Safety and Security, "DOT Status Report," 1998.

23. White House Commission on Aviation Safety and Security, "Final Report to President Clinton."

24. Chris Hansen, "Boarding Pass? Gore Commission on Aviation Safety and Security Has Done Nothing to Make Flying Safer," NBC *Dateline,* September 15, 1997.

25. Roger W. Cobb and Marc Howard Ross, "Agenda Setting and the Denial of Agenda Access: Key Concepts," in Cobb and Ross, eds., *Cultural Strategies of Agenda Denial* (University Press of Kansas, 1997), pp. 35–36.

26. Adam Bryant, John H. Cushman Jr., and Christopher Drew, "Safety Stalled, a Special Report: In Bid for Airline Security, Echoes of Unmet Promises," *New York Times,* August 13, 1996, p. A1.

27. Cobb and Ross, "Agenda Setting and the Denial of Agenda Access," p. 35.

28. Ibid.

29. White House Commission on Aviation Safety and Security, "Final Report to President Clinton."

30. Brian M. Jenkins, "Aviation Security in the United States," in Paul Wilkinson and Brian M. Jenkins, eds., *Aviation Terrorism and Security* (London: Frank Cass, 1999), pp. 102–03, 111.

31. *Hearing of the Senate Judiciary Subcommittee on Administrative Oversight and the Courts, Administrative Oversight of the Investigation of TWA Flight 800,* May 10, 1999.

32. Ernest Hollings, August 1, 1996, FDCH political transcripts.

33. "Report of Congressman James A. Traficant Jr. to the Transportation and Infrastructure Subcommittee on Aviation on the TWA Flight Investigation," July 15, 1998.

34. NTSB, *Hearing on TWA Flight 800,* December 12, 1997.

35. Ibid.

36. See www.ntsb.gov/Recs/mostwanted/aviation_issues.htm.

37. Elaine Scarry, "The Fall of TWA 800: The Possibility of Electromagnetic Interference," *New York Times Review of Books,* April 9, 1998, pp. 59–76. Scarry was able to connect EMI to two later crashes involving Swissair and EgyptAir planes.

38. See NTSB, *Aircraft Accident Report . . . TWA Flight 800,* adopted August 23, 2000.

39. Ibid.

40. P.L. 104-264.

41. P.L. 106-181.

42. *Federal Register,* daily ed., May 7, 2001, vol. 66, no. 88, pp. 23085-131.

43. Sylvia Adcock, "NTSB Renews Calls to Regulators; Urges Vapor Removal from Tanks," *New York Newsday,* May 16, 2001, p. A14.

44. Gary Stoller, "U.S. Knew of Wiring Flaws Years before TWA Crash," *USA Today,* June 14, 2001, p. 9B.

45. Matthew L. Wald, "FAA Tests System to Avoid Fuel Explosions," *New York Times,* December 13, 2002, p. A28.

46. Adcock, "NTSB Renews Calls to Regulators."

47. Frank Eltman, "Victims of TWA Flight 800 Remembered Five Years after Fiery Crash," Associated Press, July 18, 2001.

48. Bill Adair, "Experts: TWA Riddle Has Made for Safer Jets," *St. Petersburg Times,* August 23, 2000, p. 1A.

49. Cost estimates are based on Grunwald, "FBI Role in TWA Case Draws Senate Scrutiny"; Andy Pasztor, "Air Disaster's Legacy—Probe of TWA Crash Leaves Puzzles but Also Produces Stricter Jetliner Standards," *Wall Street Journal,* August 22, 2000, p. B1.

Chapter Seven

1. See thomas.loc.gov.

2. Eric Nalder and others, "Airlines Reluctant to Screen for Bombs," *San Jose Mercury News,* November 7, 2001, p. 1A.

3. Remarks of Norman Mineta before the travel and tourism industry's Unity Dinner, March 6, 2002.

4. Data taken from www.opensecrets.org.

5. Partially drawn from Malcolm Gladwell, "Safety in the Skies," *New Yorker,* October 1, 2001, pp. 50–53.

6. Donna Rosato, "Stepped-Up Security: In the Past, It Faded Out," *USA Today,* September 9, 1996, p. 3B.

7. Ibid.

8. Leslie Wayne and Michael Moss, "Bailout for Airlines Showed the Weight of a Mighty Lobby," *New York Times,* October 10, 2001, p. A1.

9. Walter V. Robinson and Glen Johnson, "Airlines Fought Security Changes despite Warning," *Boston Globe,* September 20, 2001, p. A1.

10. Ibid.

11. Robert H. Hast, "Security: Breaches at Federal Agencies and Airports," statement before the Subcommittee on Crime, House Committee on the Judiciary, May 25, 2000 (GAO/T-OSI-00-10).

12. "Aviation Security: Long-Standing Problems Impair Airport Screeners' Performance," June 2000 (GAO/RCED-00-75).

13. Aaron Davis, "Anatomy of a Security Breakdown," *San Jose Mercury News,* February 1, 2002, p. 1A.

14. Keith O. Fultz, "Aviation Security: Technology's Role in Addressing Vulnerabilities," statement before the Committee on Science, House of Representatives, September 19, 1996 (GAO/T-RCED/NSIAD-96-262).

15. Using a branch of economics called game theory, students of elections and war note that, when fighting a battle on many fronts, an optimal strategy is to deploy resources, sometimes randomly, in such a way as to make all strategies for the opponent equally costly.

16. FAA, "FAA Advises Air Travelers on Airport, Airline Security Measures," press release, APA 65-01, October 8, 2001.

17. White House, "Remarks by the President at Signing of Aviation Security Legislation," press release, November 19, 2001.

18. P.L. 107-71.

19. The TSA has subsequently been moved to the newly created Department of Homeland Security.

20. Prepared remarks of Jane Garvey before the World Aero Club, January 22, 2002. This statement can be contrasted with Norman Mineta's "no weapons, no waiting" motto.

21. Jodi Wilgoren, "Rep. Dingell Is Forced to Strip after Hip Sets off Airport Alarm," *New York Times,* January 9, 2002, p. A20.

22. P.L. 107-71.

23. Tracy Watson, "Next Week: All Bags Screened," *USA Today,* January 11, 2002, p. 1A.

24. Frank Vehlen, testimony before House Subcommittee on Aviation, *Hearing, Checked Baggage Screening Systems: Planning and Implementation for the*

December 31, 2002 Deadline, December 7, 2001. The initial law was even weaker than most thought. Contrary to initial news reports and popular belief, actual screening of every bag by these machines was not required by December 31, 2002. What was required was that the machines be deployed by that date, not that they actually screen all bags by that date.

25. House Committee on Transportation and Infrastructure, press release, October 17, 2001.

26. DOT, "Initial Findings of Review of Argenbright Security, Inc.," press release, OIG-3-01, October 16, 2001.

27. David Firestone, "Company Vows Better Screening in U.S. Airports," *New York Times,* November 9, 2001, p. A1.

28. DOT, "Transportation Secretary Mineta Announces Recruitment Targeting 30,000 Federal Security Workers," press release, DOT 19-02, March 4, 2002.

29. DOT, "Secretary Mineta Announces Beginning of Security Screening Program; BWI First to Deploy Federal Screening Personnel," press release, DOT 44-02, April 24, 2002.

30. Association of Flight Attendants, "Some Airlines Skimping on Security Searches," press release, January 24, 2002.

31. Blake Morrison and Alan Levin, "Let New Agency Handle Unruly Fliers, FAA Says," *USA Today,* January 11, 2002, p. 8A.

32. Ibid.

33. FAA, "FAA Sets New Standards for Cockpit Doors," press release, APA 01-02, January 11, 2002.

34. Those in favor of arming pilots were ultimately successful; guns will be allowed in the cockpit due to the passage of the Homeland Security Act in late 2002.

35. Alan Levin, "Security Upgrades Coming into Focus," *USA Today,* January 18, 2002, p. 3A.

36. Glen Johnson, "Flight Crews Say Checks Unfairly Target Them," *Boston Globe,* February 4, 2002, p. A16.

37. Joe Sharkey, "Business Travel: A One-Time Top Executive Says Airline Security Has Often Been Secondary to Not Ruffling Customers," *New York Times,* January 23, 2002, p. C8.

38. Blake Morrison, "Tests Show No Screening Improvements Post-Sept. 11," *USA Today,* March 25, 2002, p. 4A.

39. Kenneth Mead, DOT inspector general, statement before House Committee on Appropriations Subcommittee on Transportation, April 17, 2002. By way of comparison, the NTSB's budget is around $70 million.

40. Ricardo Alonso Zaldivar, "Congress Rethinks Screening Deadline," *Los Angeles Times,* April 18, 2002, p. A12.

41. Ibid.

42. Andy Pasztor, "Airline Industry's New Focus on Security May Slow Accident Prevention Efforts," *Wall Street Journal,* December 31, 2001, p. A3; Jonathan D. Salant, "Some Aviation Concerns Set Aside," Associated Press, October 22, 2001.

Chapter Eight

1. The risk order of buses, trains, and planes varies from year to year, but in general ground transportation is far more dangerous than travel by air. See National Safety Council, *Injury Facts, 2002,* p. 128.

2. An exception, of course, is a plane crash that kills a celebrity or well-known individual.

3. Bill Adair, *The Mystery of Flight 427: Inside a Crash Investigation* (Smithsonian Institution Press, 2002), p. 182.

4. BBC, "TWA Flight 800," 1997.

5. Fred Bayles and Robert Davis, "Doubts Shadow Flight 427 'Party' Inquiry," *USA Today,* March 23, 1999, p. 13A.

6. Mary Schiavo, *Flying Blind, Flying Safe* (Avon Books, 1997), p. 205.

7. Adair, *The Mystery of Flight 427,* p. 186.

8. National Safety Council, *Injury Facts, 2002.*

9. See "Statement of Arnold Barnett," *Aviation Safety: Issues Raised by the Crash of ValuJet Flight 592,* Hearing before the Subcommittee on Aviation of the Committee on Transportation and Infrastructure, June 25 (GPO, 1996), pp. 363–73.

10. Barry Glassner, *The Culture of Fear: Why Americans Are Afraid of the Wrong Things* (Basic Books, 1999).

11. National Safety Council, "NSC Statistics: What Are the Odds of Dying?" (www.nsc.org/lrs/statinfo/odds.htm [May 1, 2002]).

12. Gina Kolata, "When Is a Coincidence Too Bad to Be True," *New York Times,* September 11, 1994, sec. 4, p. 4.

13. Arnold Barnett and Alexander Wang, "Airline Safety: The Recent Record," NEXTOR Research Report 98-7, Cambridge, Mass., May 1998.

14. Lisa Burgess, "Aviation Experts Draw up Safety Recommendations," *Journal of Commerce,* January 12, 1995, p. 3B.

15. Matthew Wald, "Clear Agreement Elusive on Fixing 737's Rudders," *New York Times,* February 24, 1995, p. B7.

16. Adair, *The Mystery of Flight 427,* p. 96.

17. Matthew Wald, "Two Downed 737's Make a Nightmare, and a Mystery," *New York Times,* August 20, 1995, sec. 4, p. 4.

18. U.S. Code, title 49, subtitle 2, chap. 11.

19. NTSB, "NTSB Adopts Revised Final Report on 1991 Crash of United Airlines Flight 585 in Colorado Springs, Co.; Calls Rudder Reversal Most Likely Cause," press release SB-01-12, June 5, 2001.

20. NTSB Aviation Accident and Incident Data System (nasdac.faa.gov).

21. "Statement of Arnold Barnett."

22. Ibid.

23. To allay these criticisms, USAir brought in new personnel to check its operating standards and procedures. See Douglas Frantz, "USAir Revises Fuel-Tank Checks to Reassure Public over Safety," *New York Times,* December 3, 1994, p. 1; "Safety Check: USAir Takes Steps to Reassure the Nervous Passenger," *Pittsburgh Post-Gazette,* November 23, 1994, p. C2.

24. Adair, *The Mystery of Flight 427*.

25. Matthew Wald, "FAA Cites Problems with Airline and Oversight," *New York Times*, May 18, 1996, p. 7; Adam Bryant, "FAA Files Show Early Lapses by ValuJet," *New York Times*, May 20, 1996, p. B10.

26. Schiavo, *Flying Blind, Flying Safe*, pp. 84, 90.

27. Matthew Wald, "FAA Shuts Down ValuJet, Citing 'Serious Deficiencies,'" *New York Times*, June 18, 1996, p. A1.

28. N. R. Kleinfield, "260 Die in Queens Crash; 6 to 9 Missing as 12 Homes Burn; U.S. Doubts Link to Terrorism," *New York Times*, November 13, 2001, p. A1.

29. To be sure, runway collisions and air traffic control are not ignored by the FAA. But movement on these issues has been extremely slow.

30. Associated Press, "FAA Nominee Says Safety, Not Security, Will Be Top Priority," *Wall Street Journal*, September 4, 2002, p. A6.

31. H.R. 4466.

32. For a discussion of the evolution of airline regulation, see Anthony E. Brown, *The Politics of Airline Deregulation* (University of Tennessee Press, 1987), pp. 5–10.

33. Terry M. Moe, "The Politics of Bureaucratic Structure," in John E. Chubb and Paul E. Peterson, eds., *Can the Government Govern?* (Brookings, 1989).

Index